GUINNESS WORLD RECORDS 2013

GUINNESS WORLD RECORDS™

GAMER'S EDITION

British Library Cataloguing-in-Publication Data: a catalogue record for this book is available from the British Library.

ISBN:
9781904994954

Check the official **GWR Gamer's Edition** website at:
www.guinnessworldrecords.com/gamers for record-breaking gaming news as it happens, plus exclusive interviews and competitions.

GAMER'S EDITION 2013

EDITOR-IN-CHIEF
Craig Glenday

SENIOR MANAGING EDITOR
Stephen Fall

GAMING EDITOR
Gaz Deaves

LAYOUT EDITORS
Eddie de Oliveira,
Lucian Randall

EDITORIAL CONSULTANTS
Rob Cave,
Freddie Hoff

INDEX
Chris Bernstein

PROOFREADING
Matthew White

DESIGN
XAB Design,
London UK

VP PUBLISHING
Frank Chambers

DIRECTOR OF PROCUREMENT
Patricia Magill

PUBLISHING MANAGER
Nick Seston

PUBLISHING EXECUTIVE
Charlie Peacock

TALENT RESEARCHER
Jenny Langridge

PICTURE EDITOR
Michael Whitty

DEPUTY PICTURE EDITOR
Fran Morales

PICTURE RESEARCHER
Steven Lawrence

ORIGINAL PHOTOGRAPHY
Richard Bradbury,
James Ellerker,
Paul Michael Hughes,
Ryan Schude

PRINTED BY COURIER CORPORATION IN THE USA

CONTRIBUTORS

Dan Bendon
Matt Bradford
Shaun Cunneen
Brendan Drain
Joseph Ewens
Ellie Gibson
Kirsten Kearney
Kevin Lynch
Johnny Minkley
Kathryn Notley
Martin Robinson
Chris Schilling
Tommy Tallarico
Wesley Yin-Poole

GUINNESS WORLD RECORDS

Global Managing Director:
Alistair Richards

SVP Americas:
Peter Harper

SVP Japan:
Frank Foley

Country Manager (Japan):
Erika Ogawa

President (Greater China):
Rowan Simons

PROFESSIONAL SERVICES

EVP Finance, Legal, HR & IT:
Alison Ozanne

Finance Managers:
Neelish Dawett,
Scott Paterson

Accounts Payable Manager:
Kimberley Dennis

Accounts Receivable Manager:
Lisa Gibbs

Head of Legal & Business Affairs:
Raymond Marshall

Legal & Business Affairs Executive:
Michael Goulbourn

Head of IT:
Rob Howe

Web Applications Developers:
Imran Javed,
Anurag Jha

Desktop Support:
Ainul Ahmed

Head of HR:
Jane Atkins

Office Manager (UK):
Jacqueline Angus

HR & Office Administrator (US):
Morgan Wilber

Office Manager (Japan):
Kazami Kamioka

TELEVISION

SVP Programming & TV Sales:
Christopher Skala

Director of Television:
Rob Molloy

TV Distribution Manager:
Denise Carter Steel

TV Content Executive:
Jonny Sanders

LICENSING & COMMERCIAL

VP Commercial:
Paul O'Neill

Brand Licensing Managers:
Chris Taday,
Samantha Prosser

Commercial Director (Greater China):
Blythe Fitzwiliam

COMMUNICATIONS

SVP Global Communications:
Samantha Fay

Marketing Director (US):
Stuart Claxton

PR Manager (US):
Jamie Panas

PR & Marketing Executive (US):
Sara Wilcox

Brand Manager (Germany):
Olaf Kuchenbecker

Marketing Manager:
Justine Bourdariat

Senior PR Manager:
Amarilis Whitty

PR Manager:
Claire Burgess

PR Executive:
Damian Field

UK & International Press Officer:
Anne-Lise Rouse

Director of Digital Media:
Katie Forde

Video Content Manager:
Adam Moore

Community Manager:
Dan Barrett

Online Editor:
Kevin Lynch

Designer:
Neil Fitter

Creative & Brand Executive (Japan):
Momoko Cunneen

Front-End Web Developer:
Simon Bowler

Digital Executive (US):
Megan Etzel

Digital Executive (Japan):
Takafumi Suzuki

PUBLISHING SALES

VP Publishing Sales (UK and international):
Nadine Causey

Publishing, Sales & Product Director (US):
Jennifer Gilmour

Senior National Accounts Manager (UK and international):
John Pilley

Sales & Distribution Executive: (UK & international):
Richard Stenning

RECORDS MANAGEMENT

SVP Records:
Marco Frigatti

Head of Records Management Operations UK:
Andrea Bánfi (Hungary)

Head of Records Management US:
Mike Janela

Head of Records Management Japan:
Carlos Martínez (Spain)

Head of Records Management Greater China:
Wu Xiaohong

Business Development Manager (UK):
Hayley Nolan

Business Development Manager (US):
Amanda Mochan

Business Development Manager (Japan):
Kaoru Ishikawa

Operations:
Benjamin Backhouse (UK),
Kirsty Bennett (Australia),
Jack Brockbank (UK),
Fortuna Burke (UK),
Shantha Chinniah (UK),
Michael Empric (USA),
Jacqueline Fitt (UK),
Asumi Funatsu (Japan),
Manu Gautam (UK),
Johanna Hessling (USA),
Tom Ibison (UK), Olaf Kuchenbecker (Germany),
Aya McMillan (Japan),
Anna Orford (France),
Kimberly Partrick (USA),
Pravin Patel (UK),
Philip Robertson (USA),
Chris Sheedy (Australia),
Athena Simpson (USA),
Elizabeth Smith (UK),
Kristian Teufel (Germany),
Louise Toms (UK),
Carim Valerio (Italy),
Gulnaz Ukassova (Kazakhstan), Tarika Vara (UK), Lorenzo Veltri (Italy)

Commercial:
Dong Cheng (China),
Danny Girton, Jr. (USA),
Ralph Hannah (UK/Paraguay), Annabel Lawday (UK), Takuro Maruyama (Japan),
Talal Omar (Yemen),
Terje Purga (Estonia), Lucia Sinigagliesi (Italy), Seyda Subasi-Gemici (Turkey)

Publishing Manager
Jane Boatfield

Deputy Picture Editor
Laura Nieberg

ABBREVIATIONS & MEASUREMENTS: Guinness World Records Limited uses both metric and imperial measurements. The sole exceptions are for some scientific data where metric measurements only are universally accepted, and for some sports data. Where a specific date is given, the exchange rate is calculated according to the currency values that were in operation at the time. Where only a year date is given, the exchange rate is calculated from December of that year. "One billion" is taken to mean one thousand million.

Appropriate advice should always be taken when attempting to break or set records. Participants undertake records entirely at their own risk. Guinness World Records Limited has complete discretion over whether or not to include any particular record attempts in any of its publications. Being a Guinness World Records record holder does not guarantee you a place in any Guinness World Records publication.

GUINNESS WORLD RECORDS 2013

GUINNESS WORLD RECORDS™

GAMER'S EDITION

Contents

1

2

3

4

5

6

7

8

9

10

11

12

13

Introduction

HERE WE ARE FOR OUR ACTION-PACKED SIXTH EDITION OF *GWR GAMER'S*. AS EVER, WE'VE PACKED OUR PAGES WITH HUNDREDS OF RECORDS, ESSENTIAL FACTS AND THE VERY LATEST NEWS AND ACHIEVEMENTS FROM THE WORLD OF GAMING.

We've seen the start of the eighth generation of videogames consoles with the arrival of the Wii U from Nintendo as well as the Western debut of the PS Vita, the most powerful hand-held games console. But it's not just the world of gaming that's changed since 2011: the *Gamer's Edition* is now better than ever. This year we've gone all-out to bring you first-hand reports of some of the biggest things happening in gaming right now. You'll find our special features dotted throughout the book covering all kinds of cool stories, so keep your eyes peeled to find out about cloud gaming, the greatest games soundtracks, female game characters and loads more.

Everyone loves a good fantasy fight club, so this year we've taken some of our favourite gaming stars and pitted them against rivals from other series to see who would win. Check out the "VS" feature dotted around the book, where you'll see a selection of iconic heroes and villains go head-to-head with one another, their attributes ruthlessly rated by our experts.

Who's the best?

We've dug through our vast library of games to give you some ideas on what to play next: on some of our spreads you'll find a list of similar games that excel in their class. You may not agree with what we've picked but that's okay because we love arguing about games almost as much as we love playing them.

We've also asked our contributors to

COLLECT CALL

GWR's picture editor Michael Whitty has once again been travelling the world to bring you the most striking records. You'll see some of his photographers' best shoots at various points throughout the book. When he went in search of Brett Martin's (USA) collection of memorabilia (see pp.18–19) he emailed us this shot when he arrived. "I think I've found the right house," Michael reported. The ever-popular Mario keeps on breaking records – turn to pp.120–121 to find out more.

PEDAL TO THE METAL

Turn to p.127 to find out how Jann Mardenborough (UK) made the fairy-tale leap from gamer to real driver. It was *Gran Turismo* (Polyphony Digital, 1997–present) that got him noticed by a real driving team. Petrol heads of all kinds will find a favourite game featured on pp.130–137.

LEAGUE OF HIS OWN

Jacob Gaby (UK) might love it, but it's not just football that makes for a good sporting sim. That said, there's a couple of classic soccer games in the Sports chapter (pp.156–169) this year. But you'll also find *Madden NFL* (EA, 1988–present, pp.162–163) and basketball in the shape of EA's *NBA* franchise (pp.160–161). And if you want to find out what Jacob scored, shoot straight to p.157.

GAME ON
Game jams challenge programmers to develop a playable game within a time limit. The **largest game jam in a single venue** featured 299 students in a 48-hour event at the University of Bedfordshire in Luton, UK, on 14–16 September 2012. Watched over by GWR's Gaz Deaves, they created a prototype with the 2012 theme "The Pride of London".

LITTLE RECORDS
At 124 mm (4.88 in) tall, Mark Slevinsky's (USA) arcade game is even smaller than the old Game Boy, which towers over it at 148 mm (5.8 in). But it's not all small – the latest news from regular-sized kit can be found in Hardware, pp.20–39.

give their own votes for our *Gamer's* Awards 2013. See which games of 2012 got their wholehearted approval on pp.12–13.

Interactive
Your view counts too: we're back with a new and improved reader poll section. This year, we've doubled the categories and received thousands of votes from all over the world. Turn to pp.184–191 to find out about the most visually stunning games of all time, then for the

MUCH MARIO
Nintendo's *Super Mario Kart* (1992) super fan Leyla Hasso (UK) will be pleased with the plentiful appearances of the iconic plumber in this year's book. He crops up in features on collections, game-themed weddings (pp.40–41) and, of course, in the *Super Mario Kart* coverage on pp.134–135.

world's most wicked gaming villains take a look at pp.192–193.

Some things remain the same – our quiz is back for another year. You can test your game-related knowledge with the questions down many of the right-hand pages. The answers are on p.214 but don't peek until you've tried them first! All in all, this is a packed book for a year packed with new hits and old favourites – so get reading and have some fun!

WILL POWER
You'd be doing well to beat multiple tournament winner Will Johnson (USA) at his professional game of choice – *Call of Duty* (Infinity Ward/Treyarch, 2003–present). Shooters have a chapter of their own – is your favourite there? See pp.44–55.

WHAT PERCENTAGE OF AMERICAN HOUSEHOLDS PLAY VIDEOGAMES – 41%, 72% OR 86%?

GUINNESS WORLD RECORDS

How to be a Record-Breaker

HAVE YOU LOOKED AT ANY RECORDS IN THIS YEAR'S *GAMER'S EDITION* AND THOUGHT "EASY! I COULD DO THAT"? IF YOU HAVE, GUINNESS WORLD RECORDS WANTS TO HEAR FROM YOU. AND NEXT YEAR... *YOU* COULD BE HERE!

KEEP ON RUNNING

Need some inspiration for your record-breaking subject? If you've got lots of stamina and plenty of time, you could try to set a record for staying power. The **longest videogames marathon playing on a tablet computer** stands at 26 hours and was achieved by 26 people using Samsung's Galaxy Tab 8.9 in Los Angeles, California, USA, on 6 June 2012. GWR's Freddie Hoff was on hand to present the certificate.

1 APPLY ONLINE

Head over to **www.guinnessworldrecords.com** and check the competition before selecting "Set a Record". You'll need to register and choose a challenge that is measurable, breakable (or a significant first), and that can be verified.

2 PRACTISE!

If we like your idea we'll send you the rules for your category. Everyone is judged by the same criteria, and if we reject your proposal, we'll say why. When you get the go-ahead, rehearse your moves until you're ready to show us your stuff.

3 GATHER EVIDENCE

When you're ready for your big moment, video your attempt and assemble any supporting evidence. Two independent witnesses should watch your attempt and they will be asked to write witness statements.

4 WRITE TO US

Check the guidelines again and be sure to post GWR everything needed to verify your claim. Our record team will pore over your material and if you are successful we'll send you a certificate – and you may even get in *Gamer's Edition*!

CHALLENGERS

There is another way to set a record – online. Simply go to **www.guinnessworldrecords.com/challengers** and either click on PICK A CHALLENGE or, for something new, SUGGEST A CHALLENGE. The principle is the same whichever way you do it – practise your game, follow the guidelines and upload a video as proof. Each week, GWR adjudicate attempts and you could be a world record-breaker!

BAND AID

Gamers play in all sorts of genres to set their records. Shooters, RPGs and driving games are all excellent sources for world-beating feats. Try speed-running your favourite adventure, using all the glitches allowed under GWR rules, or set a puzzler score so high the computer resets the counter. You could even combine your attempt with raising money for charity. That's what Patrick Young (USA) did when he fundraised for the American Heart Association. In the process he also set a record for the **longest videogame marathon playing *Guitar Hero***. His epic fret twiddle, from 23 to 26 February 2012, lasted 72 hr 17 min. It was called "Hero for the Heart" and took place in the Horizons School Theatre Auditorium in Atlanta, Georgia, USA.

TEAM WORK

Groups can break records as much as individuals. The **most documented tournament wins for a gaming team** stands at 1,111, set by Empire Arcadia (USA) on 8 July 2012. While the team's line-up has changed since they started competing in 2004, all wins were achieved by current members. Records by Isaiah "Triforce" Johnson (left, standing at the "Arc Shrine" wall) include the **fastest time to achieve a perfect score on *Tetris DS*** (Nintendo, 2006), at 8 hr 10 min 22 sec on 19 August 2008.

COLLECT A RECORD

If you don't want to defeat the most bosses in the shortest time or score the highest number of goals in a soccer sim, don't worry. GWR monitor many different types of record. You might want to be like Brett Martin (USA) and collect a vast amount of videogame memorabilia (find out just how many items Brett has acquired on pp.18–19).

TWO FOR ONE

You have to be a fairly committed gamer to go for a marathon as long as Chris Gloyd and Timothy Bell's (both Canada). Between 12 and 17 March 2012 they set simultaneous records for the **longest videogame marathon** and **longest videogame marathon playing an FPS**, at 120 hr 7 min. They played the *Resistance* series (Insomniac Games, 2006–present) in Toronto, Canada. The main series titles and spin-offs have sold some 8 million copies.

ON CLOUD NINE

We at GWR recognize achievements by industry insiders as well as fans. Gaikai co-founder and veteran developer David Perry (USA) accepted the record for the **most widespread cloud gaming network**. Gaikai had successfully served online games to 88 countries as of July 2012. Read more about Cloud Gaming on pp.88–89.

GET YOUR DANCING SHOES ON

Still stuck for a record? Try getting together more people than the 10,730 participants who danced in the **largest simultaneous dancing game routine**. Led by choreographer Hakim Ghorab (France), they grooved to "DJ Got Us Fallin' in Love Again" by Usher feat. Pitbull on the Xbox 360's *Dance Central 2* (Harmonix Music Systems, 2011) in Paris, France, on 26 November 2011. Check out more dance moves on pp.74–75 and pp.80–81.

GUINNESS
WORLD RECORDS
CERTIFICATE

The world's most widespread cloud gaming network is Gaikai (USA) which has successfully served online games to 88 countries, between November 2008 and July 2012

GUINNESS WORLD RECORDS

Awards Round-up

As creative boundaries in the gaming industry continue to be broken, here is GWR's pick of the most impressive videogame accolades of 2012.

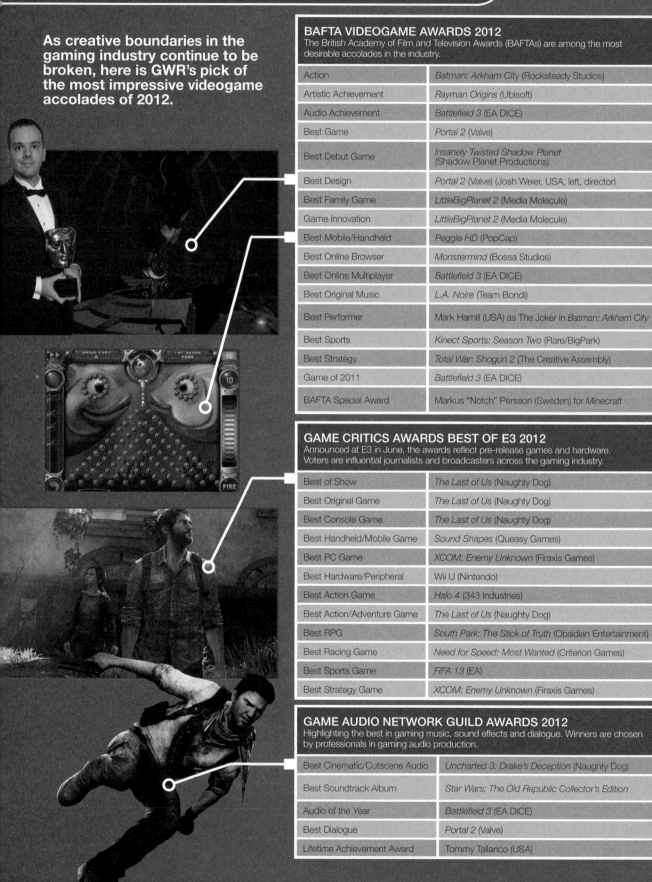

BAFTA VIDEOGAME AWARDS 2012

The British Academy of Film and Television Awards (BAFTAs) are among the most desirable accolades in the industry.

Action	*Batman: Arkham City* (Rocksteady Studios)
Artistic Achievement	*Rayman Origins* (Ubisoft)
Audio Achievement	*Battlefield 3* (EA DICE)
Best Game	*Portal 2* (Valve)
Best Debut Game	*Insanely Twisted Shadow Planet* (Shadow Planet Productions)
Best Design	*Portal 2* (Valve) (Josh Weier, USA, left, director)
Best Family Game	*LittleBigPlanet 2* (Media Molecule)
Game Innovation	*LittleBigPlanet 2* (Media Molecule)
Best Mobile/Handheld	*Peggle HD* (PopCap)
Best Online Browser	*Monstermind* (Bossa Studios)
Best Online Multiplayer	*Battlefield 3* (EA DICE)
Best Original Music	*L.A. Noire* (Team Bondi)
Best Performer	Mark Hamill (USA) as The Joker in *Batman: Arkham City*
Best Sports	*Kinect Sports: Season Two* (Rare/BigPark)
Best Strategy	*Total War: Shogun 2* (The Creative Assembly)
Game of 2011	*Battlefield 3* (EA DICE)
BAFTA Special Award	Markus "Notch" Persson (Sweden) for *Minecraft*

GAME CRITICS AWARDS BEST OF E3 2012

Announced at E3 in June, the awards reflect pre-release games and hardware. Voters are influential journalists and broadcasters across the gaming industry.

Best of Show	*The Last of Us* (Naughty Dog)
Best Original Game	*The Last of Us* (Naughty Dog)
Best Console Game	*The Last of Us* (Naughty Dog)
Best Handheld/Mobile Game	*Sound Shapes* (Queasy Games)
Best PC Game	*XCOM: Enemy Unknown* (Firaxis Games)
Best Hardware/Peripheral	Wii U (Nintendo)
Best Action Game	*Halo 4* (343 Industries)
Best Action/Adventure Game	*The Last of Us* (Naughty Dog)
Best RPG	*South Park: The Stick of Truth* (Obsidian Entertainment)
Best Racing Game	*Need for Speed: Most Wanted* (Criterion Games)
Best Sports Game	*FIFA 13* (EA)
Best Strategy Game	*XCOM: Enemy Unknown* (Firaxis Games)

GAME AUDIO NETWORK GUILD AWARDS 2012

Highlighting the best in gaming music, sound effects and dialogue. Winners are chosen by professionals in gaming audio production.

Best Cinematic/Cutscene Audio	*Uncharted 3: Drake's Deception* (Naughty Dog)
Best Soundtrack Album	*Star Wars: The Old Republic Collector's Edition*
Audio of the Year	*Battlefield 3* (EA DICE)
Best Dialogue	*Portal 2* (Valve)
Lifetime Achievement Award	Tommy Tallarico (USA)

DEVELOP INDUSTRY EXCELLENCE AWARDS 2012

Presented at trade information specialist Develop's annual conference in Brighton, UK, the awards represent a diverse range of games producers.

Grand Prix	Mind Candy, overall prize for growth and games
Best Use of a Licence	*Batman: Arkham City* (Rocksteady Studios)
Best Independent Studio	CCP
Best In-House Studio	The Creative Assembly (Sega)
Best New Studio	Bossa Studios
Best Use of Online	*World of Tanks* (Wargaming.net, 2010)
Best Tools Provider	Epic Games, the Unreal Engine 3
Publishing Hero	Valve and the Steam platform
Best Visual Arts	*Rayman: Origins* (Ubisoft) (Michel Ancel, right, designer)
Best Use of Narrative	*Dear Esther* (thechineseroom)

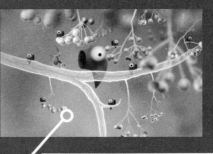

INDEPENDENT GAMES FESTIVAL 2012

Flying the flag for one-man coding shops and micro-developers, the Independent Games Festival Awards provide a showcase for breakthrough talent.

Seumas McNally Grand Prize	*Fez* (Polytron)
Audience Award	*Frozen Synapse* (Mode 7 Games)
Best Mobile Game	*Beat Sneak Bandit* (Simogo)
Best Student Game	*Way* (CoCo & Co)
Excellence in Audio	*Botanicula* (Amanita Design)
Excellence in Design	*Spelunky* (Mossmouth)
Excellence in Visual Arts	*Dear Esther* (thechineseroom)
Microsoft XBLA Award	*Super T.I.M.E. Force* (Capybara Games)
Nuovo Award	*Storyteller* (Daniel Benmergui, Argentina)
Technical Excellence Award	*Antichamber* (Demruth)

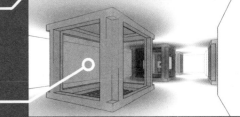

GAME DEVELOPERS CHOICE AWARDS 2012

This elite ceremony is held at a conference in San Francisco, California, USA, and is presided over by some of the greatest minds in the business.

Lifetime Achievement	Warren Spector (USA)
Game of the Year	*The Elder Scrolls V: Skyrim* (Bethesda Softworks)
Best Narrative	*Portal 2* (Valve)
Best Game Design	*Portal 2* (Valve)
Best Technology	*Battlefield 3* (EA DICE)
Best Visual Arts	*Uncharted 3: Drake's Deception* (Naughty Dog)
Best Debut	*Bastion* (Supergiant Games)
Best Handheld/Mobile Game	*Superbrothers: Sword & Sworcery EP*
Best Audio	*Portal 2* (Valve)
Best Downloadable Game	*Bastion* (Supergiant Games)

GAMES SELECTED FOR THE APPLE DESIGN AWARDS 2012

iPhone Developer Showcase	*Jetpack Joyride* (Halfbrick Studios)
iPhone Developer Showcase	*Where's My Water?* (Creature Feep)
Mac Developer Showcase	*Deus Ex: Human Revolution* (Feral Interactive)
Mac Developer Showcase	*Limbo* (Playdead)

GUINNESS WORLD RECORDS

Gamer's Awards 2013

GWR asked its panel of expert contributors to judge the best in gaming from 2012. You won't all agree with their conclusions – that's half the fun – but you're sure to find something to fascinate you in their deliberations. GWR staff gaming fans have also selected their favourite games, which you'll find listed in the table opposite, and – if you still haven't got enough to argue about – turn to pp.184–193 to find out the results of our exclusive readers' polls.

BEST GAME
Despite all the blockbusters and sequels that have made an impact this year, it was the offbeat charm of *Journey* (thatgamecompany) that stole our critics' hearts. "If anyone ever doubted that videogames were art, *Journey* proves them wrong," said Joseph Ewens. Chris Schilling was even more emphatic: "Genuinely moving, with a stunning orchestral score and one of the most inventive multiplayer setups I've ever encountered." Despite the restricted options in interacting with other players, for many the experience was touching. The minimalist design and cinematic qualities of the piece made it Matt Bradford's personal favourite. "It was like playing a Pixar movie," he said, "complete with those scenes you never get tired of watching." Not one, then, for those who like their action fast and furious and their graphics photo-realistic. But as an unusual gaming experience that offers something different, this was a worthy winner for a company founded in 2006 with the intention of creating meaningful games.

BEST GAME RUNNER-UP
Dan Bendon was among those who nominated BioWare's *Mass Effect 3* (see pp.146–147) as his personal favourite: "The perfect end to a fantastic trilogy." Not everyone who bought the game was so satisfied, with the conclusion leading to a passionate online fan campaign to have the developer change the final elements. Kirsten Kearney thought controversy was inevitable: "With millions of players so heavily invested in a character and adventure they crafted for themselves, the passion from the gaming community was incredible."

"Commander Shepard and his BioWare crew pulled off the finale with gusto."

Matt Bradford on *Mass Effect 3*

BEST FIGHTING GAME

Fighting games expert Dan Bendon nominated *Skullgirls* (Reverge Labs) as his genre's pick of the year. The saucy, all-girl fighter was first available on the PSN. "I don't think anyone really expected greatness from a downloadable fighting game but that is exactly what *Skullgirls* delivered," said Dan. "A unique setting, bizarre fighters and a smart fighting engine left me wanting more."

BEST GRAPHICS

Irrational Games' *BioShock Infinite* (pp.54–55), scheduled for a 2013 release, has the finest graphics as far as consultant Wesley Yin-Poole is concerned: "The atmosphere Irrational packed into its underwater dystopia was felt in every overturned dressing table, every message sprawled on every wall and in every stomp of a Big Daddy."

BEST SHOOTER

Wesley Yin-Poole had no hesitation in making *Borderlands 2* (see pp.50–51) both the overall winner in the shooters genre and his personal favourite of the year. "Gearbox made everything better with the sequel, increasing the game world, improving the weapon variety, upping the enemy variants and refining the single player. The best co-op FPS RPG ever. With this game, it's all about the fun. There's nothing quite like simultaneously wielding a rocket launcher and a mini-gun for extra special damage per second against Pandora's monsters and machines. And laughing maniacally while you do it."

BEST DEVELOPER

Valve was a popular choice, Matt Bradford noting that while the company didn't release much this year, fans were able to get a large number of cheap games and indie gems through their Steam platform. "Thanks to them, the Steam 'Summer Sale' is now a highly anticipated gamer holiday."

TOP TEN

	GWR STAFF FAVOURITES
1	*Mario/Super Mario*
2	*Grand Theft Auto*
3	*Tetris*
4	*Gran Turismo*
5	*FIFA*
6	*World of Warcraft*
7	*Call of Duty*
8	*The Legend of Zelda*
9	*Sonic the Hedgehog*
10	*Angry Birds*

Our runners-up were: Diablo, Donkey Kong, Left 4 Dead, Lego Star Wars, Metal Gear Solid, Need for Speed, Pokemon, Resident Evil and Temple Run.

BEST RPG

Kirsten Kearney had a hard time choosing her favourite game of the year – *Guild Wars 2* (ArenaNet) just inched out ahead of *Fez* (Polytron) as much as anything for its overall size, though both were tremendously appealing. When it came to selecting the best game in the RPG category, however, there was no such problem. It was only ever going to be ***Xenoblade Chronicles*** (Monolith Soft, 2010, shown above). "The unsung hero. What a game!" she said. "With western RPGs taking centre stage over the last few years, *Xenoblade Chronicles* quietly popped up and was an absolute masterwork of everything that's great about the Japanese RPG, renewing hope for the genre."

MANN CO.
WE SELL PRODUCTS AND GET IN FIGHTS

UPDATE

There's no shortage of goings-on in the games industry, and there have been a lot of developments since *Gamer's 2012* went to print. Here are some of the more notable stories.

HATS OFF

Back in October 2011, Valve, the makers of *Team Fortress 2* (2007), announced that content creators for the game had earned a combined total of over $2 million (£1.3 million) through the sales of user-generated hats since the online "Mann Co. Store" marketplace launched in 2010. The popularity of virtual headwear within *Team Fortress 2* has created an explosion of elaborate hats within the game, with recent estimates published on the socio-political blog The Online Society placing the value of the *TF2* hat economy as a whole at around $50 million (£32 million) annually.

FREE RADICALS

DC Universe Online (2011), Sony's superhero-themed MMORPG, was one of a growing number of online games that switched to a free2play business model, abandoning compulsory subscriptions in favour of in-game microtransactions. Within 10 days of the change in November 2011, the publisher reported that an incredible 1 million players had joined the game. The impact of the move on the developer's revenues isn't clear, but many free2play games estimate that around 20% of players are prepared to pay for in-game content of some kind.

SOPA WASHED OUT

In January 2012, the controversial Stop Online Piracy Act (SOPA) was dealt a major blow by a consortium of influential internet players including games websites Destructoid, Gamesradar and GOG.com. The bill was introduced to the US House of Representatives with the goal of reducing the availability of pirated content online. However, many web users contested that the proposal went too far in its provisions to block offending websites, potentially violating the First Amendment. Protesting sites, including Wikipedia, enacted a service blackout, effectively removing their presence from the web on 18 January 2012 to show their opposition to the proposal. Two days later, the Chairman of the House Judiciary Committee postponed the legislation to allow a less contentious compromise to be negotiated.

CRY WOLF

One of the earliest examples of an FPS, id Software's seminal World War II-set *Wolfenstein 3D* celebrated its 20th anniversary in February 2012. As a tribute to fans, the full version of the game was made available to play for free through web browsers. While the visuals in FPS games have come a long way since *Wolfenstein* hero William "B J" Blazkowicz first took the fight to Hitler's minions in 1992, the gameplay remains fresh and its influence is still felt in modern shooters.

STREET SHOOTING

Dutch advertising agency Pool Worldwide was at the centre of a storm in December 2011 when its Google Shoot View web application was shut down by Google for infringing terms of service. The game turned the existing photo database from Google Street View into a first-person shooter, allowing players to virtually explore their neighbourhoods while equipped with an assault rifle. While this FPS system lacked meaningful gameplay elements, it still proved too provocative for many internet users. The game was terminated within just four days.

FISHING FOR TROUBLE

Phil Fish (Canada), the acclaimed creator of *Fez* (Polytron, 2012), invited a world of controversy at the Game Developers Conference in San Francisco, USA, when he declared, "Your games just suck" in response to a question from a Japanese programmer about the standard of development in Japan. His climb-down via Twitter also backfired somewhat when he proclaimed, "I was a bit rough" before going on to say that Japanese games were "terrible nowadays". Despite these setbacks, *Fez* was then released to near-universal praise from critics.

UPDATE

Apple's iPhone 5 was released in the second half of 2012, while elsewhere cool was lost, games were stolen and whole countries of fans found themselves on the wrong end of sanctions.

WAR OF WORDS

Chuck Beaver, the story producer for survival-horror series *Dead Space* (Visceral Games, 2008–present), made outspoken comments in April 2012 regarding rival franchise *Gears of War* (Epic Games, 2006). He branded its storyline as "literally the worst writing in games", containing "atrocious, offensive violations of story basics". Two days later, he qualified his remarks in a statement calling *GoW* an "epic franchise that has trailblazed more than a few industry-leading player experiences and mechanics". Isn't it nice when everyone makes up after an argument?

FACE DOWN

After months of speculation, Facebook floated on the New York stock exchange. After a brief initial increase, concern about the potential for profit caused its shares to slide from a high of $38.23 at launch in May to under half that figure in September. This downward trend continued with another social networking high roller: Facebook game developer Zynga. It floated in December 2011 but suffered an even worse financial fate. The company has seen stock prices lose more than 80% of their value, from a high of $14.69 in March to $2.70 by September.

PATENTLY MINE

In March, *Minecraft* creator Markus "Notch" Persson (Sweden) won a Special Award at the BAFTA Videogame Awards in recognition of his independent development work. But in July he took to Twitter to voice his disdain at being accused of patent infringement by Luxembourg-based Uniloc over the way gamers get access to mobile versions of *Minecraft*. Persson's Mojang was one of 10 companies named in the suit, which mistitled the game "Mindcraft". The outspoken developer claimed that he would "throw piles of money at making sure they don't get a cent". He went on to brand software patents in general as "plain evil" and said that "innovation within software is basically free and it's growing incredibly rapidly. Patents only slow it down." Uniloc founder Ric Richardson (Australia) was reportedly the victim of internet hate mail as a result of the action and used his blog to defend the rights of patent holders.

AZEROTH OUT OF IRAN

World of Warcraft (2004) players in Iran awoke on 22 August to find they were no longer able to connect to the game. Initial theories that the country's censors had banned the game for promoting "superstition" were disproven when developer Blizzard Entertainment said it was cutting access to comply with trade restrictions imposed by the US government on the regime in Tehran. As a US-registered company, Blizzard was forced to terminate accounts, depriving players of their hard-earned loot.

NUN MORE BLACK

The *Hitman: Absolution* (IO Interactive) trailer sparked controversy for depicting hero Agent 47 in hand-to-hand combat against provocatively dressed nuns. At a time when the industry likes to present gaming as a maturing art form, the clip was criticized by *New Statesman* as a return to "lazy stereotypes about women in videogames". Game director Tore Blystad (Denmark) told Eurogamer that they learned "we really needed to give these characters some context and some back story. We're working ... to build these characters up before you meet them."

IT'S A STEAL!

Capcom confirmed reports that copies of its major title for 2012, *Resident Evil 6*, had been stolen and sold in Poland weeks ahead of the game's October launch. According to the developer the theft was limited to a small number of PS3 copies destined for Germany. Eurogamer reported a stolen copy of the game on eBay starting at €478 (£387; $628). Pre-launch leaks are potentially disastrous for games companies as they can reduce the level of anticipation for the release and hurt sales in the crucial first weeks when opinions are shaped.

Collectability

The largest collection of videogames memorabilia is owned by Brett Martin (USA) and was counted in Littleton, Colorado, USA, in August 2012

LARGEST COLLECTION OF VIDEOGAME MEMORABILIA

In 1989, eight-year-old Brett Martin's (USA) parents gave him a 4-cm (1.6-in) Mario holding a mushroom (shown right). Since then Brett has amassed a treasure trove of 8,030 items, many of which you can see at videogamemm.com. Here, he takes GWR on an exclusive tour of the best and rarest items in his personal collection.

More merchandise was produced for Mario than any other character – although Link remains Brett's personal favourite.

1. Mario himself was the hardest to find in the set of *Super Mario* ceramic cookie jars and banks.

2. The *Ocarina of Time 3D* official Link hat was imported from Greece, the only country where it was available at that time.

3. This *Ocarina* Link statue from E3 1997 is very fragile – few of them remain in good condition.

4. *Mario Party* statues originally stood on top of the arcade machines in Japan.

5. Brett found this statue in his local classified ads, which are not usually good hunting grounds!

6. *Mega Man* pillows were only sold online by Capcom and are rare, even in Japan.

7. The first Mario plush toy was made by Avanti in 1986. This one was imported from Japan.

8. These *Legend of Zelda* statues and figurines are Brett's favourite part of his collection.

9. There are more than 300 Mario items on this shelf alone!

10. *Pikmin* memorabilia is popular and these items have appreciated in value the most.

11. This Mario inflatable comes from a store display, and is one of Nintendo's earliest and rarest Mario marketing items.

12. The giant Mario store display plush at the back is even taller than **5** and is the only one Brett has ever seen for sale.

Contents

1

Overview

It has been an exciting year of new hardware releases, with the Wii U, 3DS XL, PS Vita and the slimmer PS3 arriving in stores, as well as major innovations in gaming. But hardware doesn't get much more innovative than Mark Slevinsky's (USA) **smallest arcade machine**. Just 124 x 52 x 60 mm (4.88 x 2.05 x 2.36 in), it's fully playable. The computer engineer built it from scratch in 2009 and wrote his own operating system, FunkOS, to program its *Tetris*, *Space Invaders* and *Breakout* clones. The machine was painted by Mark's artist wife Esther.

Biography

Johnny Minkley is a games expert for BBC radio. He also writes and presents TV shows for Sky, and reviews games for a number of publications. He has been reporting on games professionally since the days of the Dreamcast, and playing them amateurishly since the Atari 2600 era.

Wii U

THE FIRST
OF THE NEXT
GENERATION
CONSOLES TO
GET OFF THE
STARTING LINE

BLOSSOMING IDEAS

Pikmin 3 (Nintendo EAD, 2012) is the Wii U's entry in the colourful real-time strategy series that came to legendary designer Shigeru Miyamoto (Japan) while he was gardening. Eight years after *Pikmin 2* was released on the GameCube, the Wii U GamePad's screen provides the perfect technology for an enhanced experience. Players can use it as a separate, interactive map while playing with a regular Wii MotionPlus, or grasp the GamePad for greater strategic control over their Pikmin. HD, ingenious and deep, *Pikmin 3* is a complex but cute game to counteract the age of the app.

SYSTEM UPDATE

Gamers at last got to know which games they will be playing on the Wii U, successor to the Wii, the **best-selling seventh-generation console**. Some fans struggled to understand Nintendo's new vision until they finally got their hands on the GamePad. Nintendo also opted to allow the millions of existing Wii controllers out in the wild to be used with its new console. With a new, Xbox-like Pro Controller and dazzling HD graphics, the Wii U is encouraging developers to bring new games and established series on to the Nintendo platform.

The stylus may be used in addition to the analogue controls and the touch-screen to play games or draw.

The GamePad screen can be used to supplement the TV view via wireless from the Wii U, or gameplay can be streamed directly without a TV.

Weighing a hefty 1.5 kg (3 lb 6 oz), the GamePad is the **heaviest standard game console controller**.

NINTENDO LAND...

...Not a real theme park full of rides and actors dressed up as Nintendo characters, but a virtual one with 12 different "attractions" based around Nintendo franchises. There are several games within the title, which is due to be released in late 2012. Among the Nintendo legends appearing in the attractions are Donkey Kong, Zelda, Luigi and, of course, Mario.

41,980,000

Number of Wii Balance Boards Nintendo say were sold worldwide by the end of 2011. The peripheral is also compatible with the Wii U.

There is no shortage of control methods with dual analogue sticks as well as directional pads and motion sensors.

SCREEN-UPMANSHIP

The Wii changed the way we game – so much so that Sony and Microsoft released their own motion-control gadgets in an attempt to catch up. With the Wii U, Nintendo is relying on the concept of the second screen. And while its rivals offer similar features, via Vita and SmartGlass, Nintendo's is designed to be an integral part of the gameplay.

Games are supplied on disc, but the console won't support Blu-ray or DVD.

In addition to a 6.2-inch screen, the GamePad has motion control including a gyroscope.

IN WHICH YEAR WAS NINTENDO FOUNDED IN JAPAN – 1889, 1977 OR 1989?

Xbox 360

IN 2012, XBOX HELPED MICROSOFT TAKE ANOTHER STEP TOWARDS BECOMING THE CENTRE OF ALL HOME ENTERTAINMENT. ITS OPPONENTS IN THIS BATTLE ARE NO LONGER JUST SONY AND NINTENDO, BUT APPLE AND GOOGLE TOO

XBOX MARKS THE SPOT

The big Xbox announcement of 2012 was SmartGlass (see bottom right), software that works to connect users' existing smartphones and tablets to the console. By contrast, rival Nintendo products require new hardware in the shape of the Wii U GamePad. SmartGlass allows users to start watching a show on TV, then continue to watch on the move, and games can also be played on phone or tablet. It was perhaps with one eye on future Apple TV developments that Xbox Live head Marc Whitten (left) said, "Xbox SmartGlass turns any TV into a smart TV".

TOP GEAR

Turn 10's *Forza Motorsport* cemented its position as the main rival to Sony's mighty *Gran Turismo* franchise (Polyphony Digital, 1997–present). *Forza Horizon* (2012) was an adventure-fuelled spin-off, with some of the world's greatest cars leaving the confines of the race track and taking to the open roads of Colorado, USA, to race at the fictional Horizon festival. Players could race wherever and whenever they wanted, preserving the award-winning feel of *Forza* in a thrilling new landscape.

FORZA **HORIZON**

SYSTEM UPDATE

The Xbox 360 is the **best-selling HD videogames console**, with total global sales of 68.34 million as of September 2012. Microsoft's seventh-generation machine continues to advance, and has made headlines with news of significant software updates. These include the introduction of Internet Explorer, with voice search via Kinect (below), and a music streaming service.

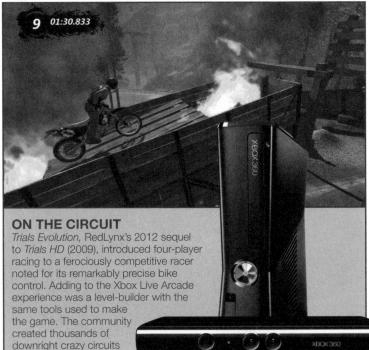

ON THE CIRCUIT

Trials Evolution, RedLynx's 2012 sequel to *Trials HD* (2009), introduced four-player racing to a ferociously competitive racer noted for its remarkably precise bike control. Adding to the Xbox Live Arcade experience was a level-builder with the same tools used to make the game. The community created thousands of downright crazy circuits to test petrol heads' skills.

ARMED FORCES

Halo 4 (343 Industries, 2012) is the eighth release in the sci-fi franchise in which humanity wages war against alien forces. The first part of a new trilogy, it saw the return of the Master Chief. *Halo*'s story is inseparable from that of the Xbox itself: *Combat Evolved* launched with Microsoft's first console in 2001. The latest game pushes the limits of the ageing hardware, taking the 360 to new visual heights. It mixes classic shooter action with a greater focus on exploration and a darker tone to the storytelling.

FEZ (POLYTRON, 2012) WAS A LONG-AWAITED XBOX 360 EXCLUSIVE. WHAT WAS THE NAME OF ITS 2D HERO?

SMARTGLASS

Microsoft's smartest decision with its new application was to allow it to work with iPhones, iPads and Android devices as well as with Windows gadgets. Users can watch TV shows such as medieval fantasy *Game of Thrones* (USA/UK) and follow the characters on a map of the fantasy realm of Westeros on their phone at the same time.

Ascend: New Gods (Signal Studios) will be among the Xbox 360 games optimized for use with SmartGlass.

The main game action takes place on the TV while players can check the map, statistics and inventory on a connected device.

PS3

IT'S BEEN ANOTHER YEAR OF STUNNING, CUTTING-EDGE GAMING EXPERIENCES FOR ALL PS3 TASTES

ON THE MOVE

The PlayStation Move, played here by actor Ryan Kwanten, endured a slow start on its launch in 2010, eclipsed by the marketing blitz that accompanied Microsoft's Kinect. But the accuracy of Sony's motion-controller always promised to deliver more substantial gaming experiences than anything Microsoft's hands-free tech could manage. It took until 2012 for developers to start exploring this properly, with *Sorcery* (The Workshop, 2012), the first fully fledged action-adventure built specifically for Move. Adopting the role of a young apprentice wizard, players were tasked with spell-casting, treasure-hunting and puzzle-solving in a charming fantasy land. What gave *Sorcery* the edge was its clever motion controls: a flick of the wrist here to let loose a bolt of destructive magic, a spin there to frantically mix a potion.

SYSTEM UPDATE

The message from Sony is clear: there's plenty of life left in the PS3 yet. In September 2012, a slimmer version of the console was released, complete with an expanded 500GB hard disk, giving the PS3 the **highest storage capacity in a videogames console**. Hardcore PS3 gamers also had plenty to celebrate, with more exclusive games to enjoy than their 360- and Wii-owning friends. Aside from the expected big hitters, Sony continued to invest in commercially risky but creatively refreshing indie projects. Vita, meanwhile, became a key piece of the PlayStation puzzle, with the "Crossplay" feature allowing gameplay to switch from PS3 to hand-held, with multiplayer action across both platforms.

EPIC JOURNEY

Game designer Jenova Chen (China) and his team shot to fame and success in 2012 with the breathtaking, unconventional *Journey* (Thatgamecompany). The game is an enchanting, beautiful trip of discovery and adventure, taking you across a shimmering desert to the summit of a mysterious mountain.

> "Nobody has the strengths that we do in gaming and entertainment."
> – Jack Tretton, President and CEO of Sony Computer Entertainment

OLD MASTERS

Alongside the brand new releases, Sony also continued to hand-pick the best-loved classics from the PlayStation back catalogue and remaster them in pin-sharp HD for a PS3 re-release. In 2012, Insomniac's *Ratchet & Clank Trilogy* (Idol Minds, 2012) and Naughty Dog's *The Jak & Daxter Trilogy* (Mass Media Inc., 2012, pictured) joined *Oddworld: Stranger's Wrath HD* (Just Add Water, 2011), which received enhanced 3D and Move support this year.

PREPARED FOR BATTLE

Some 17 years of classic PlayStation gaming was finally enough to convince Sony it had sufficient superstars to fill its own frenetic brawler. *PlayStation All-Stars Battle Royale* (SuperBot Entertainment, 2012) plundered the best of the PS, PS2 and PS3 for characters and locations in this fast-paced beat-'em-up. Sony stalwarts such as Kratos, Nathan Drake and Sly Cooper joined third-party bigwigs including *BioShock*'s Big Daddy, with online play that worked across the PS3 and the hand-held PS Vita.

SONY 3D MONITOR

In an attempt to boost interest in 3D gaming, Sony created a PlayStation-branded 3D HD monitor, which launched in the UK in April 2012. The 24-inch display and built-in stereo speakers with subwoofer were designed with gamers in mind. But at the same time, only a fraction of PS3 games released offered support for stereoscopic 3D.

"Simulview" means two players wearing 3D glasses can play on the same screen at the same time in full HD (although only in 2D).

Sony's battery-powered 3D glasses are "active shutter", which rapidly alternates the eye that can see the screen.

The bundled HDMI cable ensures gamers hooking up a PS3 can enjoy HD gaming with no loss of quality.

GUINNESS WORLD RECORDS

∃DS

ANOTHER HAND-HELD SUCCESS FOR NINTENDO – THE COMPANY THAT STARTED THE FORM WITH GAME & WATCH IN THE EARLY 1980s

THIS YEAR'S MODEL

Nintendo consoles pop up everywhere – even in museums. The Louvre in Paris, France, bought hundreds of 3DS units to replace its standard audio guides, and perhaps they might come in handy for some sneaky gaming if the *Mona Lisa* fails to entertain. Yet the 3DS is already old news just a year after launching – an XL version of the unit (see bottom right) was released in 2012. As the name implies, the model is significantly larger than the original (155 mm x 173 mm when fully open, compared with 134 mm x 138 mm on the original 3DS). The added bulk made it less portable and probably not as attractive for museum use, although gamers appreciated the increase in screen real estate.

SYSTEM UPDATE

Nintendo's latest hand-held system got off to an unexpectedly slow start at launch, but a big price cut plus the arrival of *Mario Kart 7* and *Super Mario 3D Land* (both Nintendo, 2011) ignited the public's interest and more than 15 million systems have now been sold. Nintendo released massive games, new online features and a new model of the 3DS. The Circle Pad Pro brought the flexibility of dual analogue control options to games such as *Resident Evil: Revelations* (Capcom, 2012) in response to Sony's PlayStation Vita, giving developers greater scope to create more complex home-console-style games.

VIRTUAL BOY

Nintendo's first attempt at a 3D games console was launched back in 1995. It was discontinued by the end of the year after poor sales and claims that it caused headaches and dizziness. It has since become a collector's item.

FANTASTIC FINAL RHYTHM

Final Fantasy (Square Enix) celebrated 25 years of role-playing cult success in 2012 with this cute rhythm game. Drawing on the varied in-game music that fans have grown up with, *Theatrhythm* (Indies zero) offers a simple touch-screen rhythm game. Gameplay modes include a combat system, and the game charts the series' evolution from 8-bit roots through to more recent cinematic budget-busters.

Kid Icarus (Nintendo, 1986) last appeared as an original release on the Game Boy more than 20 years ago. It was revived for the 3DS in *Kid Icarus: Uprising* (Nintendo, 2012), directed by Masahiro Sakurai (Japan), creator of Kirby. It featured support for the Circle Pad Pro, an optional extra offering more flexible control methods.

DARK AS A DUNGEON

In the year that *Diablo III* (Blizzard, 2012) thrilled PC gamers, Square Enix brought its own take on the dungeon-crawler genre on to Nintendo's portable system. *Heroes of Ruin* (n-Space, 2012) really makes the most of the system with its online features. Other players can drop in and out, and up to four gamers can undertake the quests together while also enjoying the voice chat option. As for the gameplay, the choice of four player classes means that fans can play the game more than once, a feature that goes some way to making up for the shortness of the main campaign. And for players who enjoy action-RPGs, thousands of items of loot can alter character stats, allowing for fine-tuning and the creation of a truly individual hero.

213.8 million

Nintendo platform Mii avatars created by the end of 2011, according to the company.

NINTENDO 3DS Mii

StreetPass Mii Plaza is preloaded on the 3DS and, at first, was just a nifty way to interact with other gamers, as Miis exchange information when two 3DSs come into range. Following a system update at the end of 2011, there was also greater puzzle difficulty and a new adventure in *StreetPass Quest 2*. Celebrity Miis include a Mii of Nintendo CEO Satoru Iwata (Japan) introduced to mark a year of the 3DS.

2D image of Nintendo 3DS game

Sarah

The new, wider upper screen is 800 x 240 pixels, although half of the 800 is used to render the 3D effects that make this the **first hand-held to support glasses-free 3D**. The lower screen is touch-sensitive.

The 3DS adds to the DS controls with a circle pad, an interface that responds sensitively to movement.

MORE THAN 73 MILLION MiiS HAVE BEEN CREATED IN EUROPE ALONE – TRUE OR FALSE?

PS Vita

RUSH HOUR

Gravity Rush (SCE, 2012) generated excitement among gamers with its pedigree: project lead Keiichiro Toyama (Japan) was the creator of the original *Silent Hill* (Konami, 1999). *Gravity Rush* is a stylized, third-person action title. An animated girl named Kat with the power to change gravity appears alongside a magical cartoon cat in a delightfully weird adventure. Twisting the world on its head and back again proves supremely enjoyable. And the Vita handles it all elegantly.

SYSTEM UPDATE

Sony's powerful new portable finally hit the West in 2012. Collaboration is the buzzword, as selected PS3 games can be saved and played on the move with the PS Vita, which can also act as a PS3 controller. Some original PlayStation titles are also playable on the Vita. Its main challenger is now not Nintendo, but something the original PSP never had to worry about: smartphones.

DEATHMATCHES ON THE GO

Resistance: Burning Skies (Nihilistic Software, 2012) is a sci-fi, alien-slaying FPS. The **first FPS on a portable console to use dual stick control** also has an online option to give gamers the novelty of enjoying deathmatches on the bus or even in the bath!

IT'S A SMALL WORLD

The inventive *LittleBigPlanet* (see pp.122–123) felt like it had finally found its natural home on the PS Vita. The sheer flexibility of the device, with its touch inputs and built-in cameras, meant that anyone could imagine, create and play anywhere, anytime, in its attractive universe. Gamers on both PS3 and Vita can play together, affecting each other's game, and Vita apps include a radar that shows where to grab the prizes contained in bubbles.

New in-game tools to make the most of the PS Vita's control methods include a "touch sensor" and a "touch tweaker". With these, players can make objects react to the touch-screen or rear-touch pads.

Dual analogue stick controls, an improvement on the PSP, with the second stick on the right-hand side.

Boasting a 5-in (12.7-cm) widescreen display, the PS Vita has the **largest screen on a hand-held games console**.

A touch pad on the rear is accompanied by a microphone and camera.

Swiping gestures can be used on the screen, and many games make use of them as a control method.

VITA STATISTICS

PlayStation Vita arrived in a whirlwind of publicity in Japan in December 2011, mixing the flexibility of a hand-held with the full gaming potential of a home console. It catered to all tastes, with both pricey blockbusters and affordable casual games. Key to its long-term success will be how it works in tandem with the PS3, with games that can be played across both systems seamlessly.

GUINNESS WORLD RECORDS™

Performance PC

WITH MAJOR RECENT RELEASES, PC GAMERS HAVE NOT JUST GREAT GAMES TO BE EXCITED BY IN 2013, BUT ALSO THE BEST-LOOKING ONES AVAILABLE ON ANY PLATFORM

CIVILIZED RULERS

Gods & Kings (Firaxis Games) is the first addition to *Sid Meier's Civilization V* (Firaxis, 2010) and was released in June 2012. Expansion packs have long been a core component of PC gaming and *Gods & Kings* becomes the 27th release in the multi-million-selling *Civilization* series. The game combines elements of previous titles, allowing players to found their own religion and engage in espionage. A general game overhaul improved many features, rekindling player interest in the legendary turn-based strategy which back in 1991 first encouraged players to "build an empire to stand the test of time".

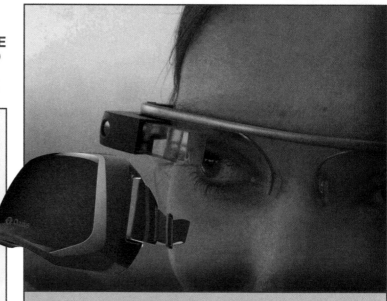

LOOKING AHEAD

The PC is evolving again with the development of wearable computing such as Google glasses. Google aim to superimpose the useful bits of mobile applications, such as mapping, over our perception of the real world to augment reality. It's a distant relation of virtual reality, that maligned gaming gimmick from the 1990s. Yet, once thought dead, VR may be making a comeback with the Oculus Rift, an immersive, stereoscopic headset designed for gaming and already championed by John Carmack (USA), the technical genius behind *Doom* (id Software, 1993) and *Quake* (id, 1996). The gadget has a wider field of vision than previous headsets and was unveiled to the press at E3 2012 with a modified version of *Doom 3* (2004).

SYSTEM UPDATE

As developers strived to squeeze more power from ageing console hardware, PCs were running the next generation of gaming. Even developers whose interest lay in selling console games showcased new titles on PCs that can still deliver visual spectacle far beyond the reach of the PS3 or Xbox 360. With 1.25 billion units in active use, Windows PCs are the **most popular game-capable devices**.

UNREAL DEVELOPMENT

Epic Games released a demo of its Unreal Engine 4 at the E3 2012 trade show in Los Angeles, USA. It could be the future of console gaming, but the video was shown on the Nvidia GeForce GTX 680 (left), the sort of card already owned by PC gamers with cutting-edge rigs. Key features of UE4 include realistic lighting, better particle effects (thousands of sparks flying from a fire) and improved flexibility for developers. But with the next PlayStation and Xbox not expected to exploit the engine properly for years, it will be PC gamers who will experience this technology first.

THE GREAT WARS

Guild Wars 2 (ArenaNet) was 2012's major MMO release. The vast fantasy-adventure won numerous pre-release awards, including the Eurogamer Expo 2011 Game of Show award, beating even *Modern Warfare 3* (Infinity Ward/Sledgehammer Games, 2011). Featuring intelligent polar bear creatures called the Kodan among its attributes, what particularly caught attention was its convention-challenging design. Most MMO titles slavishly copy Blizzard's *World of Warcraft* (2004) formula, whereas *GW2* had events that reacted dynamically to combat and to the number of players involved. It has helped to breathe new life into the genre.

Do you want to make the next PC blockbuster? One of the most ingenious inventions to arrive in 2012 was the Raspberry Pi, a £20 ($31), credit-card-sized PC designed to encourage young people to get coding. Built by a Cambridge, UK-based company whose ranks include David Braben (UK), designer of the legendary *Elite* (David Braben and Ian Bell, 1984), it can stream videos in full HD and generate graphics on a par with iOS devices.

PUMP IT UP

For serious PC gamers, every millisecond of play counts. Customized kit is pricey, but offers possibilities for enhancing everything from the HDD to the case. While DIY fans prefer to assemble their own speedy kit, most other serious gamers buy custom-built kits from specialists.

Origin (USA) gaming PCs feature an option for a complex tubed cooling system for processors using compressed gas in a similar way to air conditioners.

Laptops can be customized for gamers, but added power requires chunkier components, making them less portable.

Browser & Indie

QUICK, SLICK AND PORTABLE HARDWARE IS GIVING BROWSER GAMES AN IDEAL PLATFORM

SOUTH AMERICAN WAY

The tower defence genre is one of the most popular in browser gaming. *Kingdom Rush* (left), a 2012 release from Uruguayan developers Ironhide, is a particularly popular and critically acclaimed example. A variant on real-time strategy (RTS), tower defence games require players to build and maintain static defences against waves of enemies looking to assault their stronghold. *Kingdom Rush* boasts colourful environments, plenty of tactical depth and a balanced difficulty curve to make it a popular title for browser gaming fans. Such was the game's success that it quickly made the leap from browser to mobile – iPad and iPhone versions are now available, offering a potentially lucrative future for the trio of South American friends (above) who started Ironhide in 2010 – from left, Alvaro Azofra, Gonzalo Sande and Pablo Realini.

SYSTEM UPDATE

PC gaming isn't just about spending a fortune on a souped-up computer. Many gamers are moving away from full-featured, powerful PCs to smaller, lighter netbooks and ultrabooks that combine portability, long battery life and a low price tag. Browser gaming is a perfect match for these machines, providing great gaming experiences that you can play on almost any computer. The speedy computer books are also ideal for sampling the independent scene, with its plethora of innovative web games. Many indie developers start off by hosting their games on browser gaming sites such as Kongregate, in order to gain gamer feedback.

INDIE KID

Mike Bithell (UK) was lead designer at Bossa Studios, whose browser-based game *Monstermind* won a BAFTA in 2012. But he also spent a year developing his own personal platform/puzzler project. *Thomas Was Alone* (2012, shown below on an Acer Aspire S3) was, according to Mike, "a minimalist game about friendship and jumping". Beautifully simple visuals, an engaging storyline narrated by author Danny Wallace and inventive design made this one of the year's most charming games.

VILLE-IANT

The variety available to browser-based gamers has never been wider, but there are still some genres that rise above the rest. The hugely successful 'Ville games (see pp.84–85) from social developer Zynga are among the most popular in history. The latest entry in the franchise, simply entitled *The Ville*, was released in June 2012 and quickly hit a peak of 50 million monthly active users. The game tasks players with building and running a happy home, socializing with neighbours and taking part in mini-games. As with most Zynga titles, Facebook integration is an essential part of the experience.

SOCIAL SURVIVAL

One-button platformer *Edmus* (Pouchmouse, 2011) draws inspiration from popular survival games such as *Canabalt* (Semi Secret Software, 2009). Players navigate a fast and treacherous path in pursuit of a high score, but it's the game's social features that stand out: other players' attempts from the same day are shown alongside yours for comparison.

As you advance through *Edmus*, other players will slowly drop away, and if you're the best that day only *your* character will be visible by the end.

The speedy Samsung Series 5 Chromebook works well with portable gaming: it has a battery life of 8.5 hours, 2 GB of RAM and weighs just 1.48 kg (3 lb 3 oz).

IT'S BEEN ANOTHER YEAR OF EXCITEMENT AND INNOVATION AT APPLE'S ENORMOUS GAMES STORE

AVIAN SPACE

Angry Birds Space (Rovio), the fourth title in the hit series, was released in March 2012. That same month Apple announced that the original was the **best-selling paid-for iPhone app** of all time. *Space* added new characters, abilities and gravitational physics, played out upon the game's starry-skied setting. This brought in an element of strategy, and helped keep the series at the top end of the chart.

PURPLE PROSE

In 2012, the notoriously cagey Apple revealed tantalizing details of the origins of one of the world's most advanced smartphones. It had begun with the code-name "purple project" in 2004 and a *Fight Club*-style poster in Apple reminded employees that the first rule of the "purple project" was that you didn't *talk* about the purple project. A whole floor, the "purple dorm", was locked down in the Apple campus (pictured right) and up to five badge-reading doors had to be passed to enter. Apple iOS head Scott Forstall (USA) recruited the company's "superstars" without saying what they were going to work on – just that they would give up weekends and evenings for two years. Details of the top-secret process emerged during Apple's bitter legal row with Samsung.

SYSTEM UPDATE

Even before the new model was launched in September, the iPhone remained the world's **best-selling smartphone** in 2012. A selection of exclusive games kept the iOS App Store relevant in the face of competition from Android devices and the PS Vita. With iOS 6 on the way, older Apple devices will benefit from features that include Apple's own maps, in a further break from Google and gmaps.

Real Racing 3 (Firemint, 2012) is one of the games optimized for the iPhone's new 16:9 full widescreen display.

The iPhone 5 features an extended 4" touch-screen, a faster processor and a slimmer, lighter form. Boasting a new screen resolution of 1136 x 640, the iPhone 5 is capable of "full console quality" visuals, according to EA's Rob Murray. These credentials were demonstrated at the live unveiling of the phone.

Apple claims the phone's new touch-screen technology makes it more responsive – a must for gamers – with a brighter and clearer display.

A KIND OF MAGIC

The classic fantasy card game *Magic: The Gathering* finally came to tablet computers with the 2013 edition of *Duels of the Planeswalkers* (Stainless Games, 2012). *Magic 2013* has the features of the Xbox Live Arcade and PC version with touch-screen controls and portability. The game also features a wide range of new decks to build and customize.

111,501

Games on the App Store, as of 20 August 2012. If you played each for 30 minutes, it would take you seven years to complete them all.

DECK MANAGER

PLAYER STATUS

CAMPAIGN

Creatures with protection from red reduce damage dealt by red sources to 0.

ONE VISION

The new iPad, launched in 2012, contained a major additional feature: the retina display. With 2,048 x 1,536 pixels, the sharp, new display makes the iPad the **highest-resolution tablet**. While hardcore gamers might still prefer dedicated hand-helds, Apple's huge library makes the iPad more of a contender with games such as *Infinity Blade Dungeons* (Epic Games) announced specifically for the new iOS devices.

Retina screen boasts 3,145,728 pixels, exceeding the 2,073,600 pixels of an HD TV.

WHEN DID APPLE'S APP STORE FIRST OPEN?

GUINNESS WORLD RECORDS™

Android

LEADING SHARE

Having secured a 59% smartphone market share in 2012 – and with 900,000 devices purchased and activated every day – Android is the world's **fastest-growing operating system**. Exclusive titles allow it to stay competitive with Apple and keep the new Windows Phone at bay. The arrival of the Samsung Galaxy S III in 2012 brought big screens and faster processors for even better gaming experiences. The announcement in 2011 of the new Qualcomm Snapdragon processors promises to keep Android devices at the forefront of phones and tablets.

GOOGLE'S OPERATING SYSTEM FOR MOBILE DEVICES CONTINUES TO GROW AND CHALLENGE APPLE'S STRONGHOLD

SYSTEM UPDATE

Android handsets are currently the home of cloud gaming, with OnLive's service working particularly well as a result of the controls offered by the Sony Ericsson Xperia Play. But with the addition of a simple app, it's possible to link the fully featured DualShock 3 controller (as used on the PS3) to any Android handset. This helps create a high-performance, portable games console, allowing gamers to play major titles via OnLive. It's easy to see why some gamers are attracted by big-budget console gaming on small-scale screens. The only snag is the reliance on a speedy broadband connection to be able to stream video and audio in real time.

HARDWARE HEROES

In contrast to Apple's focus on the iPhone, iPod Touch and iPad, there are now hundreds of devices running the Android OS. Here's our pick of the latest exciting inventions.

The latest in Asus' Transformer range, the Asus Transformer Pad Infinity is part laptop, part tablet. It comes with a brand new Snapdragon S4 chip, 1920 x 1200-resolution screen – which outperforms most HD televisions – and connects to Asus' signature keyboard. This effectively turns the Infinity into an Android netbook for faster typing and surfing.

At the other end of the tablet spectrum to the Asus Infinity, the Kindle Fire is a low-cost, portable e-reader that is also used for playing games. The OS that runs on the device is now developed separately from the rest of the Android family. Even with its lower spec it can run plenty of mobile games, of which *Angry Birds* (Rovio, 2009) is one of the most popular.

MINING FOR SUCCESS

Although it's now also available for iOS, *Minecraft – Pocket Edition* (Mojang, 2011) was a coup for both Android as a whole and handset manufacturer Sony Ericsson. Available exclusively at launch for the Experia Play phone, but quickly rolled out across all Android devices, this mini version of the dig-and-build sandbox sensation makes it possible for gamers to take their pickaxes on the move, and it allows local multiplay, too. A robust set of features stands the game well apart from the traditional mobile cash-ins.

400 million

Number of Android devices activated worldwide, as of 7 August 2012.

SOCCER SENSATION

One-man developer Simon Read (UK) has been working on football titles for the PC since 2002. Inspired by *Footballer of the Year* (Gremlin Graphics, 1986) on the Sinclair Spectrum, he brought his addictive mix of on-pitch action and off-pitch simulation to Android devices this year – and promptly hit the big league. *New Star Soccer* (New Star Games, 2012) starts you out as a non-league player, then encourages you to grow quickly into an international superstar, dealing with the pressures of fame and wealth.

At launch, the Galaxy S III phone ran on the "Ice Cream Sandwich" version of Android, with a subsequent update to "Jelly Bean". Sweet teeth abound!

It weighs 3 g (0.10 oz) more than its predecessor, but the screen is 1.27 cm (0.5 in) bigger at 12 cm (4.8 in). The iPhone 5, by comparison, has a 10.2-cm (4-in) display.

The S III has a quad-core Cortex-A9 processor and up to 2GB RAM of memory in some versions.

The "official device" for the London 2012 Olympics, Samsung's long-anticipated sequel to the S II is a veritable powerhouse of a smartphone. Work began on the phone in late 2010, and it was launched with much fanfare in May 2012 in London, UK. During the 2012 Olympics and Paralympics, a special "contactless payment" edition sponsored by Samsung and Visa was given to British athletes such as cyclist Victoria Pendleton and wheelchair basketballer Jon Pollock.

WHAT WAS THE FIRST PHONE TO FEATURE THE ANDROID OPERATING SYSTEM?

GUINNESS WORLD RECORDS

You are cordially invited to

Gamer Weddings

Tying the knot makes a change from fragging and battling bosses.
Kevin Lynch meets the players who met their match in a game.

Desirai Labrada and John Henry from Florida, USA, met over Xbox Live while playing *Halo 2* (Bungie Studios) on its release in 2004. Fast forward to 17 January 2009 at an Orlando convention and Desirai was walking up the aisle to a rendition of the *Halo 3* (2007) menu music to be married to John by a man dressed in Master Chief's armour. Guests received a purple candle in the shape of a *Halo* plasma grenade.

Tables for Desirai and John's guests were named after game maps. After exchanging vows, the newlyweds had a bride-versus-groom *Halo* tournament in place of the first dance and their honeymoon included a visit to Bungie Studios, home of *Halo*'s developers.

Gamers have as many details to get right as any wedding planner. *Minecraft* (Mojang, 2011) fan Asia Ramirez set off her dress with a turquoise necklace shaped like the diamonds in the game while fiancé Matt Dunn wore a *Minecraft*-inspired tie. He had proposed live on stage at Minecon 2011 in Las Vegas, USA, with Mojang helping to make the surprise. Guests at their April 2012 ceremony in California, USA, encountered chickens and other in-game animals and even a cardboard version of its green Creeper enemies. The reception was distinctly blocky, with pixelated trees, squared animals and customized bottles to drink from

GROOM

BRIDE

Lovely Princess Peach would never be willingly given away by the villainous Bowser. At least, she wasn't until the day Bowser was played by the father of Super Mario fan Bobbi VanZante. "It's kind of part of the game," Bobbi explained of her 2011 marriage in Iowa, USA, for which she wore a Princess Peach wedding dress. "Bowser and all his buddies steal Princess Peach." As the couple emerged from Mario's castle, fiancé Elijah Slagter was resplendent as the famous plumber himself. Friends helped construct a setting for the wedding based on the game's landscape, building a castle and making turtle shells from bicycle helmets. Even Donkey Kong made a guest appearance as Mario rescued his bride-to-be.

Traditional ingredients of a proposal include knee-bending, eye-gazing and nervous, dry-throated stammering. But Gary Hudston (UK) dispensed with such embarrassment, turning instead to the modding community of mind-mangling puzzler *Portal 2* (Valve Corporation, 2011). He marked girlfriend Stephanie Harbeson's (USA) 21st birthday by concealing his big question in a one-off version of the game. Contributors gave their time for free and creators Valve Corporation helped out with technical work.

Gary oversaw three custom levels delivered in a straight style which led Stephanie to a chapel. On the way lasers drew a red heart on the floor and the end proposal was made by Ellen McLain (USA), voice of lovable villain GLaDOS, in front of rotating rings. "You can say 'No'. I'm sure he'll get over it ... eventually," she said. Fortunately, the answer was a resounding "Yes".

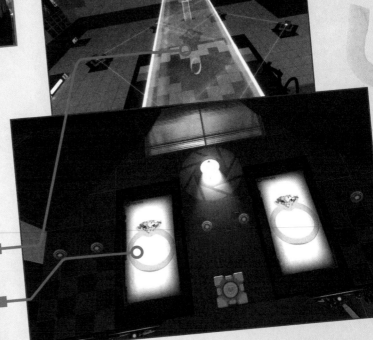

"Do you take this avatar to be your digitally wedded wife?" A Japanese Nintendo DS fan and blogger known only as Sal9000 said "Yes" in November 2009 and married Nene Anegasaki. Young, pretty and smart, student Nene was quite a catch – the catch being that she was one of three computer characters in Japan-only dating simulator *LovePlus* (Konami, 2010). The game lets players go on moonlit strolls, dance in discos and have a – sort of – conversation with a virtual love interest via a voice-recognition system.

The wedding of Sal9000 and Nene was livecast on a Japanese video site from the Tokyo Institute of Technology. In attendance were a live audience, a real priest, a master of ceremonies and the bride's in-game friend – who made a speech.

Contents

Overview

A first-person shooter – or FPS – is any videogame in which the player points, aims and fires a weapon from a first-person perspective. The most successful shooter series of all time is *Call of Duty* (see pp.46-47), with its nine main titles released between 2003 and 2012. FPS expert Will "BigTymer" Johnson (USA, see p.46) is the **highest-earning *Call of Duty* player**. Between 2009 and 2012, Will made $135,000 (£83,000) from four different *CoD* titles on the Major League Gaming Pro Circuit.

Biography

Eurogamer news editor **Wesley Yin-Poole**'s infatuation with shooters began with *GoldenEye 007* (Rare, 1997). Since then, he has feasted on almost every shooter, including all of the *Halo* (Bungie, 2001–present) games. His favourite FPS is *BioShock* (2K Boston, 2007), which inspired him to read all 1,168 pages of Ayn Rand's objectivist dystopian novel *Atlas Shrugged*.

Shooters Intro

How to spot this genre

HAS GOT:
- A "one last chance after death" perk
- Iron sights for pixel-perfect precision
- A point at which the player watches helplessly as they die in an explosion
- Either a first-person (FPS) or third-person (TPS) perspective of the protagonist

HASN'T GOT:
- A perk forcing enemies to play Phil Collins' "Against All Odds" through a boombox
- The option to negotiate with terrorists, using a *Mass Effect*-style conversation wheel
- A multiplayer mode that rewards polite players with XP

King of War

EA made inroads into *Call of Duty*'s (Activision, 2003–present) position as king of the shooters with the release of *Battlefield 3* (2011). Swedish developer DICE offers a slower style of competitive multiplayer that rewards considered team play across huge maps. In *Battlefield 3*, you're just as likely to be sniped from a mile away as you are to be obliterated by a jet fighter. The PC version of *Battlefield 3* was the most critically acclaimed FPS of 2011, with a metascore of 89% based on 61 reviews. It finished one percentage point ahead of the Xbox 360 version of *Call of Duty: Modern Warfare 3* (Infinity Ward, 2011).

Point and shoot

Since id Software's seminal *Wolfenstein 3D* (1992), shooters have been about two things: aiming a targeting reticule and pressing fire. That said, the genre has evolved considerably over the last 20 years. Powerful computing hardware has enabled developers to create realistic visuals that accurately replicate real-world warfare, with robust competitive multiplayer modes fuelled by improved internet speeds. But

FASTEST COMPLETION OF *SERIOUS SAM 2*

Aleš "Ewil" Horák (Czech Republic) and Bart "TheVoid" de Waal (Netherlands) completed *Serious Sam 2* (Croteam, 2005) in 2 hr 38 min 55 sec. The tool-assisted speed run ended on 31 July 2011 and it took the tag-team a whopping four years to perfect their levels.

FIRST FREE-TO-PLAY CONSOLE FPS

Sci-fi shooter *DUST 514* (CCP Games, 2012) is freely available to download from the PlayStation Store, although you can buy virtual items and boosters to augment the game. Microsoft, Nintendo and Sony have long resisted F2P on their hardware, preferring a more traditional model requiring players to pay upfront. But now Sony have blazed a trail that many believe signals the future of console gaming.

5,000,000
Copies of *Battlefield 3* sold in its first week on sale, according to EA.

all shooters, at a base level, work as they did when id's co-founder John Romero and lead programmer John Carmack (both USA) coined the term "death match" and established the rules of the genre that dominates gaming.

War games

One type of shooter stands head and shoulders above all others: the military FPS. Games in this sub-genre see the player assume the role of a modern soldier in a theatre of war set across multiple countries and real-world conflicts. They feature short, bombastic campaigns designed to train up the player for the main course: competitive multiplayer. It is here that these games live or die – experience points, red dot sights and perks are now essential features of the successful FPS. Games that steer from this course quickly find their servers empty.

These elements were popularized by the *Call of Duty* series, which shows no sign of relinquishing its position as the **most played shooter** (see p.46). Infinity Ward and Treyarch alternate development duties, focusing on the *Modern Warfare* and *Black Ops* series respectively. Millions play *Call of Duty* games every month on PC, Xbox Live and PlayStation Network, addicted to their fast pace and the fragging that benefits from the series' trademark smooth, 60-frames-per-second visuals.

Ops and away

Black Ops broke entertainment launch records upon its 2010 release. *Modern Warfare 3* went one better, becoming the **highest-grossing entertainment launch** (see p.47). And signs point to *Black Ops II* trumping them both in November 2012, in a genre that continues to break records.

WHICH FASCIST DICTATOR IS A BOSS IN *WOLFENSTEIN 3D*?

FASTEST COMPLETION OF *BLACK OPS*

Oliver Smith (UK), aka "TheLongshotLegend", completed *Call of Duty: Black Ops* in just 2 hr 54 min 28 sec on 26 May 2011 in Hitchin, Hertfordshire, UK. The 19-year-old played the game in the "Recruit" mode – one of four difficulty settings in the *Call of Duty* series.

FASTEST COMPLETION OF *METROID PRIME* (EUROPEAN PAL)

William "Pirate109" Tansley (UK) took a mere 1 hr 7 min to complete *Metroid Prime* (Retro Studios, 2002) on 29 August 2011 in Horsham, West Sussex, UK. William was playing the European PAL version of the fifth entry in the *Metroid* series and the 22-year-old gamer reckons that he made 15–20 seconds of errors during his run. William's strategy was to place bombs on the floor, switch to "morph ball mode" and use the explosion blast to jump high.

GUINNESS WORLD RECORDS™

Call of Duty

A DRAMATIC RECREATION OF LIFE AS A SOLDIER, THE SERIES THAT BEGAN WITH WORLD WAR II NOW BATTLES IN THE FUTURE

MOST PLAYED SHOOTER

As of 31 March 2012, the *Call of Duty* franchise (Infinity Ward and Treyarch, 2003–11) had approximately 40 million monthly active users, predominantly playing *Modern Warfare 1–3* (Infinity Ward, 2007–11) and *World at War* and *Black Ops* (Treyarch, 2008–10). The *CoD* community exceeds the combined real-world populations of New York, London, Tokyo, Paris and Madrid. Pictured here is the latest title in the series, *Black Ops II* (Treyarch, 2012).

LARGEST PRIZE POT FOR A *CALL OF DUTY* TOURNAMENT

An incredible $1 million (£618,000) prize pool was up for grabs at the *Call of Duty* XP tournament in 2011. The final of *Modern Warfare 3* was held in front of thousands of fans on 3 September 2011 in Los Angeles, USA. OpTic (USA) won with the team pictured above: Blake "Vengeance" Campbell, Joe "Merk" Deluca, Will "BigTymer" Johnson and Matt "NaDeSHoT" Haag. They defeated Infinity (UK) to claim the $400,000 (£250,000) first prize. After picking up their prize, an OpTic team member said, "No college debt – that's how I feel, baby!"

FLASH ◀◀ BACK

The first *Call of Duty* game was launched in 2003 and was developed by Infinity Ward for publisher Activision. *Call of Duty*, which used a modified version of gaming engine id Tech 3, was set during World War II and was Activision's answer to EA's popular *Medal of Honor* series.

LARGEST GAMING LAWSUIT

Former Infinity Ward executives Jason West and Vince Zampella (both USA, shown above) sued Activision over royalties and bonuses totalling $1 billion (£646.8 million) in March 2010. Activision countersued but the two sides settled out of court in late May 2012 in an undisclosed agreement.

DEAD OPS ARCADE

Find your way to a hidden twin-stick top-down shooter in *Call of Duty: Black Ops* (Treyarch, 2010). Hit the triggers alternately and quickly to break free from the torture chair in the main menu, find the keyboard on the computer against the wall, interact with it and type **3ARC UNLOCK**.

POWER UP!

HIGHEST-GROSSING ENTERTAINMENT LAUNCH

Within 24 hours of its launch on 8 November 2011, *Call of Duty: Modern Warfare 3* (Infinity Ward/Sledgehammer Games, 2011) had sold 6.5 million copies in the USA and UK. The record sales generated $400 million (£250 million), according to the game's publisher, Activision. After five days, it had grossed $775 million (£482.2 million) and within 16 days it was the **fastest entertainment property to gross $1 billion** (£641.6 million), beating the previous 17-day record set by *Avatar* (USA, 2009), the 3D movie by James Cameron.

FASTEST COMPLETION OF "STAY SHARP"

"Stay Sharp" is a challenge mode in *Call of Duty: Modern Warfare 3*. On 17 December 2011, Ibrahim Agil (USA) completed it in a record 18.5 seconds in Santa Rosa, California, USA.

GAME OVER

It nearly was "game over" for a 13-year-old *Black Ops* fan from Devon (UK) who was attacked in real life by a rival gamer in September 2011. The boy had "killed" his grown-up adversary in the online game, and then taunted him about it. The boy suffered no serious injuries and the man later admitted a charge of assault.

BEST-SELLING SHOOTER

According to VGChartz, *Call of Duty: Modern Warfare 3* has sold a phenomenal 28.25 million units, as of July 2012 – most of them (14.26 million) on the Xbox 360. This puts it fractionally ahead of *Black Ops*, which has shifted 27.74 million.

Modern Warfare 3's critical response is not quite as impressive. Across all platforms, it scored a Metacritic average of 81% – behind predecessors *Modern Warfare 2* on 91% and *Modern Warfare* on 88%, as of July 2012.

Henry "Black" Blackburn VS John "Soap" MacTavish
Battlefield 3 — *Call of Duty*

Rank	Attribute	Rank
8	Experience	7
7	Keeping it real	8
9	Number of weapons	5
8	Weaponry configurations	7
9	Hardness	10
5	Charitable work	4
6	Sniper ability	8
9	Rank	10
61		59

ONE UP

Ten million users have so far signed up to ELITE, Activision's *Call of Duty* subscription service. This allows players to track their progress and access extra social-networking features connected to the game.

With three titles in the top 10 highest-grossing games of all time, and total series sales of 134 million, *Call of Duty* is the only entertainment franchise to set opening-day records for three years running. Sales in the series exceed the worldwide theatrical box office figures for the *Star Wars* and *Lord of the Rings* movies, two of the most successful entertainment franchises of all time.

KEVIN McKIDD, THE UK ACTOR WHO PLAYED TOMMY IN *TRAINSPOTTING* (UK, 1996) AND OWEN HUNT IN *GREY'S ANATOMY* (USA, 2005–12), VOICED WHICH CHARACTER IN *CALL OF DUTY*?

GUINNESS WORLD RECORDS

Counter-Strike

TERRORISTS KILL COUNTER-TERRORISTS IN PERHAPS THE MOST PIXEL-PERFECT FPS EVER TO GRACE THE PC

100,000
As of July 2012, the number of invites issued to beta players of *Counter-Strike: Global Offensive* (Valve).

MOST UPDATED FIRST-PERSON SHOOTER
Counter-Strike: Source (2004) has been modified an amazing 450 times since 13 August 2004. Developer Valve is able to make small updates to the game through its digital distribution platform Steam. It has done so regularly ever since the game was first released. Even with *Counter-Strike: Global Offensive* (pictured) due in 2012, Valve has pledged to support *Source* as long as fans continue to play it.

BIGGEST DIGITAL GAME DISTRIBUTOR
Valve said it served in excess of 780 petabytes (one petabyte equals 1,000 terabytes) of data to players across the globe in 2011 through its distribution company Steam, double what they delivered in 2010. Steam manages more than 1,800 games directly.

By 6 January 2012, Steam – the company founded by *Counter-Strike* developer Valve in 2003 – could boast more than 40 million users. The release of *The Elder Scrolls V: Skyrim* (Bethesda, 2011) helped push Steam's total concurrent users peak to five million on 2 January 2012. It is estimated that Steam controls 70% of the digital distribution market for games.

MOST SUCCESSFUL *COUNTER-STRIKE* GAMER
Filip "NEo" Kubski (Poland) is the only recipient of two HLTV.org (*Half-Life* TV) "Player of the Year" awards, in 2007 and 2011. Earning 2,334 votes from the HLTV community, he also received the 2010 "Player of the Decade" award, with 61% of all players polled. He received more than double the votes of the next placed, Dennis "walle" Wallenberg (Sweden). NEo's 2011 achievements included his team finishing first at the World Cyber Games, where NEo received his second "Most Valuable Player" award of the year.

HIGHEST EARNING *COUNTER-STRIKE* TEAM

SK Gaming (Sweden) has won $686,000 (£442,000) since 1997, making it the most financially successful *Counter-Strike* team in eSports history. In the first half of 2012 alone, the team amassed more than $30,000 (£19,000). Their wins included the DreamHack summer tournament (left) in June 2011.

POWER UP!

VISIBLE ADVANTAGE

Professional *Counter-Strike* players recommend setting the visual quality as low as possible to ensure the best performance. In a *Counter-Strike* match, every frame counts and players want as clear a view of the action as possible. Fancy graphics just get in the way!

ONE UP

Of the best-known versions of the game, the original *Counter-Strike* (Valve, 1999) is often referred to as *1.6* by fans. *Counter-Strike: Source* is a complete remake using the Source engine. And *Counter-Strike: Global Offensive* will be all new again – and free to play. All three games attract professional players.

BEST-SELLING MOD FRANCHISE

Counter-Strike had sold well over 25 million units across its various versions and platforms as of July 2012. The first *Counter-Strike* (1999) sold 4.2 million copies. The game was modified from *Half-Life* (Valve, 1998) by fan developers Minh "Gooseman" Le (Canada) and Jess Cliffe (USA). In 2012, Le's *Tactical Intervention* (FIX Korea), a multiplayer first-person shooter, was beta tested on the PC. It featured drivable vehicles (out of which team-mates can lean and shoot), attack dogs, rappel ropes and hostages.

MOST PROFITABLE GAME COMPANY (PER EMPLOYEE)

Valve founder Gabe Newell (USA) states that his 300-person company is – on a per-employee basis – more profitable than Google and Apple. The company doesn't disclose figures, but based on Google's $216,600 (£138,991) profits per employee in the first nine months of 2011, Valve must have seen total profits of at least $65 million (£41 million). In March 2012, Newell was himself estimated to have a net worth of $1.5 billion (£970 million), ranking him 854th out of 1,226 global billionaires. Conservative estimates put Valve's enterprise value at more than $3 billion (£1.9 billion) and Newell himself owns more than half of the company.

Counter-Strike VS Counter-Strike

Source — *1.6*

Rank	Attribute	Rank
9	History	10
10	Graphics	7
6	Speed of play	8
9	Player height	6
8	Knife head shot	9
9	Radar	6
7	Brawl or mêlée	9
9	Tactical play	6
8	Goggles	6
75		67

Borderlands

A GOOD-LOOKING FOUR-PLAYER WITH THE FEEL OF ROLE-PLAYING GAMES – A WESTERN SHOOTER FOR THE SPACE AGE

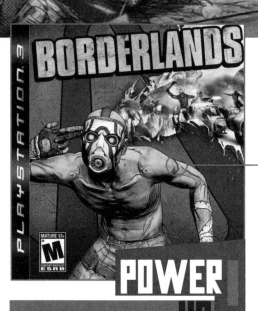

MOST GUNS IN A VIDEOGAME

Borderlands (Gearbox, 2009) features some 17,750,000 weapons, a record that will be put under pressure by *Borderlands 2* (2012), above. The sequel has a new take on the groundbreaking "procedural" system, in which the software itself creates the guns with such modifying factors as ammo type and manufacturers.

POWER UP!

FISH EGGS

Borderlands' "Fun with Barrels" Easter Egg can be found in Treacher's Landing, an island south of the Rust Commons West. It is connected to the coast via a walkway over the water. At the secret dock, shoot the barrels in the correct order and you'll see Tannis riding a fish to the accompaniment of music.

GAME OVER

A gamer called Carlo e-mailed Gearbox after his 22-year-old friend Michael John Mamaril (USA) died of cancer in October 2011. The pair had been fans of *Borderlands*, and on Carlo's request the studio recorded a special eulogy sound clip in the voice of cheeky robot mascot Claptrap. Gearbox inserted Michael into *Borderlands 2* as a non-player character.

ONE UP

Randy Pitchford (USA, above right with GWR's Gaz Deaves), co-founder of Gearbox Software, was once a magician. While a student he entertained at the Magic Castle in Hollywood. He still sometimes performs magic tricks for game journalists before interviews.

MOST ENEMY VARIANTS IN AN FPS

Borderlands 2 has more sources of potential player aggravation than any other game, with at least 300 foes to face.

Salvador VS Brick

Salvador
Borderlands 2

Brick
Borderlands 1 and 2

Rank	Attribute	Rank
7	Brute force	9
10	Number of simultaneous weapons	8
7	Fire in the hole – explosives	9
7	Brawn over brains	8
8	Local knowledge	8
7	Off-planet origins	10
8	Face only a mother could love	9
10	Unpredictability	10
64		71

FASTEST *BORDERLANDS* SPEED-RUN COMPLETION

William "Youkai" Welch (USA) completed *Borderlands* in just 2 hr 29 min 2 sec in Oregon, USA, on 24 April 2011. He played the Xbox 360 version, using the Brick character class. *Borderlands* is a particularly difficult game to speed-run, given its randomly generated weapons and the need to gain experience points.

BEST-SELLING MULTI-PLATFORM SERIES DEBUT

The games industry is not always dominated by sequels. When *Borderlands* was launched in October 2009 it was, unusually, a new franchise that became an immediate hit. Lacking the marketing clout of a single-platform launch, it still sold over half a million copies in its first month and two million copies that year. The game was Gearbox's breakout, and its success helped to convince publisher 2K Games to bankroll a sequel. As of August 2012, *Borderlands* had sold more than 4.5 million copies.

A limited edition of *Borderlands 2* costing £100 ($156) was issued in a hard-plastic scale replica of the sci-fi loot chests featured in the game. Gearbox showed off the chest being modelled by Pancake the dachshund!

ON WHICH PLANET IS THE *BORDERLANDS* SERIES SET?

GUINNESS WORLD RECORDS

Halo

THE LEGENDARY, EXPANSIVE
SCIENCE-FICTION FPS
STARRING AN ARMOURED
SPARTAN SUPER SOLDIER AND
HIS ALLURING AI COMPANION

BEST-SELLING SCI-FI SHOOTER SERIES

The *Halo* series (Bungie/343 Industries, 2001–present) has sold a total of 46.61 million units, as of 20 August 2012. The *Halo* phenomenon is expected to gather pace once more with the scheduled release of *Halo 4* (343 Industries, pictured above) in November 2012. The best-selling title in the series is *Halo 3* (Bungie, 2007), with sales of 11.57 million. *Halo 2*, meanwhile, is the **best-selling Xbox videogame ever** (as opposed to the Xbox 360), with total sales of 8.49 million. The *Halo* series' position may soon come under pressure from the *Call of Duty* franchise, which is moving into sci-fi territory for the first time with *Call of Duty: Black Ops II* (Treyarch, 2012).

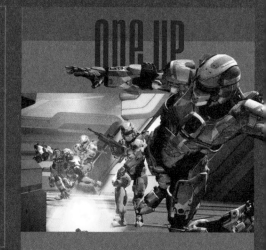

Halo 4 is the first in a new trilogy of *Halo* games planned by Microsoft-owned developer 343 Industries. *Halo 4*, *Halo 5* and *Halo 6* will collectively be known as the *Reclaimer Trilogy*. According to *Halo* lore, a Reclaimer is a person charged with activating a *Halo* super weapon and technology of the Forerunners, the ancient race that built the *Halo* rings. Microsoft have also announced that *Halo 4* will be supported by free, weekly episodes. The game's new co-op Spartan Ops mode digitally delivers episodic content – mini-missions that tell a side story of the main *Halo 4* campaign. Microsoft hope players will talk about *Halo* regularly, much like co-workers might chat about the latest TV.

FLASH « BACK

The game that became *Halo: Combat Evolved* (Bungie, 2001) was originally code-named *Monkey Nuts* and was set on a hollowed-out world. It was announced in 1999 during the Macworld Conference & Expo, and was planned as a real-time strategy game for Mac and Windows PC. Jason Jones, the project leader, changed the code-name to *Blam!* because he didn't want to have to tell his mother he was working on a project called *Monkey Nuts*. The exclamation "Blam!" is now used to censor inappropriate names in *Halo 3*.

FASTEST *HALO: REACH* COMPLETION ON "LEGENDARY" DIFFICULTY

It took Richard "RC Master" Cartwright (UK) just 2 hr 20 min 52 sec to complete series prequel *Halo: Reach* (Bungie, 2010) in Nottingham, Nottinghamshire, UK, on 27 October 2011. Richard completed the game on its hardest setting in a single segment, which he described as "the ultimate test in speed-running". He began his attempt at 7.26 a.m., having stayed up all night planning the route!

ULTIMATE KILL?

Mastering the art of "no scope sniping" will improve your effectiveness in *Halo* multiplayer. Most players zoom in while using *Halo*'s powerful sniper rifle for increased accuracy and one-hit kills from a distance. But the best players use the sniper rifle at medium distance without zooming for ultimate killing sprees. This is a sharper and more efficient sniping technique.

FIRST SHOOTER TO RUN ON TWO GAME ENGINES SIMULTANEOUSLY

Halo: Combat Evolved Anniversary (343 Industries, 2011) is a high-definition remake of the first *Halo* game, released to celebrate 10 years of the popular series. The *Anniversary* game broke the mould by being able to run across two engines at the same time. Players are able to switch – in real-time – between the original *Halo* visuals (above) and the new HD facelift (above top). The game simultaneously runs a direct port of the original *Halo* code with a new renderer layered on top.

Master Chief VS Dante

Halo — *Devil May Cry*

Rank	Attribute	Rank
10	Strength	9
10	Iron will	8
10	Weaponry	8
10	War hardiness	7
9	Costume department	7
5	Supernatural skills	9
10	Power and influence	7
3	Cheek and comedy	9
9	Potential for unleashing total carnage	8

76 — 72

Halo designers have chosen to keep concealed the face of Master Chief, aka John-117, much to some fans' frustration. In *Halo 4*, however, the designers explore the character in greater detail, examining his relationship with long-term AI companion Cortana (above), who is dying throughout the game.

HIGHEST-EARNING PROFESSIONAL *HALO* TEAM

The greatest professional *Halo* team ever is Final Boss (USA), which dominated Major League Gaming (MLG) for nearly a decade thanks to gamer Tom "Ogre2" Ryan and his now-retired twin brother Dan "Ogre1" Ryan (both USA). The team won a whopping $234,000 (£149,000) playing *Halo 3* alone, and $318,000 (£202,000) in total. Final Boss won the MLG National Championships in 2004, 2005 and 2006, earning an eight-game winning streak – the **longest winning streak in MLG history** – along the way. "Ogre2" also has the **most MLG wins in *Halo***. He has been MLG National Champion for every game in the franchise, and is the only player in MLG history to have won four National Championships. As of 20 August 2012, he has 24 tournament wins (three more than his closest competitor).

FINAL BOSS

GUINNESS WORLD RECORDS™

BioShock

THIS HIGHLY ATMOSPHERIC IMMERSIVE SHOOTER SERIES IS AS SMART AS IT IS ACTION-PACKED

HIGHEST-RATED FPS
BioShock (2K Boston, 2007) is the most critically acclaimed shooter, with a Metacritic average of 96%, as of July 2012. It was also Metacritic's 2007 game of the year, and is the ninth highest-rated videogame of all time. In addition, *BioShock* boasts an astonishing 34 perfect 100/100 Metacritic review scores.

HIGHEST-RATED FPS DEVELOPER
Irrational has an average Metacritic review score of 89% across all of its titles, as of September 2012. A total of nine Irrational games are reviewed on Metacritic, and top of the tree are the PC and Xbox 360 versions of *BioShock*. A subsidiary of 2K Games, the US-based Irrational was originally known as 2K Boston.

MOST E3 AWARDS
BioShock Infinite (Irrational Games, 2013), the third title in the *BioShock* series, scooped an amazing 75 editorial honours when it previewed at the E3 2011 trade show in Los Angeles, USA. The tally included 39 "Game of the Show" awards, among them the "Game Critics Awards' Best of Show", which is the industry's most coveted E3 gong. The "Best of Show" award is voted for by the Games Critics Awards, an umbrella organization made up of 35 North American media outlets who report on videogaming. Some of the members include newspaper *USA Today*, magazines *Wired* and *Entertainment Weekly*, and gaming websites GameSpot and 1UP. For more information on what goes on at E3, turn to page 112.

Irrational founder Ken Levine (USA) was listed in *Time* magazine's 100 most influential people in the world in 2012. The 45-year-old designer is credited by the magazine as sparking the "games as art" debate with *BioShock*. The magazine wrote, "His propensity to elevate the conversation makes the designer one of gaming's luminaries."

MOST AUDIO LOGS IN A GAME

Collectable audio logs are dictated personal diaries. They form a key part of FPS games, some of which reward gamers who manage to collect them all. The greatest number of audio logs in one game is 189, found in the underwater city of Rapture in *BioShock 2* (2K Marin, 2010), both in the main game and its *Minerva's Den* expansion pack.

Big Daddy VS Nathan Drake

BioShock — *Uncharted*

Rank	Attribute	Rank
9	Feet	6
4	"Lovable rogue" factor	9
8	Pheromones	7
9	Accessories	3
8	Weaponry	5
3	Charm	10
41		**40**

9 MILLION SALES

3 TITLES

1 TIE-IN NOVEL

D.Y.K.?

BioShock Infinite features a "1999 Mode", designed to replicate the old-school difficulty of shooters in the late 1990s. It is effectively a tougher version of the latest game in the series, in which gamers' choices have "permanent consequences".

Responding to a survey by Irrational, more than half of all *BioShock* players stated that they thought permanent decisions about their character would make the game even better.

ONE UP

Irrational launched a "Name in the Game" competition in 2011, inviting gamers to create a name to appear in *BioShock Infinite*. The contest winner was Payton Lane Easter (USA), whose fictional business "Payton Lane Easter & Sons Premium Automated Stallions" will now be immortalized. *BioShock*'s lead artists chose Mr Easter's name unanimously from over 100,000 entries.

EASTER
PAYTON LANE EASTER & SONS

POWER UP!

BOLT ON THE POOL

To succeed on the harder difficulties in *BioShock*, you need to use the environment to your advantage. For example, try using the Electro Bolt plasmid on a pool of water while enemies are standing in it. That will stun them, allowing you to finish them off with well-placed shotgun blasts.

FASTEST COMPLETION OF *BIOSHOCK*

Mirko "Cortez" Brown (Germany) completed *BioShock* in a speedy 1 hr 4 min 20 sec. The 23-year-old Mirko played the PC version of the game in 56 segments on 9 September 2008. Successful tactics he employed included "deathwarping", which tricks the game into reviving you in advanced positions after dying. Mirko found time to include a number of tricks throughout his run, and even the odd comedy blooper.

WHAT IS THE NAME OF THE BUSINESSMAN WHO BUILT THE UNDERWATER CITY OF RAPTURE?

"It's frustrating, as no one can know what the title means until they've finished playing the game."

BioShock Infinite designer Ken Levine

THE GAMING UNDEAD

Generations of consoles have come and gone, franchises have risen and fallen and genres have slipped out of fashion, but one perennial gaming truth remains: battling infection-ridden, flesh-eating, half-dead creatures is a lot of fun. We take a look at a brief history of gaming zombies over the past 30 years, and try to figure out why we still love to take on goggle-eyed beasties...

The undead serve to petrify and entertain in equal measure. From the blockbusting mother of all zombie games, *Resident Evil* (Capcom, 1996–present), to the inventive wit of *Dead Rising* (Capcom, 2006), the genre offers great variety: Nazi zombies, clown zombies, child zombies, Zamboni-wielding zombies – there's an undead antagonist for every occasion.

Zombies get everywhere. It is perhaps because they are such terrifying human objects of curiosity that they have

appeared in so many different types of game. RPG, action-adventure, shooters and even sports titles have all featured zombies over the years. UK browser-based developers Mousebreaker have a whole line of zombie sports titles, including *Match of the Dead* and *Death Penalty*, in which gamers pit their kicking wits against a hungry, undead soccer defender and goalkeeper. So beware – zombies are everywhere, and they're coming for you.

Zombie-laden videogames owe much to the seminal films of American writer-director George A Romero, whose debut title, *Night of the Living Dead* (USA, 1968), follows a group of people hiding out from a zombie horde in a farmhouse. But it is the themes and humour of *Dawn of the Dead* (USA, 1978) that have readily transferred to console games – none more so than *Dead Rising* and its 2010 sequel. Just like *Dawn of the Dead*, both these games are satirical, jumpy and set in shopping malls full of bloodthirsty creatures who trudge in and out of stores like brain-dead bargain hunters.

Here, we take a look at three of the most bizarre combo weapons that protagonist Chuck Greene (right) utilizes to defeat zombie adversaries in *Dead Rising 2*. Prepare for a zombie *mauling*...

FREEDOM BEAR & ELECTRIC CHAIR
It's double the deadly impact as Chuck takes to a heavily armed, battery-operated wheelchair, while a giant robot teddy bear has a machine gun strapped to it. This combo wipes out zombies with speed and clears a path for Chuck to move about the mall.

The realistic blood, gore and gross detail of modern-day gaming zombies is a far cry from the genre's beginnings. In 1984, Spectrum developer Sandy White (see right) was working on a follow-up to his popular ZX Spectrum title *Ant Attack* (1983), the **first isometric home computer game**. Replacing killer ants with killer zombies, Sandy created *Zombie Zombie*, the **first zombie videogame**.

That same year, *The Evil Dead* (Palace Virgin Gold, 1984), a movie tie-in game for the Commodore 64 console, was released as a free "B-side" title based on American director Sam Raimi's *Evil Dead* horror films. Capcom entered the fray in 1989 with *Sweet Home*, a Japanese zombie horror RPG for the NES. This adaptation of a Japanese horror movie was a precursor to *Resident Evil*, and signalled the beginning of Capcom's long and fruitful relationship with animated corpses.

With the arrival of fourth-generation consoles such as the Sega Mega Drive/Genesis and SNES came LucasArts' run and gun top-downer *Zombies Ate My Neighbors* (1993, released as *Zombies* in Europe and Australia). With a healthy dollop of humour – including a terrifying, gigantic, milk-bottle-squirting baby boss – this is arguably the first zombie game to replicate the sharp, black humour of classic zombie movies.

Just as *Sweet Home* paved the way for *Resident Evil*, 1994 release *Corpse Killer* (Digital Pictures), in which a Marine lands on an island populated by zombies, is reminiscent of *Dead Island* (Techland, 2011), in which a tropical paradise resort is overtaken by a zombie plague. The real turning-point in the zombie genre was *Resident Evil* in 1996 (see pp.66–67), a vivid, scary survival-horror that spawned a hugely popular series. Its success gave publishers the confidence to develop zombie games further. A year later, arcade smash *The House of the Dead* (Wow Entertainment) surfaced, and the zombie game had found a permanent and beloved place in the mainstream.

And so to the present: an abundance of not-quite-dead creatures have landed on the PS3, Wii U and Xbox 360, infecting titles such as apocalyptic FPS *Left 4 Dead* (Valve, 2008), *ZombiU* (Ubisoft, 2012), which is a reboot of Ubisoft's very first game, *Zombi* (1986), and hack and slasher *Lollipop Chainsaw* (Grasshopper Manufacture, 2012). It'll take all your gamer experience, wit and weaponry to defeat them...

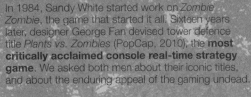

PIONEERS OF THE UNDEAD

In 1984, Sandy White started work on *Zombie Zombie*, the game that started it all. Sixteen years later, designer George Fan devised tower defence title *Plants vs. Zombies* (PopCap, 2010), the **most critically acclaimed console real-time strategy game**. We asked both men about their iconic titles, and about the enduring appeal of the gaming undead.

How did your zombie games come about?
Sandy White: I got into writing computer games through my interest in electronics when I was a kid. I built a TV tennis game from a kit, and then wanted to design my own. A few years later I borrowed an Acorn Atom computer and managed to program it to draw random cubes on to the screen. I bought a Sinclair Spectrum and converted the code over... that really was the start of *Ant Attack* [Sandy White, 1983, the **first game to allow gamers to choose between a male and a female character**]. During the development, the sprites for the ants became accidentally replaced by "boy" and "girl" sprites. The results looked uncannily like a zombie flick... *Zombie Zombie* was created.
George Fan: *Plants vs. Zombies* started out with just me and a computer. I was doing all of it at first: design, programming and concept art. It was such a different game back then! It went from fish vs. aliens to plants vs. aliens to finally *Plants vs. Zombies*; from being based in dual fish tanks to a giant crop field to the five-lane lawn setup you see today. I worked on that initial prototype for about six months until I felt I had something magical on my hands and then showed it to PopCap, who helped me form a team of talented individuals to complete the game.

Were you influenced by any zombie movies?
Sandy White: At the time, Michael Jackson's "Thriller" video was all over the place, and I'm sure that had a big influence.

Why are zombies such an enduring and popular subject of videogames?
George Fan: Zombies are the perfect videogame enemy. They naturally spawn in huge numbers, allowing for interesting combat situations, and you don't feel guilty for killing them!
Sandy White: Easy... the gore factor. They look like people, yet you can legitimately squish them any way you fancy without causing moral outrage. I feel rather sorry for the poor zombies, and am thinking of starting a society for their protection.

SPEAR LAUNCHER
As wielded here by Chuck in a fetching outfit, the Spear Launcher combines a garden leaf blower and a spear. Not only does it fire the spears, it also serves as a great device for impaling zombies and blasting them away.

PADDLESAW
Direct and to-the-point, this is a kayak paddle with two chainsaws attached to it. With the right swing technique, this popular weapon can produce a bloody, gory mess in the mall, attacking zombies to the left and to the right simultaneously.

H

YOU ARE UNDER
CLOSE SURVEIL...

ARKHAM

Overview

With a Metacritic average of 94%, *Batman: Arkham City* (Rocksteady, 2011) is the **most critically acclaimed superhero game**, and kicks off our Action-Adventure section in fine style. Typically, titles in this hybrid genre offer rich characters, vibrant worlds and consistently high excitement levels. They cast the gamer in the role of a skilled hero whose job is to overcome seemingly impossible odds and save a city or world – or even an entire galaxy.

Biography

Matt Bradford has been dazzled by videogames ever since his parents brought home an Intellivision console. Most recently, his work has appeared on gaming websites GamesRadar, Twin Galaxies and Canoe, and in the *Guinness World Records Gamer's Edition 2012*.

Action-Adventure Intro

Platinum creed

One of the leading action-adventure series is *Assassin's Creed*. Begun in 2007, Ubisoft's groundbreaking franchise is in the vein of Rocksteady's *Batman: Arkham Asylum* (2011) and Naughty Dog's *Uncharted* (2007). *Assassin's Creed II* (2009, above) is the **most completed game on PS3**, with more platinum trophy holders than any game in the history of the platform. *Assassin's Creed III* is set for release in October 2012.

Dragon's Den

From the moment gamers went toe-to-talon with the dragon Grundle in Atari 2600 classic *Adventure* (Atari, 1979, below right), the action-adventure genre has been one of the most popular and prolific in the videogame arena.

Quick thinking and fast reflexes are the ideal tools for this particular trade, as action-adventure titles typically run in real time, leaving gamers with few opportunities to rest before the next

FIRST GAME TO USE RAG DOLL PHYSICS

"Rag doll physics" is the name given to the floppy effect applied to polygonal videogame characters' deaths, generated by algorithms rather than manual programming. Based on the hit movies, *Jurassic Park: Trespasser* (DreamWorks Interactive, 1998) was the first title to introduce the "rag doll" concept to videogaming.

How to spot this genre

HAS GOT:
- Intense, real-time sequences and challenges
- Larger-than-life heroes and villains
- Hollywood-grade stories and cut-scenes

HASN'T GOT:
- Enemies who can be vanquished with hugs
- Combat that you need a scientific calculator to follow
- Either baby or pet sim names ending with the letter "Z"

fight, timed puzzle or blockbuster action sequence.

Zelda arrives

While *Adventure* is considered to be the first action-adventure game, the genre didn't attract mainstream attention until the release of *The Legend of Zelda* (Nintendo, 1986, see pp.68–69), Link's first epic for the Nintendo Entertainment System. *Zelda* combined fighting, exploration and puzzle-solving mechanics in a classic game that is still revered by fans as one of the purest examples of its kind. It cracked open the genre for other eight-bit classics such as *Metroid* (Nintendo, 1986) and *StarTropics* (Nintendo, 1990). It was also *Zelda* that laid the

groundwork for the 16-bit masterpiece sequel, *The Legend of Zelda: A Link to the Past* (Nintendo, 1991).

Polygon power

Graphic adventures such as *Beneath a Steel Sky* (Revolution Software, 1994) pushed point-and-click games into the spotlight. These back-to-basics PC/Mac games use clicks to prompt dialogue, actions and other gameplay. However,

the action-adventure genre came into its own with the arrival of 32-bit consoles. Armed with polygons and fast processors, designers took gaming one giant leap forward with classics such as *Tomb Raider* (Core Designs, 1996, see pp.64–65).

Horrifying

Meanwhile, *Resident Evil* (Capcom, 1996, see pp.66–67) popularized survival-horror, with its emphasis on

Odd couple

Steve Purcell created the characters Sam the dog and Max the rabbit in the 1980s. The dynamic duo made their debut in comics and were picked up for games by LucasArts. Purcell himself was behind the leap into computer games, and after their successful debut in *Sam & Max Hit the Road* (1993) they went on to feature in more games as well as their own TV series. Not bad for the original odd couple.

atmosphere and puzzle solving. Games such as *Thief: The Dark Project* (Looking Glass Studios, 1998, above) gave rise to the stealth genre, with a focus on strategic combat

over all-out assaults, while Rockstar's notorious *Grand Theft Auto* series (see pp.62–63) gave birth to open-world "sandbox" games in which gamers could move freely through a virtual world.

LOWEST-RATED VIDEOGAME MOVIE

It may be a legend in survival-horror gaming, but with a 1% review average on RottenTomatoes.com, the *Alone in the Dark* (USA, 2005) movie is the worst-rated videogame adaptation in cinema. It earned a paltry $5.2 million (£3 million) worldwide.

LONGEST EPISODIC GAME SERIES

Telltale Games released the Sam & Max episodic adventure series *The Devil's Playhouse* over a record 3 years 316 days. The final part of the series was "The City that Dares Not Sleep", released in August 2010.

WHAT WAS THE NAME OF THE GAMING SEQUEL TO *SAM & MAX HIT THE ROAD*?

Grand Theft Auto

MOST VIEWED TRAILER FOR AN ACTION-ADVENTURE GAME

On 2 November 2011, gamers made a mad dash to the internet to catch a first peek at Rockstar's *Grand Theft Auto V*. For 1 min 25 sec, fans were treated to a glimpse of the sequel's Los Santos setting and its mafioso lead. The trailer has accumulated 23 million views across major video-sharing sites, making it now the most watched for any action-adventure game. As of September 2012, no release date had been confirmed.

LOOT, SHOOT, STEAL OR BREAK A FEW SPEED LAWS. IN *GRAND THEFT AUTO*, THE CITY IS YOUR SANDBOX

BEST-SELLING ACTION-ADVENTURE SERIES

With more than 106 million copies of *Grand Theft Auto* games sold since its debut in 1997, the *GTA* series comfortably beats all others. As of August 2012 the latest instalment, *GTA IV* (Rockstar, 2008), has sold 19.5 million units. Regarded as the godfather of sandbox games, Rockstar's crime franchise continues to raise the bar for open-world interactivity, and for gaming controversy.

POWER UP!

HIDDEN HEART

GTA IV's largest Easter egg can be found by taking a helicopter to the uppermost platform of the Statue of Happiness and entering the door marked "No Hidden Content This Way". Once inside, you can climb up the ladder to discover a big, beating heart held in place by chains.

FLASH « BACK

Grand Theft Auto was originally pitched as a top-down (bird's-eye-view) racing game called *Race 'n' Chase*. Developed in 1995 by Scotland-based DMA Design (now Rockstar North), it was described as a "fun, addictive and fast multi-player car racing and crashing game", featuring the gameplay that would later define the *GTA* series. It was set in three real-world cities: New York, Miami and Venice.

Two-and-a-half years later, *Grand Theft Auto* was released on the PC and PlayStation. The action was relocated to fictional zones – Liberty City (based on New York), Vice City (based on Miami) and San Andreas (based on San Francisco). This version accumulated total worldwide sales of 2.32 million, and a gaming legend was well and truly born.

HIGHEST SCORE IN *GRAND THEFT AUTO IV*'s "COPS 'N CROOKS" MULTIPLAYER MODE

The "Cops 'n Crooks" mode in *GTA IV* tasks players with choosing one side of the law and either escorting or stopping a criminal VIP en route to their final destination. The highest overall individual score for ranked matches, as of 11 June 2012, is 100,726,804, set by a gamer going by the name of xlPhoeniX.

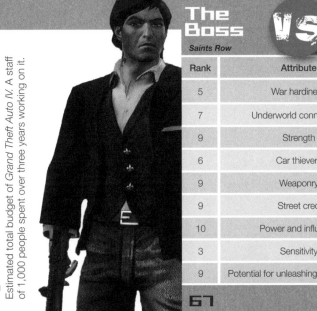

The Boss
Saints Row

VS

Niko
Grand Theft Auto

Rank	Attribute	Rank
5	War hardiness	9
7	Underworld connections	8
9	Strength	9
6	Car thievery	9
9	Weaponry	7
9	Street cred	8
10	Power and influence	7
3	Sensitivity	4
9	Potential for unleashing total carnage	8
67		**69**

$100 million

Estimated total budget of *Grand Theft Auto IV*. A staff of 1,000 people spent over three years working on it.

WHICH GTA GAME BECAME THE BEST-SELLING TITLE OF ALL TIME ON THE PLAYSTATION 2?

MOST CRITICALLY ACCLAIMED SANDBOX VIDEOGAME

Rockstar's open-world opus *Grand Theft Auto IV* reigns supreme as the highest-rated sandbox videogame. The game holds a 97% average on review site Gamerankings.com and a 98% average on Metacritic, placing it firmly at the top of its genre. It is also the second highest-rated game overall, behind *The Legend of Zelda: Ocarina of Time* (Nintendo, 1998).

ONE UP

Singer-drummer Phil Collins once took a bullet for *Grand Theft Auto* – virtually, of course. He starred in a three-mission storyline in *Grand Theft Auto: Vice City Stories* (Rockstar, 2006) for the PSP. At the game's end, Phil "performed" his 1981 hit single "In the Air Tonight".

FIRST "ADULTS ONLY" CONSOLE GAME

Grand Theft Auto: San Andreas (Rockstar, 2004) became the first console game to be rated AO ("Adults Only") on 20 July 2005, when a sexually charged mini-game called *Hot Coffee* was found buried within its code. Although *Hot Coffee* was inaccessible from the main game, its existence on the retail disc provoked North America's Entertainment Software Ratings Board (ESRB) into upgrading its original "Mature" (M) rating to AO. As a result, the game was banned by several retailers.

Tomb Raider

FROM ANCIENT CRYPTS TO LOS CITIES, THERE' NO PLAC LARA CROF WON'T GO FO ADVENTURE. OR REVENG

1996

1999

2000

2006

2008

BEST-SELLING VIDEOGAME HEROINE

With nearly 30 million copies sold worldwide over multiple console generations – from the PlayStation to the Nintendo Wii – *Tomb Raider* is the best-selling videogame series with a female lead. According to its original publisher Eidos, the first game, *Tomb Raider* (Core Designs, 1996) remains Lara Croft's most lucrative title, with nearly 8 million copies sold. Numerous accusations of sexism have been levelled at Croft's designers, although, curiously, her anatomy wasn't meant to turn out as it did. Creator Toby Gard (UK) intended to increase her chest size by 50%, but accidentally cranked up her measurements to 150% instead!

LARGEST COLLECTION OF *TOMB RAIDER* SCREENSHOTS

If you're seeking a picture of Lara Croft in action, the place to go is "Katie's *Tomb Raider* Site", a fan-run website that is home to at least 10,000 in-game screenshots. Its owner, Katie Fleming (USA), is one of North America's biggest *Tomb Raider* fans, and her short stories and films, all inspired by Lara Croft's adventures, have won her awards and acclaim from *Tomb Raider*'s creators since she started writing them in 2000.

2013

Lara VS Ezio

Lara — *Tomb Raider*

Ezio — *Assassin's Creed*

Rank	Attribute	Rank
8	Weaponry	8
7	Strength	7
6	History skills	9
9	Geography skills	6
8	Costume department	9
4	Back-up personnel	8
9	Nobility	7
8	Education	6
9	Tolerance of trauma	8
9	Athleticism	8
77		**76**

Developer Toby Gard (UK) was responsible for both the creation and the physical appearance of Lara Croft. While he has suggested that his employers Core Designs wanted to play up Lara's glamour, Gard has said, "Compared to the burly men shooting guns, she had a real appeal. She was mysterious and had a danger about her. This gave her a real difference to other female game characters."

FASTEST GLITCHLESS COMPLETION OF *TOMB RAIDER III*

On 28 May 2009, speedrunner Shaun "Mman" Friend (UK) put Lara Croft through her paces to set the fastest glitch-free completion of *Tomb Raider III* (Core Design, 1999), in 2 hr 4 min 10 sec. The super-fast run saw Lara travel an incredible in-game distance of 20.95 km through 19 levels, travelling from Area 51 to the Lost City of Tinnos.

FLASH BACK

Tomb Raider's leading lady was originally to be a South American explorer named Laura Cruz. Publisher Eidos, however, wanted a more "UK-friendly" moniker and backstory and therefore selected the name Lara Croft from a listing in an English telephone book.

MOST REAL-LIFE STAND-INS FOR A GAME CHARACTER

Perhaps unsurprisingly for a videogame heroine who quickly became an enormous global star, *Tomb Raider*'s Lara Croft is the character with the most official real-life stand-ins. British actress Rhona Mitra, TV presenter Nell McAndrew and UK gymnast and model Alison Carroll (pictured below) are among the 10 women hired as the official face of Lara Croft.

Although never an official model, UK celebrity Katie Price was another stand-in: along with three other models, she was brought in to promote *Tomb Raider* at the 1996 European Computer Trade Show.

RAREST ACHIEVEMENT IN *LARA CROFT AND THE GUARDIAN OF LIGHT*

The PC version of *Lara Croft and the Guardian of Light* (Crystal Dynamics, 2010) contains 12 "achievements" that can be unlocked by performing in-game challenges. By 11 June 2012, only 1.7% of players of this downloadable title had unlocked the "Tomb Raider" achievement, which requires players to hunt down all the relics, weapons and artefacts scattered throughout the game.

Lara Croft and the Guardian of Light was the first game in the series not to feature "Tomb Raider" in its title.

WHICH HOLLYWOOD STAR PLAYED LARA CROFT IN THE *TOMB RAIDER* FILMS?

Resident Evil

THE VIRUS OUTBREAK THAT DEFINED A GENERATION OF SURVIVAL-HORROR

MOST INCORRECT 3DS GAME BOXES DISTRIBUTED

In a mistake that excited game collectors worldwide, the first print run of *Resident Evil: Revelations* (Capcom, 2012) carried a conspicuous typo on its box art, spelling the subtitle as "Revelaitons". The publisher claimed in a statement that 90,000 copies were shipped with the erroneous packaging immediately following the game's January 2012 release.

BEST-SELLING SURVIVAL-HORROR GAME

Having been narrowly beaten to the record by *Resident Evil 4* (Capcom, 2005) in last year's *Gamer's*, *Resident Evil 5* (Capcom, 2009) is now the best-selling survival-horror title. As of 30 August 2012, it had sold 7.9 million copies across all platforms. Little wonder, then, that the *Resident Evil* series also holds the record for the **best-selling survival-horror series**.

Capcom is confident that the latest release, *Resident Evil 6* (2012), will keep the franchise at the top of the genre. They anticipate shipping 7 million units in 2012 alone. Executive producer Hiroyuki Kobayashi described the new game as "dramatic horror".

POWER UP!

HERBAL REMEDY

Max out your green herb supply in *Resident Evil: The Mercenaries 3D* (Capcom, 2011) by emptying your inventory of all green herbs, locating a new one, and pressing **Y** and **A** together with the default controls to pick it up. This will confuse the game into resetting your green herb count to 300.

ONE UP

Originally launched as *Biohazard* in Japan, the landmark horror series became known as *Resident Evil* for its North American debut. Capcom made the change to avoid potential copyright battles and lawsuits with another *Biohazard* game, and a New York-based punk-metal band of the same name. Chris Kramer, Capcom's senior director of communications, said he didn't like the American title at the time, describing it as "super-cheesy".

FASTEST COMPLETION OF *RESIDENT EVIL 4*'s "ASSIGNMENT: ADA"

Gamer Robert "Sunblade" Brandl (Germany) dodged the undead in *Resident Evil 4* for the Wii to set the fastest recorded completion of "Assignment: Ada", at 5 min 48 sec. Ada, right, offers a bonus mission wherein players must evacuate an island with five samples of the Las Plagas parasite.

MOST PROLIFIC LIVE-ACTION VIDEOGAME MOVIE STAR

American actress Milla Jovovich has played the role of Alice in five *Resident Evil* films in 10 years, making her more prolific than any other videogame movie star. Her character has been transformed dramatically through the series, from an Umbrella Corporation lab rat to a fearless, mutant-slaying saviour of humanity.

MOST "CAREER XP" IN *RESIDENT EVIL: OPERATION RACCOON CITY*

As of June 2012, PlayStation 3 gamer WESKER-666 had earned the most career experience points (XP) in *Resident Evil: Operation Raccoon City* (Six-Slant Games/Capcom, 2012), with a total of 17,142,572. The game follows a crack team of zombie-busting Umbrella Corporation mercenaries.

FASTEST-SELLING SURVIVAL-HORROR GAME

Resident Evil 5 moved 1.18 million copies globally in its first two weeks on sale, beating all other survival-horrors. The sequel became one of Capcom's biggest launches ever, and the title's continued success has made it the top-selling game in the *Resident Evil* franchise.

Many of the original *Resident Evil* developers returned to work on the fifth instalment of the series, which is set in Africa and features the perennial antagonist Arnold Wesker.

WHAT IS THE NAME OF THE FIRST MUTAGENIC VIRUS DEVISED BY THE UMBRELLA CORPORATION?

USS

GUINNESS WORLD RECORDS

The Legend of Zelda

LOADED WITH ADVENTURE AND FULL OF HEART, HEROIC LINK'S JOURNEYS ARE THE STUFF OF GAMING LEGEND...

MOST PROLIFIC ACTION-ADVENTURE GAME CHARACTER

Starring in 16 official *Legend of Zelda* games, three CD-i spin-offs, and making cameo appearances in all three *Super Smash Bros.* (HAL Laboratory, 1999–2008) titles, *Super Mario RPG: Legend of the Seven Stars* (Square,1996) and *SoulCalibur II* (Project Soul, 2003), Link (pictured here in battle) is the most prolific action-adventure mascot in the genre. Nintendo's iconic Hyrulean has been collecting hearts and saving princesses across every Nintendo platform since his debut in 1986.

MOST CRITICALLY ACCLAIMED VIDEOGAME

Nintendo 64 classic *The Legend of Zelda: Ocarina of Time* (Nintendo EAD, 1998) holds the honour of being the highest-rated game ever, with a Gamerankings.com review average of 97.48% and an extraordinary Metacritic score of 99%. Link's debut for the 64-bit system is also the **best-selling action-adventure game on a Nintendo platform**, with over 7.6 million copies sold on Nintendo consoles worldwide, as of 30 August 2012. It was remade for the Nintendo 3DS in 2011 and has sold an impressive 2.7 million units, holding a Metacritic score of 94%.

LARGEST BEAD SPRITE

Kevin Gillespie (USA) decided to show his appreciation for *The Legend of Zelda* by creating an exact, pixel-by-pixel replica of the title screen from the NES classic, using 57,344 tiny perler beads. The finished sprite measures some 1.25 m (4 ft 1 in) across and, according to Gillespie, weighs 2.3 kg (5 lb).

FASTEST COMPLETION OF *THE LEGEND OF ZELDA: A LINK TO THE PAST*

On 5 June 2003, Rodrigo Lopes (Brazil) sped through Hyrule's Light and Dark World dungeons to finish Link's 16-bit outing in 1 hr 36 min 43 sec. *A Link to the Past* (Nintendo EAD, 1991) features the villain Agahnim (right) and was the first *Zelda* game for the Super Nintendo Entertainment System (SNES), and the third instalment in the *Zelda* series.

HIGHEST LEVEL SCORE IN *LINK'S CROSSBOW TRAINING*

Using steady aim and razor-sharp reflexes, hunter "ribasalp" (Brazil) earned 725,977 points in Level 3 of *Link's Crossbow Training* (Nintendo EAD, 2007) for the Nintendo Wii, setting the top cumulative level score for the motion-controlled action game. *Crossbow Training* utilizes the Wii Zapper, a gun peripheral, and has sold 4.95 million units worldwide as of 30 August 2012.

Legend of Zelda creator Shigeru Miyamoto named the titular princess after the writer Zelda Fitzgerald, wife of celebrated American novelist F Scott Fitzgerald. In a 2006 interview with videogames expert Todd Mowatt, the Nintendo legend explained: "She was a famous and beautiful woman from all accounts, and I liked the sound of her name."

RAREST *LEGEND OF ZELDA* GAME

If you've never played *BS Zelda no Densetsu* (Nintendo, 1995), you likely never will. Developed for the BS-X Satellaview console in Japan (BS-X), it could only be played during weekly satellite "broadcasts", which started in August 1995. The total number of subscribers to the BS-X service peaked at 116,378 in March 1997.

FLASH «BACK

Link starred in three games for the Philips CD-i console: *Link: The Faces of Evil* (Animation Magic, 1993), *Zelda: The Wand of Gamelon* (Animation Magic, 1993) and *Zelda's Adventure* (Viridis, 1994). The CD-i, an "interactive multimedia CD player", only sold 570,000 units and was discontinued by manufacturer Philips in 1998.

Samus VS Link		
Metroid		*The Legend of Zelda*

Rank	Attribute	Rank
8	Strength	7
9	Hair	9
6	Life longevity	8
9	Intelligence	7
9	Agility	8
9	Power of outfit	5
3	Sword skills	10
7	Hero status	9
9	Weaponry	9
10	Puzzle-solving	8
79		80

Uncharted

SECRET SOCIETIES, HISTORICAL MYSTERIES AND LONG-LOST TREASURES ARE ALL IN A DAY'S WORK FOR NATHAN DRAKE

ONE UP

Nathan Drake takes inspiration from real-life explorers and swashbucklers. Above is T E Lawrence, whose early-20th-century Middle East exploits were noted in *Uncharted 3: Drake's Deception* (Naughty Dog, 2011). "Lawrence of Arabia" is not alone: *Drake's Fortune* (Naughty Dog, 2007) follows the trail of 16th-century navigator Sir Francis Drake, while *Among Thieves* (Naughty Dog, 2009) references the 14th-century Venetian merchant Marco Polo.

WOW

One of the must-have titles for the launch of the PlayStation Vita in 2011, *Golden Abyss* (SCE Bend Studio) is a showcase for the power of the newest hand-held. The gameplay makes use of the touchscreen, rear touch pad and gyrometer, but the real draw is the SGX543MP4+ graphics unit, which allows more than 260,000 polygons to be animated in every frame of play. The results are crisp, clear graphics, the likes of which have never been seen on hand-held consoles before.

FIRST PS3 GAME TO OFFER A PLATINUM TROPHY

In July 2008, Sony added trophy support to its PlayStation Network, allowing PS3 gamers to earn virtual mementos for their in-game achievements. On 4 August 2008, developer Naughty Dog patched their *Uncharted: Drake's Fortune* (2007) to make it the first retail game to offer a platinum trophy – the rarest of its kind, and awarded for obtaining all bronze, silver and gold trophies in an individual game. Every subsequent PS3 retail release has included this feature.

> "Drake is a thief... a good-natured scoundrel in the same vein as Han Solo or Indiana Jones – those great Harrison Ford roles."
> – Justin Richmond, game director, *Uncharted 3*

EAGLE-EYED PLAYERS CAN FIND "THE STRANGE RELIC" IN EVERY UNCHARTED GAME. THESE EASTER EGGS ARE A REFERENCE TO THE ORBS IN WHICH FRANCHISE OF GAMES CREATED IN 2001 BY NAUGHTY DOG?

BEST-SELLING PLAYSTATION VITA GAME

When Sony needed a star for its PS Vita launch, it was *Uncharted: Golden Abyss* to the rescue. Developed under the watchful eye of creators Naughty Dog, the spin-off debuted with the PS Vita in Japan on 17 December 2011. As of August 2012, this fourth entry in the *Uncharted* saga had sold 580,000 copies worldwide, firmly cementing Nathan Drake as PS Vita's leading man.

LARGEST PS3 BETA

By the time the last shot was fired in the PlayStation Network multiplayer beta of *Uncharted 3: Drake's Deception*, some 1.53 million unique users had taken part in the trial. From 28 June to 14 July 2011, more than 22 million matches were played, racking up an amazing 362 years of game time.

FASTEST-SELLING PS3 NARRATIVE ADVENTURE

In its first two weeks of release in November 2011, *Uncharted 3:* *Drake's Deception* sold more than 1.7 million copies. The epic sequel debuted in Europe, where it was supported by Sony UK's largest marketing campaign to date – estimated at £5 million ($7.82 million).

MOST CASH EARNED IN *DRAKE'S DECEPTION* MULTIPLAYER

PlayStation 3 gamer Saian24 (France) is the richest in *Uncharted 3: Drake's Deception*'s multiplayer universe, earning a virtual total of $208,796,551 (£166,086,000) online by June 2012. Cash is awarded after every multiplayer match and can be used to buy advantages in the game.

Nathan Drake *Uncharted*	VS	Prince of Persia *Prince of Persia*
Rank	**Attribute**	**Rank**
10	Climbing skills	9
9	Useful friends	7
8	Troves of treasure	9
4	Time-lord control	9
7	Self-reliance	8
9	Indiana Jones ability	6
9	Traveller class	7
56		**55**

HIGHEST TOTAL SCORE IN *UNCHARTED 3: FORTUNE HUNTER*

Uncharted 3: Fortune Hunter is a promotional third-person action game found within Sony's PlayStation Home online environment. It challenges visitors to rack up points in a deadly obstacle course inspired by *Uncharted 3*'s Yemen multiplayer map. As of June 2012, the top cumulative score for all levels was 563,675. It was set by PS Home resident KINGSNOOPY26.

GUINNESS WORLD RECORDS

KICKSTARTER

Crowd-funding is a new way for games developers to raise money for their projects by tapping the pocket power of thousands of fans online. It's already resulted in some multi-million-dollar games being greenlit. One of the largest websites promoting this alternative to the corporate misery of begging "the man" for money is Kickstarter.com, where high-profile projects *Double Fine Adventure* and *Wasteland 2* attracted gamers in 2012.

The route for developers is simple. Set a target figure and fix a deadline to amass the pledges. In return, backers of successful ideas – movies, comics, albums and theatrical productions as well as games – receive rewards according to their generosity, with the goodies often including one of the finished products.

Pledgers are not charged until the target figure is reached. So be warned, aspiring games makers: miss the deadline and you get nothing.

DOUBLE FINE ADVENTURE

Veteran American videogame designer Tim Schafer (USA) is shown left, with Double Fine Productions game producer Greg Rice. Schafer was finding it hard to interest publishers in his brand of point 'n' click adventure, so he launched *Double Fine Adventure* through Kickstarter, with in-game artwork (below) among his pledge

rewards. The results were astonishing.

As the man behind *Grim Fandango* (LucasArts, 1998) and *Day of the Tentacle* (LucasArts, 1993), Tim Schafer was already well-known, but even such an established star found Kickstarter an attractive alternative to realize his gaming vision.

He also asked film-makers 2 Player Productions to film the production progress, with Kickstarter funding both projects. Double Fine opened for Kickstarter pledges on 8 February 2012 and was due to close on 13 March, yet backers met Schafer's target of $300,000 (£192,000) for the game and $100,000 (£64,000) for the documentary in a matter of hours.

Double Fine Adventure was Kickstarter's second multi-million-dollar project, with pledges of $3,336,372 (£2,127,420) from 87,142 investors, more than eight times their goal. It was the **most money raised for a crowd-funded videogame**.

THE *DOUBLE FINE* EFFECT

In the month before *Double Fine Adventure*, the Videogames category averaged 629 pledges per week, according to Kickstarter. After the launch this figure rose to an average of 9,755 per week, excluding those made to *Double Fine Adventure* itself. The game bought in more than 60,000 first-time backers to Kickstarter.

WASTELAND 2

Brian Fargo (USA) of inXile Entertainment turned to Kickstarter to fund the sequel to his influential 1988 RPG *Wasteland* (Interplay Productions). Frustrated by his experience of mainstream publishers and inspired by the success of *Double Fine Adventure*, Fargo first sounded out fan forums before the inXile team set the goal of $900,000 (£574,000). Fargo himself vowed to put in an extra $100,000 (£63,300). By the deadline of 17 April 2012, they had raised $2,933,252 (£1,870,370) from 61,290 backers. Fargo pledged to invest 5% of profits from the game into other Kickstarter schemes.

MYTHIC

Not all Kickstarter projects have had positive results. In April 2012, Little Monster Productions launched a project called *Mythic*. They promised an "action/strategy-based RPG brought to you by the same team that left Activision/Blizzard" in a pitch with images purporting to be concept art. But web-savvy gamers soon discovered that the images came from other websites and crowd-funding turned to crowd-exposure via social websites Reddit, SomethingAwful.com and RockPaperShotgun.com. The project was withdrawn before deadline with pledges of just $4,739 (£3,021). Little Monster insist their project was legitimate. With enthusiasm for Kickstarter high, however, it is almost inevitable that scammers will try to take advantage of the goodwill of backers.

MYTHIC: The Story Of Gods And Men (Canceled)
A Video Games project in Hollywood, CA by Little Monster Productions (deleted) · send message

83
BACKERS
$4,739
PLEDGED OF $80,000 GOAL

FUNDING CANCELED
Funding for this project was canceled by the project creator on April 28.

PLEDGE $5 OR MORE
0 BACKERS
An exclusive desktop WALLPAPER for your PC, Mac, tablet or mobile device, along with our heartfelt thanks. Choose with or without the logo. Be a part of the revolution! BONUS... will also receive an air high five from random member of our team! ;-)
Estimated Delivery: Jun 2012

PLEDGE $10 OR MORE
37 BACKERS
A copy of MYTHIC, along with all the big

ABOUT THIS PROJECT

OUYA CONSOLE

Hardware projects have also been kickstarted. Ouya was a new, open-source console that was set at $950,000 (£606,000) but closed on 9 August 2012 with more than $8.5 million (£5.8 million) pledged – the **most money pledged for a Kickstarter gaming project**.

FUNDING THE FUTURE

The question for gamers remains how much enthusiasm Kickstarter will be able to sustain with developers in the longer term, especially for newer studios. In a recent interview for Forbes.com, Tim Schafer revealed his own secret for success: "Backing the project is part of the entertainment itself – *'I'm taking part in something that feels like an event.'*… I think this can continue if people can make sure each Kickstarter feels special." The message is that game-makers need to keep on coming up with compelling ideas and fun ways to back them through Kickstarter or other sources of crowd-funding.

Casual Gaming

Contents

4

Overview

Casual games are all about simple, fun gameplay that doesn't take long to learn – whether you're playing in short bursts or long sessions, there's something here for everyone. Elizabeth "Kitty McScratch" Bolinger (USA), seen here in four different dance poses, is the **most prolific dancing game high scorer**. She achieved this by topping the boogie leaderboard for more than 85 different songs on *Dance Central*, *Just Dance* and *Just Dance 2*.

Biography

Ellie Gibson describes herself as a hardcore casual gamer. She is a big fan of everything from *Diner Dash* (GameLab, 2003) to *Draw Something* (Omgpop, 2012), and has spent more hours matching similarly coloured objects into groups of three than she cares to count. She is also a recovering *FarmVille* addict.

Power to the people

Casual games are designed to appeal to a mass audience. They tend to work on basic principles and have simple control systems.

They are built around the idea of "pick up and play", which means they are usually games players can enjoy in short bursts, without having to finish a tutorial. You

MOST DOWNLOADED MOBILE GAME SERIES

Angry Birds (Rovio, 2009) celebrated its second birthday in December 2011 with *Birdday Party*. The series passed the 1 billion download mark early in 2012 – that's a copy for every one in seven people on the planet. Rovio had made 51 games before *Angry Birds* hit, but it wouldn't have a long wait for another successful title. *Angry Birds Space* (Rovio, 2012) raced to 100 million downloads in 76 days, becoming the **fastest-selling smartphone game** of all time.

HIGHEST SCORE ON *JET BOAT BARNEY*

Jet Boat Barney, a flash game developed for the iconic UK TV series *Blue Peter*, was played at the first Games Britannia expo in Sheffield, UK. On 5 July 2012, 11-year-old Dan Ingoldsby set a record with a 1,619-metre jump in a final on stage watched by his classmates and teachers.

How to spot this genre

HAS GOT:
• Cute, colourful graphics
• Fun ways to interact with friends
• A fool-proof control system

HASN'T GOT:
• A high price tag
• Complex button inputs to produce combos
• Guns

PAC-Man

With its simple and colourful mechanics, it has been said that *PAC-Man* (Namco, 1980) inspired the casual genre. It still attracts record-breakers – on 30 January 2012, Brice Tugbenyoh (USA) racked up 491,020 points, the **highest score on *PAC-Man Championship Edition DX*** (Namco Bandai Games, 2010).

don't need a lot of gaming experience or advanced skills to play most casual titles.

These games have been around a long time, but it's only in recent years that the genre has taken off. This was partly down to new hardware such as the Nintendo Wii and DS. Now gamers can flick their wrist as if holding a real tennis racket or draw on a screen with a stylus.

Net appeal

The growth of the internet also gave the genre a boost, especially with people who might never own a console or pick up a joypad. Then came blockbuster social gaming titles such as *FarmVille* (Zynga, 2009, see pp.84–85) and *Words with Friends* (Newtoy, 2009, see pp.78–79). But it was the arrival of the iPad, iPhone and other mobile gaming platforms that really caused an explosion in the number of casual titles being created and played.

Casual gaming has come of age in the last few years. Niklas Hed (Finland) of Rovio had his "eureka!" moment when he saw his mother burn the Christmas turkey, distracted by the pre-production version of *Angry Birds*. "She doesn't play any games. I realized: this is it."

Just let it shine

LONGEST KARAOKE VIDEOGAME MARATHON
Karaoke king Julian Hill (UK, above) showed off his impressive vocal talents and spectacular stamina by playing *SingStar* (London Studio, 2007) for an astonishing 24 hr 21 min in support of Great Ormond Street Hospital, a children's hospital in London, UK, on 13–14 April 2012. Julian livestreamed the entire attempt, taking requests from internet users for songs to perform in exchange for donations to the charity.

HIGHEST *BEJEWELED BLITZ* SCORE
Games instantly playable in a browser, such as *Bejeweled* (PopCap, 2001), popularized casual gaming. On 6 August 2011, Lee Chen Wei (Singapore) set a *Bejeweled Blitz* (PopCap, 2010) score of 804,200 points.

MOST *CUT THE ROPE* NO.1 SPOTS
Cut the Rope (2010) has been downloaded more than 100 million times and developers ZeptoLab claim that 30 million people play the game every month. The most prolific high scorer on the iPhone leaderboards is "Purple Dream". As of June 2012, he held four out of a possible 11 No.1 spots, on the Tool Box, Cosmic Box, Magic Box and Valentine Box boards.

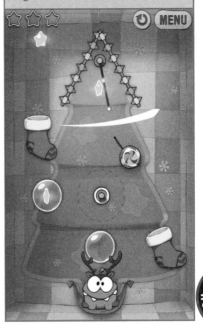

WHAT IS THE NAME OF THE 2011 SEQUEL TO *CUT THE ROPE*?

Games with Friends

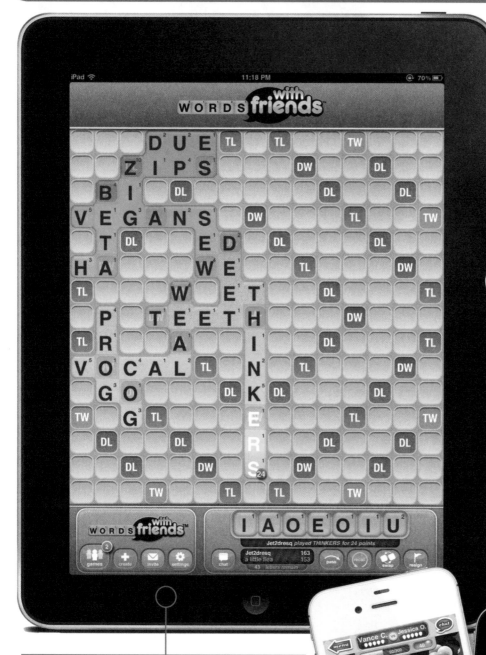

WHETHER YOU'RE A CHESS MASTER OR A WORD WIZARD, IT'S ALWAYS MORE FUN TO PLAY WITH FRIENDS

MOST POPULAR ONLINE WORD GAME

Words with Friends (Newtoy, 2009) was being played by a record 15 million people every month as of 13 August 2012. *Scramble with Friends* (Zynga with Friends, 2012) was in second place with 5 million monthly users, while the figure for *Hanging with Friends* (Zynga with Friends, 2011) stood at 2 million. *Words with Friends* was the sixth most recommended game of any kind by Facebook users in 2011.

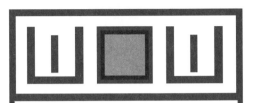

Words with Friends features a random opponent option, which can result in a long-term friendship or even romance. That's what happened to Stephen Monahan and Britney Hilbun from Texas, USA, who fell in love after being drawn by the game. Stephen went on to propose, using his own version of the board to spell out "Britney, will you marry me?" and the letters "I-L-U-V-Y-O-U".

MOST VIEWED ONLINE WORD GAME VIDEO

"Scramble with Friends Match (2700 points, 1 Round)" was uploaded by YouTube user thedotnetkid on 3 April 2012. By 19 September of the same year, it had been watched 307,764 times. The video shows thedotnetkid racking up an amazing 2,740 points in a single round.

40%

Words with Friends players who would date someone they met playing the game, according to a survey by Zynga.

D.Y.K.?

Newtoy, the developer later acquired by Zynga, was set up by brothers Paul and David Bettner in 2008. They had previously been working at Ensemble Studios on *Halo Wars* (2009) and left after Microsoft said it planned to shut down the studio once the game was complete. The brothers didn't even have an office to begin with – they wrote *Chess with Friends* in their local library in McKinney, Texas, USA. When American singer-songwriter John Mayer tweeted "*Words with Friends* is the new Twitter" in October 2009, the game went viral among his millions of followers.

FIRST ASYNCHRONOUS IOS GAME

Newtoy, the original developer of the *...with Friends* series, released its first game in November 2008. *Chess with Friends* was the first to allow players to compete against each other without being online at the same time – asynchronous play. The feature paved the way for *Words with Friends* and *Draw Something*. But the original is still popular. As of August 2012, more than 300,000 people were still playing the game on Facebook every month.

MOST REVIEWED WORD GAME

Words with Friends has been reviewed an incredible 1,425,842 times on the Google Play and iOS app stores, earning an average rating of four-and-a-half stars and four stars respectively.

ONE UP

Serious *Words with Friends* players learn all the valid two-letter words. There are more than you think and they can be worth a lot of points. Plus, they give your opponent fewer options. Here are some to start you off: FI, KA, JO, QI, XI...

Just Dance

HAPPY

FUNKY

CR

THIS TOE-TAPPING FLOOR-FILLER OF A SERIES SHOWS NO SIGN OF HANGING UP ITS DANCING SHOES

GOOD

GOOD

BEST-SELLING DANCING GAME SERIES

Boogie-game franchise *Just Dance* (Ubisoft, 2009–present) remains huge, with more than 25 million copies sold. *Just Dance 3* (Ubisoft, 2011) is the series' best-seller, with 11.42 million units shifted across all platforms. The series' popularity has been boosted by launches in Korea and Japan, where more than half a million games have been shifted. *Just Dance*'s biggest rival, *Dance Dance Revolution* (Konami), has been around since 1998, but lags behind with sales of 21.39 million.

OLDEST SONG TO FEATURE IN A DANCING GAME

Perennial Christmas favourite "Jingle Bells", which appears in *Just Dance Kids 2* (Ubisoft, 2011), was written by James Lord Pierpont (USA) in 1857 and was originally titled "One-Horse Open Sleigh". It is performed in the game by the Just Dance Kids, but has previously been covered by dozens of artists including Frank Sinatra, Louis Armstrong, Ella Fitzgerald (all USA) and The Beatles (UK). "Jingle Bells" also became the **first song played in space** when, on 16 December 1965, it was broadcast during NASA's Gemini 6A space flight.

ONE UP

Just Dance 4 (Ubisoft) was scheduled for an autumn 2012 release on the Wii U. The game features the new "Puppet Master Mode", which lets the player holding the Wii U controller choose which routines the other four players must perform. He or she can switch routines in real time, create choreographies and select playlists. The Wii U controller also allows players to write live on-screen dedications, and take snapshots and videos of dance routines to share online.

POWER UP!

WAGGLE DANCING
If you're feeling lazy but still fancy racking up the points, this is the ideal trick. Don't bother shaking your whole body when playing the Wii version of *Just Dance* – simply waggle the remote as fast as you can. You might even find that you end up with more points than you'd get by playing the game properly!

080

MOST DANCING MINUTES LOGGED

As of 6 August 2012, *Just Dance 3* players were
clocking up 23 million minutes of dance time each day,
according to Ubisoft. The game's 49 tracks include
"I Don't Feel Like Dancin'" by the Scissor Sisters.

The record for the **largest simultaneous dance
game routine** is held by *Dance Central* (Harmonix,
2010) with 10,730 participants in Paris, France, on
26 November 2011.

According to personal training website
Fitnessblender.com, an average-sized
woman in her twenties burns six calories per
minute, or 380 calories in an hour, by playing
Just Dance 2. The site calculated that if
you played the game for 90 minutes
every day, you could lose 500 g
(17.63 oz) in just one week.

FIRST GAME WITH PLAYER-CHOREOGRAPHED DANCE ROUTINES

Just Dance 3 for the Xbox 360
features a "Just Create" mode, which
allows players to video themselves
performing moves they have created
using the Kinect camera. They can
then challenge their friends to copy
their choreography and share routines
online. The mode was demonstrated
in the trailer for *Just Dance 3* by
Harry Shum, Jr. (USA), who plays star
dancer Mike Chang in the hit US musical
comedy-drama TV show *Glee*.

BEST-SELLING THIRD-PARTY Wii GAME

As of 6 August 2012, some
9.28 million copies of Ubisoft's *Just
Dance 3* had been sold for the Wii,
making it more successful than any
Wii game *not* developed and designed
by Nintendo, who produce the vast
majority of Wii titles. *Just Dance 2*
(Ubisoft, 2010) is right behind its
sequel with 9.24 million Wii copies
sold, while *Just Dance* has sold
6.78 million. Total franchise sales of
28.61 million make *Just Dance* the
best-selling third-party Wii series.

Wii.

Wi-Fi connection
Pay & Play

INCLUDES 45 NEW TRACKS SUCH AS:
S.O.S. Rihanna | Rockafeller Skank Fatboy Slim | Hot Stuff Donna Summer
The Power Snap! | When I Grow Up The Pussycat Dolls | I Got You (I Feel Good) James Brown

JUST DANCE 2
MORE TRACKS · MORE FUN

3
www.pegi.info

LICENSED BY
PAL (Nintendo)

Draw Something

A GREAT GUESSING GAME WITH AN ARTY TWIST THAT YOU CAN PLAY AGAINST FRIENDS. CAN YOU TELL WHAT IT IS YET?

FASTEST-GROWING MULTIPLAYER MOBILE GAME

In the 50 days following its launch in February 2012, Pictionary-style *Draw Something* (Omgpop, 2012) had been downloaded 50 million times, according to parent company Zynga. At peak times, players were creating more than 3,000 drawings per second. The **fastest-growing mobile game** overall, however, is *Angry Birds Space* (Rovio, 2012), released five weeks later, which reached the 50-million milestone in 35 days.

POWER UP!

ART ATTACK
To produce better *Draw Something* sketches, try putting your device on a table or any stable surface. Draw the background first and outlines last. Remember, there's no clock ticking, so take your time! If you're really serious, consider investing in a stylus for those finer details and play on an iPad with its bigger screen.

FIRST GAME TO FEATURE PLAYER-CREATED ADVERTS
Plenty of games feature advertisements, but *Draw Something* was the first to get players creating the ads. From May 2012, advertisers could buy words to insert into the choices for players. Gamers might find themselves being asked to sketch out such household names as Doritos, KFC and Nike. The National Hockey League (Canada/USA) also signed up and bought the rights to terms such as "puck" and "slap shot".

ONE UP

Dan Porter (USA), then CEO of Omgpop, said he got the idea for *Draw Something* after playing catch with his son and a friend in the park. He promised them ice-cream if they tossed the ball 100 times. "This game is like catch because we're working collaboratively together to try to achieve something."

LEAST POPULAR WORD IN *DRAW SOMETHING*
Draw Something lets you choose from a selection of words before the start of each round. The least selected word, according to Zynga, is "latrine". The most popular words are "starfish", "pregnant", "hangman", "six pack" and "boom box". The most frequently guessed are "rainbow", "catfish", "fish", "sun", "house", "god" and "tornado". The least guessed are "oar", *Metroid*", "Warhol", "pounce", "polaroid", "meathead" and "Autobots".

GAME OVER
Shay Pierce (USA) was the only Omgpop employee not to go with Zynga when they were bought out. He said that "the company's values are completely opposed to my own values, professionally and creatively", and "I can sleep soundly at night knowing that I'm not working for any employer with whom I strongly disagree." Dan Porter, CEO of Mongpop, hit back with an angry tweet, although he later apologized.

6 billion
Number of pictures created in *Draw Something*'s first six weeks.

If you like *Draw Something* try...

Max & the Magic Marker (Press Play, 2010)
Trivia Party (Lamplighter Games, 2012)
Draw a Stickman (hitcents.com, 2012)
Quarrel (Denki, 2011)
Doodle Movie Challenge (Odin's Eye, 2012)
Say What You See (Big Ideas Corporation, 2010–present)
Doodle Find (KlickTock, 2010)
Depict (Makeshift Games, 2009)
Quiz Climber Rivals (Relentless Software, 2011)
Charadium II HD (On⁵, 2011)

MOST POPULAR *DRAW SOMETHING* ARTIST
As of 27 September 2012, the most popular artist on fansite bestofdrawsomething.com was "MehlMistula", with 35,969 "likes". Among the user's subjects for their high-rating drawings was Batman. The most popular superhero subject was Ironman.

WHICH OF THESE IS NOT A ZYNGA GAME: CASTLEVILLE, CRUELLA DE VIL OR FARMVILLE?

FarmVille & CityVille

WHETHER YOU'RE A CITY
SLICKER OR A COUNTRY
BUMPKIN, THESE
SOCIAL GAMES CAN BE
GLORIOUSLY ADDICTIVE...

MOST POPULAR FARMING SIMULATOR

Online sensation *FarmVille*
(Zynga, 2009) remains the
undisputed king of farming
sims. The aim of the game is to
successfully manage and develop
your own farm by growing crops
and greenery, taking care of
livestock and trading at the in-
game market with "farm coins".
At the height of *FarmVille*'s
popularity, in the spring of 2010,
83.8 million people were playing
every month. By the summer of
2012, that figure had dropped
but was still a substantial
20.6 million.

"It's so monotonous and
yet great at the same
time. I'm obsessed."
FarmVille fan and
Hollywood star Mila Kunis

MOST POPULAR SOCIAL NETWORKING GAME

CityVille (Zynga, 2010) launched on
2 December 2010 and quickly out-
grew *FarmVille*, attracting 290,000
players on its first day. A month
later it had become the most
popular Facebook app ever, and
the biggest social network game,
with 84.2 million monthly players.

POWER UP!

CASH COTTON

Looking to earn cash quickly in
FarmVille? Fill your fields with
cotton. It costs 90 coins to plant, takes
12 hours to grow and sells for 201 coins.
That works out at 9.75 coins of profit per
hour, making cotton the most lucrative
crop in the game. The least profitable
crop is eggplant, which only makes
1.02 coins per hour.

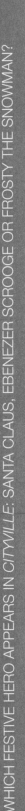

BIGGEST PETITION AGAINST A SOCIAL GAME DEVELOPER

In March 2011, Zynga launched the "English Countryside" expansion for *FarmVille*, inviting an English farmer and his sheep to London, UK, for promotional duties. The expansion enabled players to own two farms, but crops could only grow on one farm at a time, while the other remained on pause. Outraged players petitioned to keep both farms active. After 12,000 signatures, an expansion was released allowing the pause mode to be turned off.

The **biggest petition against any game developer** consisted of 60,103 signatures aimed at *Diablo III* (2012) developers Blizzard after concerns that the game was overly influenced by the *World of Warcraft* universe.

MOST PEOPLE PLAYING A CITY SIMULATOR IN 24 HOURS

The busiest day in the history of city sims was 28 February 2011, when a total of 20,297,542 people logged in to play *CityVille*. The game's busiest month was June 2011, with 71,151,588 players – equivalent to the combined populations of New York, Los Angeles and New Delhi!

Celebrity fans of the 'Ville games include *The Amazing Spider-Man* star Emma Stone (USA). Speaking on a US talk show, she admitted becoming so addicted to *FarmVille* that she ended up deleting her Facebook page! Other celebrities rumoured to enjoy the farm include Wyclef Jean and Avril Lavigne.

MOST POPULAR VIRTUAL FARMING CROP

Virtual farming is a concept that stretches back to the likes of *Sim Farm* (Maxis, 1993), but it was the internet that allowed gamers to see what everybody else was planting. According to data from Zynga, 50.4 billion White Grape crops have been planted in *FarmVille* since the game's launch in 2009, making it easily the most popular virtual plant, as of August 2012. The most popular tree is the apple tree, with more than 381 million planted.

MOST EXPENSIVE *CITYVILLE* ITEM

CityVille's costliest in-game item is the Geodesic Rainforest, at a cool 5,000,000 City Coins. City Coins are an in-game currency that are usually acquired through normal gameplay, but they can be bought in bulk for real money if the player chooses. Employing this method to purchase the Geodesic Dome would set back the player an extraordinary $3,333.33 (£2,140).

4 trillion

Number of crops harvested in *FarmVille* between June 2009 and June 2012.

In March 2012, American writer, TV presenter and "domestic goddess" Martha Stewart launched her very own kingdom within *CastleVille* (Zynga, 2011). It featured the largest building ever seen in the game, modelled after Stewart's real-life home in Bedford, New York, USA. The celebrity add-on also offered new animals, such as a Friesian horse and a black sheep.

BIGGEST SOCIAL GAME DEVELOPER

American developers Zynga remain firmly at the top of social gaming, with 259,943,459 active monthly users on Facebook alone, as of August 2012. Three new games were announced by Zynga developer Mark Skaggs in June 2012: *The Ville*, billed as Zynga's "most social game to date", allowing players to design their own homes and interact with friends; *ChefVille*, in which players can build their dream restaurant and earn real recipes as rewards; and the much-anticipated *FarmVille 2*.

Casual Cards

FROM SOLITAIRE TO SNAP, CASUAL CARD GAMES ARE A MODERN SPIN ON AN OLD TRADITION. HOW WELL CAN YOU BLUFF?

LONGEST COMPUTER CARD GAME MARATHON

Card game enthusiasts Laura Rich (UK, right) and Kathleen Henkel (USA, inset) took their passion to extremes when they both completed a 30-hour marathon on *Solitaire Blitz* (PopCap, 2012). Organized by the game's developer in aid of "charity: water", the record attempt took place on different sides of the Atlantic. Laura played in London, UK, while Kathleen was in New York City, USA, with livestream link-ups keeping the two locations connected throughout.

MOST POPULAR APP STORE CASUAL CARD GAME

As of 6 August 2012, *Texas Poker* (Kamagames, 2012) had an average rank of No.5 across nine of Apple's international App Store game charts. The title's popularity might have something to do with its accessibility – it is playable in 19 languages, including Arabic, Norwegian and Vietnamese. Model Carmen Electra is the official face of the game.

MOST PLAYED FACEBOOK GAME

With 6.8 million players logging on to play each day, *Zynga Poker* is Facebook's most popular game. The number of people playing each month stands at 34.5 million, as of 6 August 2012. Launched in July 2007 as *TexasHoldEm Poker*, it was the first game ever released by Zynga. Today it is the **largest free2play online poker game**. The real-life game is hugely popular on the international professional poker scene.

GAME WITH MOST FACEBOOK "LIKES"

Facebook's most popular game page belongs to *Texas HoldEm Poker* (Zynga, 2007). As of 6 August 2012, the number of Facebook users who had clicked "like" on the game's page stood at 64,055,254. The only page with more fans is Facebook itself! The number of hands of cards played stands at a whopping 55 million. According to the game's creators, someone hits a Royal flush – five cards of the same suit in sequence, starting with an ace – once every 15 seconds.

ONE UP

In December 2008, Capcom released a special card deck themed on *Super Street Fighter II Turbo HD Remix* (Backbone, 2008) for the Xbox version of casual card game *UNO* (Carbonated Games, 2006). It featured Sagat's stage background and level music, along with *Street Fighter* character art and move animations. Best of all, the deck included a special Hadoken card, which players could use to force each other to pick up extra cards. Hadoken is a special attack move in *Street Fighter*.

FLASH « BACK

The original Solitaire card game was first played in the mid-1700s. It became popular in English society during the late 19th century, when Queen Victoria's (UK) husband, Prince Albert (Germany), was known to be a fan. Today there are more than 100 Solitaire variations, or more than 1,000 if you include those versions which feature minor gameplay variations.

BEST-SELLING STANDALONE SOLITAIRE GAME

Solitaire Overload (Telegames, 2007) for the Nintendo DS was released on 24 October 2007. By 6 August 2012, more than 400,000 copies had been sold around the world. Billed by Nintendo as "the most comprehensive and feature-rich compilation of Solitaire games ever released for a portable gaming system," it includes 101 different versions of the game.

Options	
Foundation	Same suit
Tableau	Alternate colors
Empty tableau	Any card

Accept and restart game

Cancel | Default

Game   Preference   Options

HIGHEST TURNOVER FOR A SOCIAL GAMES DEVELOPER

The most successful developer of social games is Zynga, which made $1.14 billion (£732 million) in revenue in 2011. The company was established in San Francisco, California, USA, in July 2007. As of 6 August 2012, more than 54 million people were playing a Zynga game every day. Zynga has over 60 apps on Facebook, more than any other social gaming company. Pictured here is Zynga's general manager, Lo Toney (USA).

WELCOME TO THE WORLD'S LARGEST CASINO

zynga

OPEN ALL NIGHT

ALL YOU CAN PLAY

FEATURI... SOC...

GUINNESS WORLD RECORDS

CLOUD GAMING

Cloud gaming is part of a wider computing innovation whereby users can access the data storage and processing power of vast farms of computer servers – collectively known as "the cloud" – maintained at a variety of locations around the world. These servers hold multiple copies of their data, so if one malfunctions or falls out of action the information can be retrieved from another server elsewhere. If you have a web-based e-mail account, you are already using cloud computing – these messages are stored on remote servers and can be accessed from any internet-connected device, anywhere on the planet.

DrawSomething

You're guessing!

CLOUDS ON THE MOVE

As videogaming grows to encompass new types of games and new types of gamers, so too does the accompanying technology. A new breed of games devised specifically for mobile devices include Scrabble variant *Words with Friends* (Newtoy, 2009), and – for the more artistically minded – *Draw Something* (Omgpop, 2012; see pp.82–83). While these games are still downloaded on to a mobile device, the data they require is passed on to users via remote servers.

CLOUDING YOUR SCREENS

Who said there's never anything good on TV? A new breed of televisions made by Samsung, among others, will have cloud-based gaming as a built-in feature, which potentially gives them valuable access to the gaming market. What's more, film- and TV-streaming service Netflix uses cloud technology, as does music streamer Spotify and file-sharing site Dropbox.

"We've got an audience of 1.5 million who are coming in every month checking it out."
– Bruce Grove, head of OnLive UK

Why should we be excited by cloud gaming?
When server farms deal with all the processing power and storage, players can concentrate on the important stuff: gaming.

If a game's on the server, how do we play it?
That's the beauty of cloud gaming – a player only needs a device that is capable of displaying the visuals and amplifying the audio. It might even be a gadget you already have – a smartphone, tablet or feature-rich TV.

Who supplies these games?
Subscription services could provide a delicious all-the-titles-you-could-ever-want buffet. It's the route that cloud gaming provider OnLive appears to be pursuing and its main rival, Gaikai, could easily follow.

What's in it for the publisher?
They save on physical production costs and they have control over updates – players may not even notice games being tweaked on the server. There will also be less piracy – after all, players can't copy something to which they have no access!

Is there a catch?
Currently, yes: speed. Both OnLive and Gaikai require a minimum 2 mps connection and upwards of 5 mps to deliver the 720p HD experience most gamers expect as standard – and double that to achieve the 1080p+ HD visuals well-equipped gamers already enjoy. Everything depends on a reliable connection to the internet. Lose that and there's no game at all.

What about us high-end gamers?
For those who get their thrills from the fast-response gaming of *Call of Duty* multiplayer and other top-rank shooters, every millionth of a second is important. The greater the distance between the player and the server farm the greater the lag, though recent experiments have shown cloud gaming systems are edging closer to their console counterparts on some titles.

HIGHEST-RATED CLOUD GAMES FOR PC	
BioShock (OnLive)	96%
Mass Effect 2 (Gaikai)	94%
Batman: Arkham Asylum (OnLive)	91%
Batman: Arkham City (OnLive)	91%
Braid (OnLive)	90%
Deus Ex: Human Revolution (OnLive)	90%
Sid Meier's Civilization V (OnLive)	90%
World of Goo (OnLive)	90%
Fallout (OnLive)	89%
FIFA 12 (Gaikai)	89%

*Source: Metacritic.com.
Accurate as of 21 July 2012.*

TOP TEXT

> "You're going to see everything evol
> to that state because people want
> access to their data anywhere."
> – Scott Rohde, VP, Sony Worldwide Studios

CLOUD PROVIDERS
Apps for gamers on the go are available for both the iOS and Android-driven systems. OnLive is one of the cloud providers, though it has had a troubled year in 2012. The Sony Xperia Play is designed to be the phone that can play PSP games, and it boasts a slide-out control pad. It also supports OnLive so will suit gamers who want a mobile home-console experience.

But it's not all hardware. Flash-based games of the kind seen on Facebook are also cloud-based. Indeed, Gaikai's Facebook app shows that the company recognizes that a key strength of cloud gaming is that it doesn't need any specific hardware platform but can just follow its audience.

Overview

The fighting genre continues to enthrall and surprise with new ways to beat, brawl and bash opponents on screen. One recent addition to the canon is the downloadable *Skullgirls* (Reverge Labs, 2012). With a total of 11,515 frames used by its eight playable characters – an average of 1,439 per fighter – *Skullgirls* features the **most frames of animation per character**.

Biography

Still on a quest to play every fighting game ever released, **Dan Bendon** lives in a world of "delayed hyper combos" and "armour-breaking bread-and-butter cross-ups". Founder and editor of *Ready Up*, and living in Glasgow, Dan works closely with the Scottish fighting game community.

Fighting Games Intro

How to spot this genre

HAS GOT:
- Long-running, deep-seated character rivalries
- Online players that are better than you
- Patently evil corporations

HASN'T GOT:
- Easy-to-follow, cohesive timelines
- Healthy father/son relationships
- Slow-moving female characters

MOST SUCCESSFUL FEMALE *SOULCALIBUR* PLAYER

With 48 *SoulCalibur* podium placements since 2002, when she was just 10 years old, French gamer "Kayane" is a fighting games legend. Having featured in *Gamer's 2012* as the **most successful female *Street Fighter* player**, she has returned to her first love with the release of *SoulCalibur V* (Project Soul, 2012). Her recent tournament successes include a second place at the MLG Anaheim competition in June 2012, in the USA, where she lost to arch-rival "Keev" (France, shown with "Kayane"). The most successful male *SoulCalibur* player is a hotly contested title, and there is currently no outright record holder.

Fight Night

What began in 1976 with arcade title *Heavyweight Champ* (Sega), the **first fighting videogame**, has evolved into one of the most fast-moving and imaginative genres in gaming. Although *Heavyweight Champ*'s boxing glove controllers were a distinctive novelty, the game bears little resemblance to the modern fighter. A host of titles that followed it swiftly broke new ground in the fighting world of the 1980s and 1990s, including the **first 3D fighting game**, arcade title *Virtua Fighter* (Sega, 1992). *Virtua* spawned its own lucrative series of games which have sold at least 8 million copies, as of 14 August 2012.

Sucker punch

But the game that truly changed the fighting landscape was Capcom's *Street Fighter II* (1991), which moved from the arcade to a host of platforms in 1992, including the SNES, Mega Drive/Genesis and Game Boy. Not only was it a huge hit, swiftly becoming the **best-selling coin-operated fighting videogame**, but, more importantly, it was also the **first fighting game to use combos**, which are now considered an essential component

BEST-SELLING DOWNLOADABLE FIGHTER

Marvel vs. Capcom 2 (Capcom, 2009) was revamped for Xbox Live Arcade and the PlayStation Network, selling 1,035,000 copies as of 14 August 2012. The **best-selling fighting game** overall is the SNES version of *Street Fighter II* (Capcom, 1992), which sold 4.10 million copies. Fighting game pros made the Mad Catz Tournament Edition FightStick (above right) the **best-selling arcade stick peripheral**. It has sold 194,000 units, as of September 2012.

of combat. Combos – short for combinations – allow players to seize an advantage by stringing together their attacks.

Famous force

Fighting games have given us a host of beloved characters, as well as a style of play and persona to suit every gamer. There's the stoic focus of *Street Fighter*'s Ryu, the vicious rage burning in

God of War's Kratos and the charged-up prowess of the sultry shape-shifting witch Bayonetta.

Heavyweights

While the ambitious *DmC: Devil May Cry* (Ninja Theory) was disappointingly delayed, hugely anticipated titles released in 2012 included the ultimate crossover *Street Fighter X Tekken* (Dimps/Capcom) and the

beautifully dramatic *Dead or Alive 5* (Team Ninja). Surprise hits of the year included the technically impressive *Skullgirls* (Reverge Labs) and the genre-hopping *Persona 4 Arena* (Arc System Works). So choose your weapon wisely, be it twin pistols or cursed blades, arcade stick or controller – there is much to be learned, and many costumes to be unlocked.

FIRST FIGHTING GAME TO USE DIGITIZED SPRITES

Although *Mortal Kombat* (Midway, 1992) made it popular, arcade game *Pit-Fighter* (Atari Games, 1990) was the first fighting game to use digitized video of live actors as in-game sprites. Despite having paved the way for several other franchises, the game featured only three playable characters and a simplistic fighting engine. The very **first game to use digitized sprites** was arcade title *Journey* (Bally Midway, 1983), which featured the US rock band of the same name.

WHICH AUSTRALIAN POP STAR APPEARED IN THE LIVE-ACTION *STREET FIGHTER* FILM?

MOST CRITICALLY ACCLAIMED PORTABLE FIGHTING GAME

PSP title *Tekken 5: Dark Resurrection* (Namco, 2006), an update to the arcade version of the game, had a Metacritic score of 88% as of 14 August 2012. It features wireless multiplayer and several bonus game modes from previous *Tekken* titles. With an astonishing Metascore of 98%, the **most critically acclaimed fighting game** of all is the Dreamcast version of *SoulCalibur* (Namco, 1999).

Street Fighter

CAPCOM'S
SEMINAL 2D
FIGHTING
SERIES – A
PIONEER OF
THE GENRE

MOST DLC CHARACTERS
IN A FIGHTING GAME

The PS Vita release of *Street Fighter X
Tekken* (Capcom, 2012) featured 12
additional characters not seen on other
platforms. *Street Fighter* and *Tekken*
each provided six classic heroes from
their worlds. Shortly after release, all
12 were made available as paid-for DLC
for the home console editions of the
game. This expanded the potential cast
from an already impressive 38 characters
on the Xbox 360 and 43 on the
PlayStation 3, to 50 and 55 respectively.

POWER UP!

BEST-SELLING iOS FIGHTING GAME

Street Fighter IV (Capcom, 2010) successfully transferred the gameplay to an iOS version that sold 615,000 copies. The surprise iPhone rendering of its complex moves saw it become the **most critically acclaimed iOS fighting game** with a Metacritic score of 84%. The game used simplified move mechanics to make the most of the touch-screen controls of the iPhone. It was followed by *Street Fighter IV Volt* (Capcom, 2011), featuring more characters and an online multiplayer mode.

SHADY CHARACTER

Dudley and Guile are the two *Super Street Fighter IV* (2010) characters who have hidden taunts. Press the down button and both heavy attack buttons simultaneously. Dudley will throw a rose that interrupts his opponent's move. Guile coolly dons the mirrored aviator sunglasses that he first removes at the start of a match.

FIRST PLAYER TO SCORE 30,000 BATTLE POINTS ON *STREET FIGHTER X TEKKEN*

By June 2012, PSN user Kaz_0519 had amassed 31,017 online battle points from playing 2,824 ranked matches on the PlayStation 3 version of *Street Fighter X Tekken*. The Japan-based player used the tag-team tactics of the game to employ a devastating mix of *Street Fighter*'s amnesiac mixed martial artist Abel (left) and *Tekken*'s blood-cursed antagonist Kazuya (right). As of September 2012, the **top scorer on *Street Fighter X Tekken*** was Zet-Familia with a whopping 40,320 battle points.

Ryu		Jin Kazama
Street Fighter		Tekken
Rank	**Attribute**	**Rank**
10	Longevity	9
9	Evil alter ego	8
5	Devil gene	10
10	Practical fighting wear	6
6	Corporate sensibility	10
9	Sheer speed	9
10	Combos	8
8	Power-ups	8
8	Way with a ready quip	7
75		75

WOW

Poison was originally an antagonist in the arcade *Final Fight* (Capcom, 1989), but when the game was released outside Japan on consoles, there were concerns about players attacking a female. Unwittingly beginning a long-running fan debate, Capcom first suggested Poison might be trans-gender before replacing the character with male fighters. Poison later reappeared as a playable character in *Street Fighter X Tekken*.

WHICH TWO ORIGINAL *STREET FIGHTER* CHARACTERS DID NOT APPEAR IN THE 1994 HOLLYWOOD FILM BASED ON THE GAMES?

GUINNESS WORLD RECORDS

Dead or Alive

OFFERING DRAMATIC BATTLES AND INTERACTIVE ENVIRONMENTS, TEAM NINJA'S FIGHTER IS MORE THAN JUST A PRETTY FACE

FIRST GAME TO FEATURE A MULTI-POINT COUNTER SYSTEM

While many games have featured "counter moves", the birth of the *Dead or Alive* franchise (Team Ninja, 1996–present) heralded a new era for the concept. The first *DoA* title, released in 1996, had a counter system that allowed players to punish any attacking move by responding with one of six different inputs corresponding to high, middle and low kicks and punches. For some titles the system was simplified but it is returning to its traditional – and highly technical – form for *Dead or Alive 5* (Team Ninja, 2012, above).

FLASH ≪ BACK

In the PlayStation game *Monster Rancher* (Tecmo, 1997), gamers generate random playable monsters by inserting music CDs into the console. However, if the original *Dead or Alive* game disc is inserted, an exclusive, playable "Kasumi" monster is unlocked. Nirvana's *Nevermind* and Beck's *Mellow Gold* albums also unlock unique monster types.

FASTEST DEFEAT OF A COMPUTER OPPONENT ON *DEAD OR ALIVE 5*

Phil Joseph (UK, pictured right with *DoA* producer Yosuke Hayashi, Japan) beat some of the world's greatest *Dead or Alive* players at an exclusive pre-release event in London, UK, on 21 August 2012. He also triumphed over an AI opponent in just 10.61 seconds. Phil's choice of character was Jeet Kune Do expert Jann Lee.

MOST *DEAD OR ALIVE* TOURNAMENT TITLE WINS

Emmanuel Rodriguez (USA) hasn't taken on his moniker of "Master" lightly: the *Dead or Alive* veteran currently holds 20 first-place titles earned in both online and offline tournaments, covering nearly every game in the series. Highlights include a $10,000 (£5,100) prize for winning the Championship Gaming Invitational in 2006 on *Dead or Alive 4* (Team Ninja, 2005).

5.6 million

Total sales for the *Dead or Alive* series, as of 31 August 2012.

D.Y.K.?

Shortly after the introduction of the "Platinum Hits" list of mid-price titles on the original Xbox, *Dead or Alive 3* (Team Ninja, 2001) became the first third-party game released by the budget label. During the lifetime of the Xbox, 135 of the console's best-selling titles, including *Halo 2* (Bungie, 2004) and *Doom 3* (Vicarious Visions, 2005), were issued as Platinum Hits and sold at less than half the original retail price.

FASTEST "TIME ATTACK" COMPLETION ON *DEAD OR ALIVE 4* ("VERY HARD")

Holding the top spot across all difficulties for the *Dead or Alive 4* "Time Attack" mode on Xbox Live, Reginald "ElectrifiedMann" Wysinger has set the fastest time on the "Very Hard" setting at 1 min 54.60 sec. Playing as opera singer Helena Douglas, Reginald beat the next best time by just under 14 seconds.

FIRST SEVENTH-GENERATION FIGHTING GAME

While the Xbox 360 now has a selection of well over 60 fighting games, *Dead or Alive 4* brought the genre to the console in its infancy back in November 2005. The game has sold some 440,000 units, as of September 2012.

Ivy *SoulCalibur*	VS	Hitomi *Dead or Alive*
Rank	Attribute	Rank
9	Intelligence	7
8	Hair	6
9	Costume department	6
6	Martial arts	10
8	Strength	8
5	Milk of human kindness	9
8	Power and influence	8
8	International connections	9
61		63

WHO IS THE FINAL BOSS OF THE FIRST *DEAD OR ALIVE*?

Devil May Cry

IF YOU'RE GOING TO BE HUNTING DEMONS, BE SURE TO KEEP YOUR COOL AND DO IT IN STYLE...

BEST-SELLING MULTI-PLATFORM HACK-AND-SLASH SERIES

Selling 12.32 million copies worldwide as of July 2012, the *Devil May Cry* series (Capcom, 2001–12) is the most popular multi-platform hack-and-slasher. The game has graced several different consoles during its 11-year lifetime, including the PlayStation 2, PlayStation 3, Xbox 360 and PC. The arrival of series reboot *DmC: Devil May Cry* from award-winning UK developer Ninja Theory in 2013 will undoubtedly see protagonist Dante's demon hunting find an even larger audience.

HIGHEST-RATED HACK-AND-SLASH GAME

Sitting at No.10 in the list of most critically acclaimed PS2 games, the original *Devil May Cry* (Capcom, 2001) also has the honour of being the highest-rated hack-and-slash game overall. The title shares its 94% Metacritic score with *God of War* (SCE, 2005), but is ranked higher as it has exclusively positive metascores, while *God of War* has a mixed review scored at 60%.

Nero VS Julie

Nero *Devil May Cry* **VS** **Julie** *Lollipop Chainsaw*

Rank	Attribute	Rank
8	Costume department	6
7	Other halves	7
8	Weaponry	7
3	Cheerleading skills	9
8	Hair	7
8	Fitness	8
9	Kick-ass fighting skills	9
8	Emotion factor	6
8	Harrowing life experience	7
67		**66**

20,099 The total number of "Bloody Palace" challenge floors playable across *Devil May Cry 2, 3* and *4*.

MOST USED *DEVIL MAY CRY* WEAPON

Weapons in *Devil May Cry* are often passed down and wielded by multiple characters. The most notable of these is the Sword of Sparda, which has been used throughout the series by Dante, Vergil, Nero, Trish, Sanctus, Arkham and Sparda himself. The sword is also used by Vergil and Trish in *Ultimate Marvel vs Capcom 3* (Capcom, 2011) and by Sanada Yukimura in *Devil Kings* (Capcom, 2005).

FASTEST SINGLE-SEGMENT COMPLETION OF *DEVIL MAY CRY 4*

A single-segment run, in which the entire game is played in one sitting, is a different challenge to the luck manipulation and repetition required for segmented speed running. Matt "Alucard" Pine completed his run of *Devil May Cry 4* (Capcom, 2008) in just 1 hr 38 min 5 sec on 18 March 2008. In the run-up to the launch of the game, the marketing was focused on the new hero, Nero, with no mention of Dante being playable at all; trailers only showed him fighting against Nero. In reality, the player takes control of Dante for just under half of the game, with the pair teaming up for the game's finale.

D.Y.K.?

Best known for his work on the *Megami Tensei* series, game designer Kazuma Kaneko designed Vergil (left) and Dante's demon forms for *Devil May Cry 3*. As part of a deal between Capcom and Atlus, Dante then appeared as a character in the enhanced release of *Shin Megami Tensei: Nocturne*.

FASTEST 100% SPEED-RUN ON *DEVIL MAY CRY*

Playing the game on "Normal" difficulty, Wesley "Molotov" Corron completed *Devil May Cry* in 58 min 27 sec on 17 June 2005. The 100% completion rules required him to complete all bonus missions, unlock every weapon and upgrade, and achieve a perfect S-rank on each level.

ONE UP

In *Ultimate Marvel vs Capcom 3*, Dante and Vergil both have downloadable costumes that enable them to take on the form of their demon father Sparda during the "Devil Trigger Hyper Combo" mode. Trish's downloadable costume, meanwhile, gives her the appearance of alter-ego Gloria. Crossover fighter *Ultimate Marvel vs Capcom 3* also features Wolverine, Captain America and the Incredible Hulk.

WHICH SUCCESSFUL GAME SERIES WAS THE ORIGINAL *DEVIL MAY CRY* INTENDED TO BE A PART OF?

GUINNESS WORLD RECORDS™

CELEBRITY GAMERS EXPOSED

It might seem like their fabulous lives are spent rolling around in giant piles of cash and hanging out with the beautiful people, but the shocking truth is that celebrities are just like the rest of us: they can't put that controller down, even if it means ruining a scene, missing a gig, or screwing up in the big game. As gaming journalist **Johnny Minkley** reveals, the next time you're owning someone on Xbox Live, it might well be Lady Gaga, sat at home, dressed as half a banana.

■ MY NAME IS... DONKEY KONG

No game causes more intense rivalry at the highest level than Nintendo's classic 1981 coin-op *Donkey Kong*. It's so brutal, they even made a documentary film about it – *King of Kong* (USA, 2007). It turns out celebs take it just as seriously as hardcore gamers. Rapper Eminem is best known for slapping down enemies with words, but when comedian Will Forte bragged about his 116,500 high score to US talk-show host Conan O'Brien in 2008, Eminem hit back in 2010, posting a photo of a 465,800-point game on Twitter – this puts him in the world top 30!

■ POLITICAL PUZZLER

Between running the country and jetting off to meet fellow world leaders, you'd think the British Prime Minister would have enough on his plate already. But it turns out David Cameron followed millions of his fellow gamers by becoming hooked on puzzler *Angry Birds* (Rovio, 2009). "It is quite addictive," he admitted to the BBC in 2012. "Sometimes when you're on these long flights to Afghanistan or wherever, and you've finished your work, you need something to relax with." Cameron claims to have completed every level.

TIER 12 MAGE

NO WAYNE! ROONEY RUINED!

Manchester United and England football star Wayne Rooney is the face of EA's *FIFA* series in the UK. Unlike some cover stars who'll happily take the money without knowing a Nintendo PlayBox from a Microsoft WiiStation, Rooney really does love his games. But he was beaten 3–0 by 17-year-old Portuguese gamer Francisco Cruz, the world champion at that time, in the *FIFA 12* player tournament at FIFA's Ballon D'or event in 2012. Cruz also beat the Spanish World Cup winner Gerard Piqué!

CABIN FEVER

Oscar-nominated Hollywood star Alec Baldwin is the oldest Baldwin brother and, by all accounts, the family's "problem gamer". He began 2011 by receiving his own star on Hollywood's Walk of Fame, and ended it by getting chucked off a plane for refusing to stop playing Zynga's *Words with Friends* (2009). Asked to turn it off for take-off, Baldwin allegedly did exactly what you might expect from a megastar: flatly refused, threw a tantrum... and then tweeted about it.

WoW, IT'S MILA KUNIS!

Blizzard's MMO titan *World of Warcraft* (2004) may well be the most popular celeb game of all. Famous fans are said to include actors Macaulay Culkin, Cameron Diaz and Jessica Simpson, and even hard rocker Ozzy Osbourne. Then there's American star Mila Kunis. She told talk-show host Jimmy Kimmel that she was very good at the game, but became so obsessed that she had to quit!

THE LEGEND OF ROBIN

Naming your children is one of life's toughest tasks – unless you're a gamer, that is. Who needs John, Jill, Simon and Samantha when there's Kratos, Robotnik and Snake for boys and Birdo, Gruntilda and GLaDOS for girls? So all credit to American acting legend Robin Williams, who named his daughter after the titular princess in *The Legend of Zelda* (Nintendo,1986). Williams named his son Cody – which some gamers interpreted as a reference to Cody from the classic Capcom brawler *Final Fight* (1989).

Contents

6

Overview

Fantasy-themed massively multiplayer online role-playing games (MMORPGs) are some of the biggest online games in the world, with millions of players worldwide logging into games such as *Rift* to cross swords, seal rifts... and get hitched. On Valentine's Day 2012, the players of *Rift* (Trion Worlds, 2011) were given the chance to get married in-game for the first time. As a bonus to the nuptial celebrations, GWR was invited into the world of Telara to witness gamers tying the knot. During the course of the first day, an extraordinary 21,879 weddings took place – the **most in-game weddings in 24 hours**.

Biography

Brendan Drain is a freelance writer and editor who is hopelessly hooked on MMOs and other online games. He has written a weekly *EVE Online* column at MMO news website Massively for more than four years, and is also the CEO of Irish indie-game development studio Brain and Nerd.

MMORPGs Intro

FASTEST-SELLING MMO AT LAUNCH

As one of the most anticipated MMOs of the year, *Star Wars: The Old Republic* (BioWare, 2011) shattered MMO launch sales records worldwide. Over 1 million units were sold within its first three days on sale, from 20 to 23 December 2011. A further million copies were sold from 24 December 2011 to 24 August 2012. This makes BioWare's first foray into massively multiplayer online role-playing gaming the fastest-selling MMO or MMORPG at launch. While *World of Warcraft*'s (Blizzard Entertainment, 2004) three expansions have each secured over 2 million launch sales, the original game took six months to sell that many units.

How to spot this genre

HAS GOT:
- Grinding for XP
- Dungeons full of bad guys
- Major achievements

HASN'T GOT:
- Single-player modes
- Balanced PvP
- Polite chat channels

FIRST VIDEOGAME ART TO WIN THE EXPOSÉ GRAND MASTER AWARD

Australia's prestigious Exposé Grand Master Award is given to one artist every year for superlative digital artwork. In 2011, *Guild Wars 2* (ArenaNet, 2012) art director Daniel Dociu (Romania) became the first person to be given the award directly for videogame concept art, although other designers who have worked on videogames have won the prize in the past.

Massive steps

Massively multiplayer online role-playing games (MMORPGs) have undergone something of a revolution, evolving from their origins as a niche hobby into one of the biggest entertainment genres. The term was coined by Richard Garriott (UK), creator of the seminal *Ultima Online* (Origin Systems/EA, 1997), which is the **first MMORPG to reach 100,000 players**. The key requisite for an MMORPG title is that hundreds of players can log on to the same game world and play together. Unlike match-based multiplayer games with levels that disappear when the match ends, MMORPG worlds remain online and players can come and go as they wish.

Fantastic!

Fantasy-themed MMORPGs are some of the most popular online games, with millions of players around the globe logging on to titles such as *World of Warcraft* (Blizzard, 2004, see pp.106–107) every month to cross swords with monsters. Sci-fi MMORPGs such as *EVE Online* (CCP Games, 2003) have similarly taken the genre by storm, offering the same massive online gaming experience but

MOST ADVANCED IN-GAME FACIAL ANIMATION SYSTEM

The SOEmote system, launched in August 2012 and integrated into *EverQuest II* (Sony, 2004), uses a player's webcam to track 64 different points on the human face. It then converts the face's movements into animation inside the game, allowing players to have their real-life emotions reflected on the faces of their virtual characters. According to the developers, this makes the experience of playing in groups even more immersive.

with different settings and gameplay.

Pay to play?

Some MMORPGs still charge players a monthly subscription fee for access, such as *Darkfall* (Aventurine SA, 2009) and *Perpetuum* (Avatar Creations, 2010). Other titles, including *Star Trek Online* (Cryptic Studios, 2010), now follow the free2play model (see pp.110–111), allowing gamers to play for free, but still charging for certain extras such as mounts, costumes and "experience potions", or access to further levels.

Recent additions to the MMORPG realm include the hit fantasy titles *Rift* (Trion Worlds, 2011) – which switched from a paid-for model to allowing free access to its first 20 levels – *TERA* (Bluehole Studio, 2011), and the sci-fi MMORPG *Star Wars: The Old Republic* (BioWare, 2011), as well as *Guild Wars 2* (ArenaNet, 2012). The MMORPG market is, indeed, massive.

While MMORPGs remain the most popular type of MMOs, other genres have also utilized massively mutiplayer features, including action games, platformers, sandbox games and FPS titles such as *PlanetSide* (Sony Computer Entertainment, 2003).

MMO WITH MOST USERS

In July 2012, *RuneScape* (Jagex, 2001) reached an historic milestone as it became the first MMO to exceed 200 million user accounts. The game, set in a medieval realm, has been through many changes and updates in its 12 years. Pictured right with his GWR certificate is Jagex CEO Mark Gerhard (South Africa).

MOST BOTS BANNED IN A WEEK

Most, if not all, MMOs are plagued with "gold farmers" who use bots – software applications programmed to perform automated tasks – to collect in-game currency to be sold for cash. No developer has gone to as much effort to get rid of bots as *RuneScape* developer Jagex, which banned an astonishing 7.7 million bots in one week in October 2011. It was estimated that 98% of all bots were disabled and barred, at an average of 1.1 million each day!

World of Warcraft

ONE OF THE ALL-TIME
FAVOURITE RPGS IS STILL
QUESTING AND EXPLORING
A VIBRANT LANDSCAPE
AFTER ALL THESE YEARS

BIGGEST MMO COMMUNITY DONATION
When a catastrophic earthquake and tsunami struck
eastern Japan on 11 March 2011, the *World of
Warcraft* community raised a staggering $1.9 million
(£1.175 million) to help out. Developer Blizzard
Entertainment offered a special in-game feathered pet,
the Cenarion Hatchling, which was bought by more
than 190,000 generous players to raise money for
the Red Cross. The total surpassed the $1.1 million
(£691,000) raised by a pet called the Pandaren Monk,
created in November 2009.

A fourth *World of Warcraft* expansion, *Mists of
Pandaria* (main picture), was released in autumn 2012.

MOST LEVEL-85 CHARACTERS
Level limits are no obstruction to Erik Marzolf
(USA), who had taken 21 different characters
to the maximum level of 85 as of July 2012.
Each of his top characters is equipped
with full end-game gear that would take an
average player well over 100 hours to accrue.

While buying and selling characters is
strictly prohibited by the game's terms of
service, characters are available through
more disreputable parts of the internet for
as much as $450 (£290). A collection similar
to Erik's could be worth $9,000 (£5,800) on
the black market.

BEST-SELLING ANNUAL MMO SUBSCRIPTION

Between October 2011 and May 2012, Blizzard sold 1.2 million annual passes for *World of Warcraft*. Each came with an exclusive rideable in-game creature, access to the *Mists of Pandaria* beta and a free copy of *Diablo III* (Blizzard, 2012, see pp.148–149). Shown here are the developer's US headquarters, guarded by a 3.65-m-tall (12-ft) brass statue of an orc riding a wolf.

Death-wing VS Arthas

Cataclysm   *Wrath of the Lich King*

Rank	Attribute	Rank
5	Leading the armies of the undead	9
8	Potential to end world	4
9	Sources of power	4
9	Size	7
8	Resistance to cold	9
9	Resistance to fire	4
8	Intelligence	6
5	Swordplay	10
61		**53**

MOST BOSS KILLS IN *CATACLYSM*

DREAM Paragon, a guild of players from Finland, was the first to eliminate 14 out of a possible 55 bosses in *World of Warcraft: Cataclysm*. As with previous releases, the 2010 third expansion pack had triggered a race among guilds to kill as many bosses for the first time as possible.

FASTEST DRAGON SOUL RAID SPEED-RUN

On 12 May 2012, top *World of Warcraft* raiding guilds Stars, DREAM Paragon, Blood Legion and Exorsus competed head-to-head in a Dragon Soul speed-run raid in another great example of gamers using their expertise to raise funds – and awareness – for charities. The Stars guild (Chinese Taipei) narrowly won the contest, beating the legendary dragon boss Deathwing with a speed-run of 1 hr 11 min 36 sec. All of Stars' winnings for the competition were donated to Save the Children.

FLASH ◀◀ BACK

In classic *World of Warcraft*, the first elite monster was Hogger, a level-11 gnoll. Gamers staged Hogger raids, with dozens of level-1 characters trying to kill him through force of numbers. Players still jokingly compare difficult raid bosses to Hogger.

WHERE DOES THE FINAL BATTLE TO KILL ARTHAS TAKE PLACE IN *WRATH OF THE LICH KING* (BLIZZARD, 2008)?

EVE Online

ONE OF THE BIGGEST SCI-FI SANDBOX MMO TITLES IS NOW ENTERING ITS TENTH YEAR

BIGGEST MMO GUILD

The biggest MMO game guild is "Goonswarm Federation", the largest territorial alliance in *EVE Online* (CCP Games, 2003) with 9,283 members as of 24 August 2012. Since each game account is limited to three characters, the alliance contains at least 3,094 separate accounts. This beats *World of Warcraft*'s (Blizzard Entertainment, 2004) largest guild "Alea Iacta Est", which peaked at an estimated 5,000 characters on 2,500 separate accounts.

LONGEST-RUNNING MMO RADIO STATION

EVE Radio began as a volunteer project during *EVE Online*'s 2003 beta, and quickly became the most popular thing to listen to while playing. Following its full launch in August 2003, the station comprises a full 24/7 schedule of music, talk-shows and events. Having run for more than nine years, *EVE* Radio is the longest-running MMO radio station in the world. Across a single week, *EVE* Radio attracts 3,000 unique listeners.

Upcoming FPS MMO *DUST 514* (CCP Games, 2012) is due to become the first console shooter linked directly to a PC MMO. *DUST* players on the PlayStation 3 will fight battles on the surface of planets in the *EVE Online* universe, and *EVE* players can even lend a hand with real-time artillery strikes from orbit. Players in both games will be able to join the same organizations and conquer territory together.

3,665 Average number of ships destroyed in *EVE Online* every day, according to CCP's Research and Statistics department.

If you like EVE Online

try...

Perpetuum
(Avatar Creations, 2010)

Evochron Mercenary
(StarWraith 3D Games LLC, 2010)

FlightGear (open source, 1997)

X3: Terran Conflict (Egosoft, 2008)

Homeworld 2
(Relic Entertainment, 2003)

Black Prophecy
(Reakktor Media, 2011)

Shattered Horizon
(Futuremark Games Studio, 2009)

Star Trek Online
(Cryptic Studios, 2010)

Star Wars: The Old Republic
(BioWare, 2011)

Vendetta Online
(Guild Software, 2004)

Frontier: Elite II (GameTek, 1993)

FLASH « BACK

When *EVE Online* was launched in 2003, it attracted only 30,000 subscribers. After competing sci-fi MMORPG *Earth and Beyond* (Westwood Studios, 2002) closed its doors in September 2004, *EVE* welcomed thousands of its players. A similar boost occurred in November 2005 when *Star Wars Galaxies* (Sony, 2003) released its unpopular "New Game Enhancements" update.

MOST SOLAR SYSTEMS IN AN MMO

In March 2009, *EVE Online* broke its own record by expanding its universe from 5,431 to 7,699 solar systems. In the Apocrypha expansion, 2,498 new, hidden solar systems were added – but these can only be reached via unstable wormholes (of which there are 70 different types) that appear randomly in space and later collapse. Beware – not only do these hidden systems *not* appear on the game's own maps, but they are also home to deadly sleeper non-player characters (NPCs).

LARGEST VIDEOGAME PvP BATTLE

On 30 October 2010, a total of 3,242 *EVE Online* players from 460 different "corporations" fought for control of the LXQ2-T star system. Players experienced severe lag but, remarkably, the server didn't crash. *EVE*'s time-dilation upgrade now allows large battles to occur lag-free, but no fight has since matched LXQ2-T for sheer size. While most MMOs have very light death penalties for accidents in battle, in *EVE Online* your ship is destroyed permanently and you have to buy a new one. The most expensive confirmed ship loss in *EVE* to date is *Bjoern's Titan*, destroyed on 20 March 2011 by a Russian fleet. The value of the ship and cargo totalled 128 billion ISK, which could have bought 355 of the 30-day game time codes then worth $6,212 (£3,826). This makes it the **most expensive MMO character death.**

CAN YOU NAME TWO OF THE FOUR EMPIRES IN *EVE ONLINE*?

GUINNESS WORLD RECORDS

free2play

MMORPG WORLDS
REMAIN INCREDIBLY
POPULAR AND CAN
BE ACCESSED FOR
NOTHING

MOST MONTHLY ACTIVE USERS FOR A FREE2PLAY PUBLISHER

Korean giant Nexon is currently the biggest publisher in the free2play market with a peak total of 86.2 million monthly active players spread over 39 games. Nexon's most popular title remains 2003's *MapleStory*, which is played all over the world. The company's total revenue for 2011 was $1.12 billion (£714.51 million), the **highest revenue for a free2play publisher**.

For publishers, the revenue from free2play games comes from selling low-price add-ons such as costumes and pets.

One Up

Worldwide MMO subscriptions peaked at an estimated 22 million accounts in 2010. That number has since slowly declined as companies converted their games to free2play or hybrid business models. Others such as *Rift* (Trion Worlds, 2011) offer never-ending free trials that limit a player's character level or the areas of the game they are able to access.

MOST SUCCESSFUL MMO CROWD-FUNDING CAMPAIGN

Innovative funding services such as Kickstarter (see pp.72–73) let developers pitch game ideas not to a few rich investors but to millions of gamers. Paizo Publishing needed funding for its tech demo of free2play MMO *Pathfinder Online*. It launched a Kickstarter campaign on 9 June 2012 and raised a total of $307,843 (£196,039), making it the most successful MMO Kickstarter campaign to date. The demo will be used to secure private investment.

FIRST COUNTRY TO BAN IN-GAME SALES

In June 2012, South Korea made virtual item sales illegal. The fine for breaking this new law was set at 50 million South Korean won (£28,000; $42,000).

MOST EXPENSIVE DLC

A virtual diamond chisel costing £50,000 ($77,000) will be available in *Curiosity: What's in the Cube?*, an MMO announced in June 2012 by industry veteran Peter Molyneux. The game features only a black cube that players hit with virtual chisels, working together to find out what's inside. The cheapest upgrade is 59p (91 US cents).

World of Warcraft has been the world's biggest subscription MMO for six years, but was almost a free2play game. Blizzard wanted to support it through in-game advertising, but decided to follow *EverQuest* (Sony Online Entertainment, 1999) and charge a monthly subscription.

FIRST MAJOR FREE2PLAY MMO CONVERSION

Based on the 1970s paper-and-dice RPG, *Dungeons & Dragons Online* (Turbine, 2006) went free2play on 9 September 2009. Gamers could, however, buy certain in-game extras, or choose to take out an all-inclusive VIP subscription which unlocked everything. Turbine claimed to have added a million users within six months, and later switched over its successful MMO *Lord of the Rings Online* (2007) to the same model, tripling the game's profits in just four months. This success led other popular subscription MMOs to adopt similar free2play and hybrid models.

MOST PLAYED FREE2PLAY MMO

Between January 2001 and June 2012, *RuneScape* (Jagex) gamers have shown themselves to be more dedicated than most with a combined total of 7,392,566,991 hours spent playing the game. At least 200 million user accounts have been created in the game since it began.

GAME OVER

MapleStory Europe suffered complete economic collapse in 2011 when hackers manipulated the in-game currency, buying every item on the game's market and ruining the entire game economy overnight. Publisher Nexon EU didn't roll the server back but deleted currency from every player who had logged in that month.

WHICH TWO PEOPLE DESIGNED THE ORIGINAL 1974 ROLE-PLAYING GAME *DUNGEONS & DRAGONS?*

GAMER'S GUIDE

Gaming events don't get any bigger or better than E3 – the Electronic Entertainment Expo. This annual trade show for the videogame industry began in 1995 and has expanded each year into its present guise as a veritable candy-store of geek. It's *the* place for developers and publishers to flaunt their new creations and be inspired by their peers. GWR's own Freddie Hoff (right) and Gaz Deaves went to E3 2012 in Los Angeles to get the buzz on the newest games, console developments and groundbreaking technologies on show.

HONOUR ROLL

At E3 2012, GWR presented 10 certificates for gaming records, including the **most guns in a videogame** (*Borderlands*, with 17,750,000) and **most videogames voiced by an individual** (261 by Steve Blum). Here, GWR's Gaz Deaves is seen presenting Sony Worldwide Studios' Scott Rohde with a certificate for the **most advanced hand-held platform game**, the PS Vita's *Uncharted: Golden Abyss* (SCE Bend Studio, 2011). Read more about the game's innovative features on page 70.

CONSOLE YOURSELF
If E3 is only for industry professionals, journalists and bloggers, why should the rest of us get excited? Well, almost all those gaming magazines you read, websites you browse and rumour mills you listen to will have sourced their information from E3. This event is a glimpse of tomorrow's gaming world, and over the past 17 years, E3 has hosted the launch of the PlayStation, Xbox and the very first *Resident Evil*, among countless other newsworthy events.

QUEUE TIPS
The most popular new-release demos and presentations attract such large crowds that a great deal of time can be spent standing in line. Planning ahead is therefore crucial. An amazing 45,000 videogame workers, investor analysts, journalists and retailers from 103 countries squeezed their way into the Los Angeles Convention Center for E3 2012.

LEFT TO THEIR OWN DEVICES
Despite a plethora of internet rumours – and a lot of crossed fingers – no major new console hardware was announced at E3 2012. There were, however, a number of significant new games unveiled. These included original titles such as *The Last of Us* (Naughty Dog) and *Watch Dogs* (Ubisoft Montreal), and eagerly anticipated sequels *Call of Duty: Black Ops II* (Treyarch) and *Tomb Raider* (Crystal Dynamics).

BIG WIGS IN GAMING
Each year, game companies hire actors to pose as in-game characters. At E3 2012, some dressed in *Resident Evil* costumes, handing out flyers and warning of impending doom – and advertising the next *Resident Evil* game in the process. Others, such as these "booth babes", paraded the hall in *Tekken Tag Tournament 2* (Namco Bandai, 2012) gear and wigs.

(HEDGE)HOGGING THE LIMELIGHT
Celebrity cameos at E3 2012 included NASCAR driver Danica Patrick, pictured here with the legendary Sonic the Hedgehog. US comedian Wayne Brady and soccer legend Cobi Jones were among the notable names who took part in a charity gaming contest.

SAY HALO TO NEW GAMES
E3 offers plenty of opportunities to play samples from new games for the first time. At the 2012 event, *Halo 4* (343 Industries), *Just Dance 4* (Ubisoft, left), *Tekken Tag Tournament 2* and *Borderlands 2* (Gearbox Software) all made their debuts.

Overview

Packed full of platforms of various shapes and sizes to jump on to and over, the platform game frequently criss-crosses with other genres, such as shooters and RPGs. French designer Michel Ancel's unique, quirky platformer made a triumphant return in November 2011 with the release of *Rayman: Origins* (Ubisoft) on the PS Vita. The game's hand-drawn style, visual humour and four-way co-operative modes made *Origins* a huge hit with reviewers. It quickly became the **most critically acclaimed PS Vita game**, with a Metacritic average of 88%, as of 2 August 2012.

Biography

Chris Schilling has been writing about games for eight years and playing them a great deal longer. He contributes to a variety of publications including *Edge*, Eurogamer.net and T3, and his current gaming ambition is to finish *Super Meat Boy* (Team Meat, 2010) without breaking any more controllers (current count: three).

MOST CROSSOVER CHARACTERS IN A PLATFORMER

Ultra-hard indie platformer *Super Meat Boy* (Team Meat, 2010) has been a huge hit on both PC and consoles and acted as an inspiration for independent games developers all over the world. In a heartwarming gesture of unity, a raft of developers agreed to have their characters featured in the game, resulting in 18 playable cameo appearances from different games series, including *Half-Life* (Valve Corporation, 1998), *Braid* (Number None, 2008), *Alien Hominid* (The Behemoth, 2004) and *Minecraft* (Mojang, 2011). The game has also been a magnet for speed gamers. Niklas "Exo" Nierling (USA) took 18 min 39 sec to complete the **fastest single-segment run of *Super Meat Boy*** on 11 October 2011. He used the PC version of the game to set a record that is a clear 3 min 36 sec faster than the time of 22 min 15 sec for the Xbox Live Arcade version.

Don't shoot

The platform game is one of the most enduring genres. While it may have been usurped in the affections of some by the first-person shooter, the rise of the App Store, indie gamers and developers and the continuing success of Nintendo has seen it enjoy a renaissance.

The earliest platform games were created in the early 1980s, though it was 1985's *Super Mario Bros.* (Nintendo, see pp.120–121) that really saw the genre blossom. The platformer went on to dominate the 8- and 16-bit console eras to such a degree that it accounted for almost a third of all games

'Fez up

With its 2012 launch, one of the oldest genres got a new angle... literally. Polytron's witty take on platform classics messed with two and three dimensions to create something new. *Fez*'s world rotated 90°, switching between 2D and 3D perspectives.

How to spot this genre

HAS GOT:
- Collapsible platforms that crumble the instant you step on them
- A damsel in distress in an inconveniently located castle
- Fire, snow, desert and jungle environments

HASN'T GOT:
- A pit that's either bottomless or filled with something other than lava or spikes
- Ice worlds without slippery surfaces
- Bald space marines with guns bigger than their biceps

released for the Sega Master System. That had dwindled to a quarter by the next generation of consoles, though gamers still avidly ran, jumped, climbed and collected.

Out of fashion
By the late 1990s, the 32- and 64-bit consoles had ushered in a new era of large, polygon-based 3D worlds. These machines offered complex controls and sophisticated experiences, but RPGs and first-person shooters were increasingly popular. Nintendo managed to move its mascot into the third dimension with the pioneering *Super Mario 64* (1996), but few other developers followed.

Rare talent
It was Nintendo's partner Rare that published many of the most critically acclaimed platformers of the time, including *Banjo Kazooie* (1998) and *Donkey Kong 64* (1999). By the next generation of consoles, the genre was no longer a market leader and even Sonic struggled to keep its momentum.

Revival
Yet with the advent of digital services, opening the way for smaller developers to reach a wider audience, the

platformer – particularly in 2D – has enjoyed a revival. Indeed, three platformers – *Braid*, *Super Meat Boy* and *Fez* – are among the highest-rated games on Xbox Live Arcade. The inclusive nature of iOS has encouraged bedroom coders to create platform games for the App Store, while *LittleBigPlanet* (Media Molecule, 2008, see pp.122–123) is taking the genre in new directions by focusing on user-generated content.

As games such as *Rayman Origins* (Ubisoft, 2011) innovate further in the genre that Mario made famous, platforming remains a force and maintains a devoted fanbase of run-and-jumpers.

Mascot wars
In the 1990s, the battle between Nintendo's Super Mario and Sega's Sonic the Hedgehog caught the imagination of developers, who produced such mascot-led platformers as *Crash Bandicoot* (Naughty Dog, 1996) and the bobcat adventures of *Bubsy* (Accolade, 1992).

HIGHEST SCORE ON *DONKEY KONG*
Veteran Hank Chien (USA) cemented his position as the undisputed champion of *Donkey Kong* (Nintendo, 1981) in May 2012, when he beat his own high score with a new record of 1,110,000. Chien, who is a New York plastic surgeon by profession, trumped rivals Steve Wiebe and Billy Mitchell (both USA), whose long-running battle for the highest score on the game formed the basis of documentary film *The King of Kong: A Fistful of Quarters* (USA, 2007).

MOST CRITICALLY ACCLAIMED iOS GAME
As of June 2012, *Super QuickHook* (Rocketcat Games, 2011) had managed to rack up an average review score of 96% on Metacritic, putting it in joint first place with *World of Goo* (2D Boy, 2010). With convincing in-game physics, its one-touch platforming action makes it well suited to the iPhone's touch-screen and lack of buttons while its retro visual and audio styling has made it an instant critical success with reviewers.

WHAT IS SONIC'S FRIEND MILES PROWER BETTER KNOWN AS?

Sonic the Hedgehog

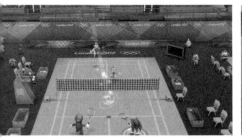

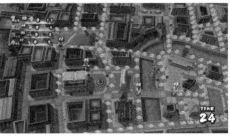

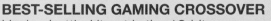

BEST-SELLING GAMING CROSSOVER

Having battled it out in the 16-bit era, gaming's most famous hedgehog and plumber put aside their differences to join forces for *Mario & Sonic at the Olympic Games* (SEGA Sports R&D, 2007). This lucrative sporting compilation, released for the Beijing Games of 2008, had sold over 12.83 million copies on Nintendo platforms as of 13 August 2012. It includes 24 Olympic events as well as more fanciful "Dream Events". The duo followed it up with a Winter Games title in 2009, and a London 2012 Games release in 2011.

HIGHEST SCORE ON *SONIC SPINBALL*

It's never too late to set your sights on becoming a world record holder on a classic videogame, as evidenced by John A Pompa (USA) of Reynoldsville, Pennsylvania. In December 2011 – 18 years after the game was a hit on the Sega Mega Drive/Genesis – Pompa smashed the record for the Blue Blur's spin-off *Sonic Spinball* (Polygames Interactive, 1993) with a whopping 15,735,000 points – a clear 2 million above the previous record, which had stood unbeaten for five years.

84.3 million

Total sales of *Sonic the Hedgehog* games and spin-off titles as of 13 August 2012.

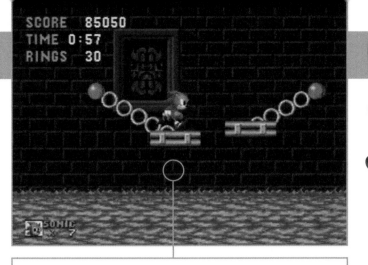

SCORE 85050
TIME 0:57
RINGS 30

FASTEST GLITCH-FREE
SONIC THE HEDGEHOG SPEED-RUN

Charles K Ziese (USA) completed the original *Sonic the Hedgehog* on 13 May 2012 in a mere 28 min 22 sec. Pittsburgh-based gamer Ziese holds a number of *Sonic*-related records on score site Twin Galaxies, as well as speed-runs for two *Castlevania* titles and the original *Crash Bandicoot*.

BEST-SELLING GAME
ON SEGA PLATFORMS

Sonic the Hedgehog (1991) is Sega's most successful game ever. It had already sold over a million copies as a standalone release before two Sega executives approached the developer's then-president with the idea of bundling the title with the Mega Drive/Genesis. The game shifted more than 15 million units, and Sega outsold Nintendo in the West for the first time. Since his debut, Sonic has appeared in a variety of games across a total of 29 different game formats, giving him the record for the **most platforms for a videogame character**. This total includes obscure devices such as Tiger's Game.com, which sold fewer than 300,000 units, Sega's own 32X add-on (pictured) and the Neo Geo Pocket Color.

LONGEST
TAG-TEAM *SONIC*
MARATHON

The longest *Sonic* gaming marathon by a tag-team ran for a total of seven days, from 28 December 2011 to 4 January 2012. Four members of the US-based gaming collective Respawn Point played 12 games from the main *Sonic* series, from *Sonic the Hedgehog* through to *Sonic Generations* (Sonic Team, 2011), with the record attempt being streamed online.

Sonic VS Mario

Rank	Attribute	Rank
8	Hair	7
9	Speed	8
6	Manual labour skills	10
9	Heroism	9
9	Strength	8
9	Street cred	7
8	Friends and allies	9
9	Stamina	9
67		**67**

Super Mario Bros.

THE ONGOING ADVENTURES OF MARIO, THE PAUNCHY PLUMBER WHO BECAME GAMING'S GREATEST HERO

HIGHEST COIN TARGET IN A PLATFORM GAME

New Super Mario Bros. 2 (Nintendo EAD, 2012) contains more coins than any previous Mario title – thankfully so, as the game's ultimate objective of collecting one million coins represents the highest coin target in a platform game. The sequel to *New Super Mario Bros.* (Nintendo EAD, 2006) is also the **first Nintendo platform game with a simultaneous digital and retail launch**, appearing in both the 3DS eStore and shops on 17 August 2012.

FLASH《BACK

Kaette Kita Mario Bros. (Nintendo, 1986) contains one of the earliest examples of in-game advertising. Nintendo struck a deal with Nagatanien, a Japanese food company, to advertise their Mario-themed curry.

FASTEST 70-STAR COMPLETION OF *SUPER MARIO 64*

In the run-up to his record attempt, Mario fanatic Mike "Siglemic" Sigler (USA) had been speed-running *Super Mario 64* (Nintendo EAD, 1996) for more than a year, particularly focusing on the 70-star run. Seventy is the lowest number of stars required to confront the final boss without glitches. Sigler's record time of 49 min 34 sec was livestreamed as a single segment on twitch.tv on 13 June 2012. *Super Mario 64* was one of the launch titles for the Nintendo 64, and has sold a total of 11.89 million copies worldwide.

FASTEST *SUPER MARIO BROS.* MINIMALIST SPEED-RUN

John J Lundrigan (USA) completed the minimalist speed-run on *Super Mario Bros.* (Nintendo, 1985) in just 5 min 2 sec on 29 August 2011. Lundrigan used the Wii Virtual Console version of the game to set his record. His use of warp pipes helped him finish so speedily.

RAREST *SUPER MARIO* GAME

In 1991, Nintendo toured US campuses with *Nintendo Campus Challenge*. After this national tournament, all the cartridges were destroyed save one, which was retained by a Nintendo employee and sold to US collector Rob Walters at a 2006 New York garage sale. In 2009, the game was resold on eBay for $20,100 (£12,350).

HIGHEST-RATED PLATFORM-GAME SERIES

The seven games in the main *Super Mario* series have achieved a Metacritic average of 92%. The two *Super Mario Galaxy* games (Nintendo EAD, 2007 and 2010) lead the way with 97% each, closely followed by *Super Mario 64* on 94%, making *Mario* the most critically acclaimed platform game series.

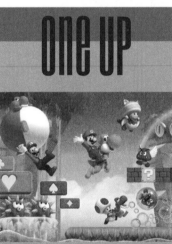

In an unprecedented step for Nintendo, two Mario platformers were scheduled for release in 2012: *New Super Mario Bros. 2* for the 3DS and *New Super Mario Bros. U* (Nintendo EAD, 2012, pictured above) for the Wii U. This represents the shortest release gap between two titles in the main series, beating the nine-month difference between the launches of *Super Mario Bros.* and sequel *Super Mario Bros.: The Lost Levels* (which, confusingly, was known in Japan as *Super Mario Bros. 2*).

FASTEST SINGLE-SEGMENT COMPLETION OF *SUPER MARIO BROS. 2*

Super Mario Bros. 2 (Nintendo EAD, 1988) was all over in a blistering 9 min 15 sec for serial speed-runner Andrew Gardikis (USA) on 13 June 2007. Gardikis also holds the record for the **fastest single-segment completion of *Super Mario Bros.: The Lost Levels*** (Nintendo EAD, 1996), with a time of 8 min 34 sec set on 26 May 2010. His run used two different characters, depending on the level: Luigi for his extra-long jumps, and Toad as the fastest on-foot sprinter.

LittleBigPlanet

CREATE UNIQUE CONTENT WITH IN-GAME TOOLS, THEN SHARE IT ONLINE

MOST DOWNLOADABLE PLATFORM GAME COSTUMES

By 17 August 2012, *LittleBigPlanet 2* (Media Molecule, 2011) featured more than 270 customizable costumes. These are themed around iconic characters from sources as diverse as *The Muppets*, *Pirates of the Caribbean* and *Final Fantasy* (Square Enix, 1987–present).

BEST-SELLING PS3 PLATFORM SERIES

Platform games aren't as popular as in the 16-bit era, but quality still finds fans. *LittleBigPlanet* (various, 2008–present) is the best-selling platform series for the PS3, with 7.60 million copies sold by 27 September 2012.

If you like *LittleBigPlanet*

try...

Minecraft (Mojang, 2011)

Ratchet & Clank Future: A Crack in Time (Insomniac Games, 2009)

Lego Batman 2: DC Super Heroes (Traveller's Tales, 2012)

ModNation Racers (United Front Games, 2010)

Freakyforms: Your Creations, Alive! (Asobism, 2011)

Max & the Magic Marker (Press Play, 2010)

WarioWare D.I.Y. (Intelligent Systems, 2009–10)

Tales from Space: Mutant Blobs Attack!!! (Drinkbox Studios, 2012)

Limbo (Playdead, 2010)

MOST BAFTAS FOR A PLATFORM SERIES

Sackgirl, Sackboy and the rest in the *LittleBigPlanet* series have won no fewer than four British Academy of Film and Television Arts awards (BAFTAs). In 2009, the original won the Artistic Achievement prize, while the PSP version (Cambridge Studio/Media Molecule, 2009) took the Handheld award a year later. Finally, *LittleBigPlanet 2* topped both the Family and Game Innovation categories at the 2012 ceremony. Even the *Super Mario* series (Nintendo, 1986–present) has managed only two BAFTAs.

21 years

The length of time it would take Sackboy to run through all the user-generated levels in *LittleBigPlanet*.

one up

On the PS Vita version of *LittleBigPlanet, the* Memorizer adds a helpful "save" function. It's simple but powerful – users can build standalone games with multiple stages and characters whose progress can be saved over time. Anything is possible, from recalling a player's music preferences to creating an entire RPG.

LONGEST PLATFORM MARATHON

The launch of *LittleBigPlanet 2* included a three-day event at the Sony Style store in New York, USA, where Sean Crowley, David Dino and Lauren Guiliano (all USA) played for 50 hours. From 17 to 19 January 2011, they tackled 237 levels, the **most user-generated game levels played in 24 hours**.

By the start of August 2012, *LittleBigPlanet* users had created more than 7 million levels and games. If they were all placed side by side, they would wrap around the Earth five times or reach almost halfway to the Moon.

FIRST PUBLIC HAND-HELD PLATFORM BETA TEST

LittleBigPlanet Vita (Sony, 2012) invited players into a beta test. Players were asked to sign up, and then e-mailed special codes to download the game, with access to a number of levels and the game's creative toolset. Everyone who took part was promised a Beta Test Vest costume download in the final game. The exclusive item was in the appropriate shape of a worker's high-visibility jacket!

COMICS AND VIDEOGAMES

Videogames and comics have a long shared history, with each crossing into the other's native territory, not always with entirely successful results. Here's our pick of the milestones of the great comics/videogame crossovers of the past 40 years.

SUPERSTAR CROSSOVER

Atari dominated the early videogame market, but founder Nolan Bushnell sold his company to Warner Communications in 1976. Warner also owned the iconic comics publisher DC, so it was inevitable that their most celebrated character, Superman, became the **first superhero to feature in a videogame** with *Superman* (Atari, 1979), designed for the Atari 2600. Crossing over in the other direction, in 1982 DC became the first publisher to produce comics to tie in to videogames. Their free *Atari Force* comic came with several classic Atari cartridges, including *Defender* (William Electronics, 1980) and *Star Raiders* (Atari, 1979).

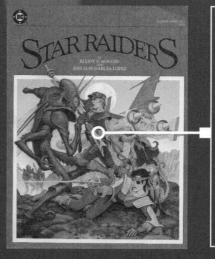

CRASH LANDING

Rushed and poorly received games in late 1982 contributed to a sharp drop in consumer confidence and the North American gaming crash of 1983. This caught DC by surprise as it had started working on a *Star Raiders* comic which was to be given away with new Atari cartridges throughout that year. With 40 pages of the project completed, DC decided to publish the story as a 64-page single volume – the **first graphic novel to feature videogame characters**.

DREAM A LITTLE DREAM

It isn't just superheroes who have made the leap from the printed page to the videogame screen: newspaper strips – including *Garfield*, *Peanuts* and *Popeye* – have all featured in various games over the years. However, the **oldest comic strip character featured in a videogame** is the sleepy-eyed child Nemo from Winsor McCay's newspaper strip *Little Nemo in Slumberland*, first published on 15 October 1905. The adaptation was titled *Little Nemo: Dream Master* (Capcom, 1990) for the NES/Famicom. A simple platform game, it had Nemo travelling through the land of dreams known as Slumberland in order to rescue its rightful ruler from the clutches of the Nightmare King.

SUPERSONIC

Some videogame characters have become bigger than the game or platform that spawned them. Sonic the Hedgehog is just such a character. Originally intended as Sega's answer to Nintendo's Mario, Sonic has achieved something that the plump plumber never has, by inspiring long-running spin-off comics on both sides of the Atlantic. The American version, published by Archie Comics, started in May 1993 and is still going strong almost 20 years later.

COMBATIVE CROSSOVER

A key feature of both comics and videogames is the crossover, a chance for different characters to test their various skills against each other. *X-Men vs. Street Fighter* (Capcom, 1996) was the landmark title that brought the fight between comics and videogames into gamers' hands. The title proved that comic characters could hold their own against their digital opponents, and it spawned a slew of similar match-ups, including the legendary *Marvel vs. Capcom 2* (Capcom, 2000).

PENNY FOR THE GUYS

Started as a hobby by Mike Krahulik (far left) and Jerry Holkins (both USA) in 1998, Penny Arcade, a simple webcomic about videogames, has become something of a sensation. The writers chronicle the gaming interests of their respective alter-egos Gabe and Tycho, who have even starred in their own videogames. In addition to the ongoing strip, Krahulik and Holkins have also set up a charity, Child's Play, which provides videogames for sick children, and a biennial convention, Penny Arcade Expo (PAX). They even appeared in *Time* magazine's list of the 100 most influential figures shaping our world in 2010.

A SENSE OF DREDD

By the year 2000, videogame companies were buying comic publishers. Rebellion Developments, founded by brothers Jason and Chris Kingsley (all UK) and most famous for various *Aliens vs. Predator* titles, purchased the iconic British sci-fi comic *2000 AD*. The company has subsequently created a number of games based on *2000 AD* characters such as Judge Dredd and Rogue Trooper.

HEROES AND VILLAINS

For a long while, no major comic publisher was interested in licensing out their characters for an MMO title. Developers Cryptic Studios and publisher NCSoft broke new ground with *City of Heroes* (Cryptic, 2004). The game, which enables players to become either the hero or villain of their dreams, is still going strong. It can also be seen as an influence on DC, which launched MMO title *DC Universe Online* (Sony, 2011).

BATMAN: BAR RAISER

Batman: Arkham Asylum (Rocksteady, 2009) and its 2011 sequel *Batman: Arkham City* – the **best-selling game based on a comic** (with sales of 7.19 million as of September 2012) – have raised the bar in comic-related videogames. Melding beat-'em-up, puzzle and stealth elements, the *Arkham* titles appeal to a broad range of gamers – and not just to comic fans who also play games.

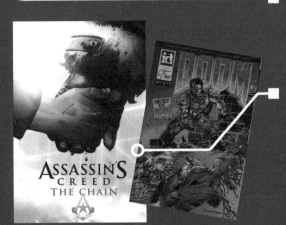

*DOOM*ED

In the 1990s, some comics based on games – such as *Doom* in 1996 – were criticized for falling short of the games that inspired them. Today, many comic creators are also gamers and want to create comics that add to the world of the game to which they are linked. Karl Kerschl and Cameron Stewart (both Canada) are two such pros. Their acclaimed work on the comic *Assassin's Creed: The Fall* saw the debut of Daniel Cross, who took a key role in *Assassin's Creed: Revelations* (Ubisoft, 2011). *The Chain* followed in 2012 as the sequel to *The Fall*.

Overview

The line between sim racing and real racing is increasingly blurred: Jann Mardenborough (UK) won the 2011 GT Academy, an initiative set up by Nissan and PlayStation to bring together the best *Gran Turismo* gamers and give them a chance to drive a professional racing car. Jann, who was 19 at the time of his triumph, making him the **youngest GT Academy winner**, now has an international racing licence and drives for Nissan in the Blancpain Endurance Series.

Biography

Martin Robinson is *Eurogamer's* Features Editor, and he's obsessed with all things on wheels – indeed, his very first word was "car". Actually, it was "duck", but seeing as there aren't many videogames about those any more he decided to dedicate himself to the racing genre.

Racing Intro

Hasty hog

Sumo Digital's 2010 kart-racer features every gamer's favourite hedgehog and a host of SEGA celebrities, including Doctor Eggman, Tails, Jacky Bryant and Billy Hatcher. In 2012, speed demon Sam Fetherstonhaugh (UK, right) beat stiff competition at the Games Britannia show in Sheffield, South Yorkshire, UK, to claim the record for the **fastest first-course lap on *Sonic & SEGA All-Stars Racing*** with a time of 41.074 seconds. Sam's sister Sophie came in second place, in a live final held on-stage with commentary from the game's executive producer, Steve Lycett (UK).

Keeping it real

From taking on swarms of the undead, to lining up headshots in some exotic corner of the globe or bounding through a technicolour wonderland, games often have a deliberately loose grip on reality. Most driving games, however, aim to recreate a real-world experience. While it's challenging to replicate the danger and physical exertion of combat through a plastic controller, it's somewhat easier – if not entirely precise – to simulate what it takes to wrestle several hundred horsepower around a ribbon of tarmac. Virtual racing

Wanted!

The seminal *Need for Speed* series has been developed by a number of companies since 1994, most recently Criterion. According to publisher EA, more than 100 million games have been sold worldwide, making *Need for Speed* the **best-selling racing game series**. Scheduled for November 2012, *Most Wanted* – the 19th *NfS* title – revisits the 2005 game.

FIRST 3D DRIVING GAME

Popular myth cites *Night Driver* (Atari, 1976) as the very first driving game rendered in 3D and from a first-person perspective, but it was in fact preceded – and inspired – by *Nürburgring 1*. This obscure arcade title was developed in 1976 by Dr Reiner Foerst (Germany), an engineer with expertise in driving simulation. While its visuals, with white bollards marking out a road on a black background, now seem basic, it was a significant milestone in the genre. Dr Foerst's groundbreaking racer was housed in a stylish, if rather simplistic, cabinet. He developed two follow-ups in 1976, *Nürburgring 2* and *Nürburgring 3* (pictured right), with each cabinet looking more sophisticated than its predecessor.

HIGHEST SCORE ON *FREEWAY FURY*

Thailand's Thanapat Voraphaphun set a new high mark for online smash-'em-up *Freeway Fury* (Crazy Monkey Games, 2010) with a run of 438,047 points on 24 May 2012.

has been pursued with increasing realism since 1974, when Atari title *Gran Trak 10*'s abstract, top-down take on driving kick-started the genre.

Artistic driver's licence

In the four decades since *Gran Trak 10*, racing games have accelerated from pixelated tours to high-definition cinematic experiences such as the Kinect-enabled *Forza Motorsport 4* (Turn 10 Studios, 2011). It's not all about life-like accuracy, of course, and some of the best and most memorable driving games have no concern for tyre pressures or wheel cambers. Nintendo's *Mario Kart* series (1992–present) has done this best, and most successfully, offering a sweet tour through the Mushroom Kingdom, even if the joy of a drifting kart with a whooping Mario at the wheel is often undermined by having a red shell stuffed up your exhaust pipe. Then there's the kooky, two-wheeled acrobatics of *Trials Evolution* (RedLynx, 2012).

Auto appeal

Whether you're bouncing along the sun-kissed sand of Koopa Beach or threading an F1 car through the needle streets of Monaco in a Grand Prix, the appeal is much the same. It's all about mastering the machinery to prove you're the greatest and the fastest. This genre remains at the forefront of console technology, producing some of the most exhilarating new games around.

MOST CRITICALLY ACCLAIMED RACER

The original *Gran Turismo* (Sony, 1997), which sold 11.15 million units, remains the highest-rated racing game of all time, according to Metacritic. As of 27 September 2012, it had an average score of 96% – just 1% above *Gran Turismo 3: A-Spec* (Polyphony Digital, 2001), the series' PlayStation 2 debut. The highest-rated non-*Gran Turismo* game is Firemint's *Real Racing 2* (2010) for iOS on 94%, and a point behind that is Criterion's *Burnout 3: Takedown* (2004).

ON WHICH CONSOLE DID THE FIRST *SUPER MARIO KART* APPEAR?

THE XBOX'S RACING PHENOMENON TAKES DRIVING SIMULATORS TO A NEW LEVEL OF REALISM, SPEED AND AUTHENTICITY

FASTEST SPEED IN A SIMULATED REAL-WORLD CAR

The greatest speed attained in a simulated version of a genuine car available in real life is 272.2 mi/h (438 km/h), achievable in *Forza Motorsport 4* (Turn 10 Studios, 2011) with a fully upgraded and tuned McLaren F1 car. The Bugatti Veyron falls just shy at 271 mi/h (436 km/h). *Gran Turismo* gamers can reach 302 mi/h (486 km/h) with the awesome Red Bull X series cars, but these vehicles are not manufactured in real life.

MOST DETAILED CARS IN A CONSOLE GAME

While car manufacturers compete to see who can get the most power out of their cars, videogame makers have their own "arms race", and it's counted in polygons. *Forza Motorsport 4* contains the most detailed car models of any console game; its 800,000 polygons that go into each vehicle comfortably oust the 500,000 that make up *Gran Turismo 5's* (Polyphony Digital, 2010) steeds. The figure also eclipses the 300,000 polygons that *Forza Motorsport 3* employed. Many of those polygons come to good use in *Forza Motorsport 4's* Autovista mode, a virtual showroom wherein it's possible to get up-close and personal with a selection of these dream machines.

FASTEST CLASSIC LE MANS LAP IN *FORZA 4*

British *Forza* fan Shaun Arnold has proven to be the fastest at tackling the iconic Le Mans circuit. The 20-year-old gamer lapped the French track in just 2 min 58.85 sec in the rotary-engined Mazda 787B. The real-world track, famous for hosting the 24 Hours of Le Mans race, has been altered several times, but no driver has completed it in less than three minutes.

BEST-SELLING XBOX DRIVING SIM SERIES

Forza has firmly established itself as the premier driving experience on Microsoft's consoles, and it has the sales to back up the hype. Since the series launched in 2007, some 12.45 million units have been shifted – and, as of 4 September 2012, a total of 11.4 million of those have come on the Xbox 360. This is an impressive feat, but it still has some way to go if it wants to match PlayStation-exclusive rival *Gran Turismo*, which boasts total series sales of 64.86 million games to date, making it the overall **best-selling driving sim series**.

HIGHEST-RATED RACING SERIES

The original *Gran Turismo* (Polyphony Digital, 1998) may be the **highest-rated racing game**, but *Forza* (Turn 10 Studios, 2005–present) remains the most critically acclaimed series, with all four main releases sitting above 90% on Metacritic. The original Xbox game from 2005 is tied with *Forza Motorsport 3* (2009) on 92%, while nestling behind is 2011's *Forza Motorsport 4* (pictured) at 91%. The series' Xbox 360 debut, *Forza Motorsport 2* (2007), comes in at 90%.

MOST CRITICALLY ACCLAIMED RACING SIMS ON XBOX 360	
Game	Metascore
Forza Motorsport 3 (Turn 10, 2009)	92%
Forza Motorsport 4 (Turn 10, 2011)	91%
Forza Motorsport 2 (Turn 10, 2007)	90%
Trials Evolution (RedLynx, 2012)	90%
Burnout Revenge (Criterion, 2006)	89%
Burnout Paradise (Criterion, 2008)	88%
Joe Danger: Special Edition (Hello Games, 2011)	88%
Need for Speed: Hot Pursuit (Criterion, 2010)	88%
Project Gotham Racing 3 (Bizarre Creations, 2005)	88%
DiRT 3 (Codemasters, 2011)	87%

According to Metacritic, as of 4 September 2012.

TOP TEN

WHAT DOES THE ITALIAN WORD "FORZA" MEAN IN ENGLISH?

Formula 1

THE LATEST DRAMA IN THE WORLD OF FORMULA 1 IS REFLECTED IN THE MOST CUTTING-EDGE RACING SIM

BEST-SELLING F1 GAME
F1 2010 sold 2.06 million copies and paved the way for its 2011 sequel (above). Developers Codemasters took the licence from Sony and ended a four-year drought with an HD sim series that was also the first multi-platform F1 game since 2003. As of 13 September 2012, *F1 2010*'s closest sales rival, *F1 2011*, had sold 1.89 million copies.

FASTEST LAP OF THE F1 2011 INDIAN GRAND PRIX
Multiple record-breaker Justin Towell (UK) lived the dream when he became a Formula 1 superstar at the 2011 Golden Joystick Awards in London, UK. In front of a crowd of onlookers, Justin posted an incredible 1-min 20.38-sec lap of the Buddh International Circuit, as used for the inaugural Indian Grand Prix in 2011 (shown inset, above). A keen racer, Justin also set the **fastest completion of SEGA Rally Championship (Desert Course)** with a time of 2 min 30.73 sec on 29 January 2009.

D.Y.K.? Most gamers will never get to play the most realistic Formula 1 sims ever made. These are driven in cockpits mounted on hydraulics, developed at a cost of millions by the world's top teams for drivers to learn new circuits and engineers to test new components. Such is the secrecy surrounding the technology that you have as much chance of finding yourself behind the wheel of a real F1 car as getting into the lab to try one of the latest manufacturer simulators!

FLASH《BACK

When Sega wanted to get into F1 sponsorship in the 1990s, it sealed a last-minute deal with Williams over McLaren. The 1993 season featured Williams cars driven by Alain Prost (France, below in cockpit with cartoon legs painted underneath) and Damon Hill (UK, seated at wheel) plastered with Sega and Sonic logos. McLaren's response was to mark every victory that season by placing a picture of a flattened hedgehog on the side of Ayrton Senna's (Brazil) car.

MOST CRITICALLY ACCLAIMED F1 CONSOLE GAME

The best Formula 1 games are ultra-realistic simulators on which even the slightest error can prove to be costly. You might think that this kind of gameplay would appeal more to PC enthusiasts than to console gamers. But then came *F1 2010* for consoles (below), providing enough depth for even the most hardcore racers to get revved up about. Scoring 84% on Metacritic as of 13 September 2012, *F1 2010* remains in pole position with games critics. Even its 2011 sequel has failed to overtake it.

FIRST F1 VIDEOGAME

F-1 (Namco, 1976) was simple but intriguing, with players sliding a cutout image of a car across a projected backdrop animation. The *Monaco GP* (Sega) series began in rudimentary arcade form in 1979 and lasted for 13 years across four releases, making this the **longest-running F1 series**. Its fame came in 1989 with the Mega Drive port of *Super Monaco GP* (Sega, top), which was successful enough to receive a 1992 sequel endorsed by renowned F1 champion Ayrton Senna.

WHAT WAS THE NAME OF CODEMASTERS' ENDURING SERIES OF GAMES FEATURING MINUSCULE MOTORS?

GUINNESS WORLD RECORDS

Super Mario Kart

THE ORIGINAL MULTIPLAYER RACER STAYS IN POLE POSITION, YEAR AFTER YEAR

CERTIFICATE

The most world records held by a female player on Super Mario Kart (Nintendo, 1992) is 30, achieved by Leyla Hasso (UK) in London, UK, between January and August 2012

GUINNESS WORLD RECORDS

MOST *SUPER MARIO KART* RECORDS (FEMALE)

Thirteen-year-old Leyla Hasso (UK) wasn't even born when *Super Mario Kart* (Nintendo EAD) was released on the SNES in 1992, but that hasn't stopped her from climbing to the top of the female time trial circuit in the game. As of 19 September 2012, Leyla held 30 out of 40 possible time trial records on the PAL version of the game, including her speedy completions of the Donut Plains 1, Choco Island 1, Bowser Castle 2 and Rainbow Road tracks. She holds 26 more records than her closest rival, Tanja Brönnecke (Germany). *Kart* gaming certainly runs in Leyla's family: her uncle, Sami Çetin (UK), holds several *Super Mario Kart* records.

TOP TEN

BEST-SELLING RACING GAMES

Game	Sales
Mario Kart Wii (Nintendo EAD, 2008)	32.40 million
Mario Kart DS (Nintendo EAD, 2005)	22.04 million
Gran Turismo 3: A-spec (Polyphony Digital, 2001)	14.88 million
Gran Turismo 4 (Polyphony Digital, 2004)	11.36 million
Mario Kart 64 (Nintendo EAD, 1996)	11.15 million
Gran Turismo 2 (Polyphony Digital, 1999)	9.87 million
Super Mario Kart (Nintendo EAD, 1992)	8.76 million
Gran Turismo 5 (Polyphony Digital, 2010)	7.85 million
Need for Speed: Underground (EA Black Box, 2003)	7.20 million
Mario Kart: Double Dash!! (Nintendo EAD, 2003)	6.95 million

According to VGChartz, as of 19 September 2012.

91.64 million Total sales of the *Mario Kart* series, as of 19 September 2012.

FLASH ◄◄ BACK

An early test version of *Mario Kart 64* (Nintendo EAD, 1996) was known as *Super Mario Kart R*. It featured a slightly different character line-up, with Magikoopa making an appearance as a playable driver, and it also included a track called Toadstool Turnpike – a course that would be renamed as Royal Raceway for the final, published game.

FASTEST SINGLE-SEGMENT SPEED-RUN OF *MARIO KART Wii*

Quick laps are impressive, but single-sitting runs – uninterrupted timed sessions on games – require a different skill-set altogether. Jose Karica of Panama has the stamina and concentration to succeed: he managed a run-through of *Mario Kart Wii* (Nintendo, 2008) on "hard" difficulty in an exceptional 1 hr 7 min 9 sec.

POWER UP!

UNLOCK 'EM UP

Some of *Mario Kart 7*'s unlockables are highly desirable: take the "Golden Kart Parts", the ultimate way to bling your ride. They're tough to attain, though. If you want the Golden Wheels you're going to have to beat every cup in every class. If you want the Golden Glider you'll have to StreetPass 100 people or collect 10,000 coins. Finally, if you want the Gold Kart you'll have to have at least 20,000 coins. You'd better start collecting!

BEST-SELLING RACING GAME

The most popular racing title is *Mario Kart Wii* (Nintendo EAD, 2008), with staggering overall sales of 32.40 million as of 19 September 2012. It's way ahead of *Mario Kart DS* (Nintendo EAD, 2005), the second most popular game, with total sales of 22.04 million.

MOST WATCHED RACING-GAME-THEMED VIDEO

Popular French comedian Rémi Gaillard went further than most in his tribute to *Mario Kart*. In a stunt that's as dangerous as it is comical – not to mention illegal – Gaillard took to the streets dressed as Mario, behind the wheel of a kart. Imitating the game, he darted between cars and threw loose banana skins on to the road. His antics have earned him an astonishing total of 48,910,491 views on YouTube, as of 19 September 2012. The video was uploaded in December 2008.

BEST-SELLING RACING GAME ON 3DS

After selling 1 million copies in its first week on sale in Japan alone, *Mario Kart 7* (Nintendo EAD, 2011) went on to become by far the most popular racing game on the Nintendo 3DS, having shifted some 6.14 million units globally as of 19 September 2012. But it's still only the second most popular game on the hand-held – *Super Mario 3D Land* (Nintendo 3AD/Brownie Brown, 2011) takes the record for **best-selling 3DS game** with 6.60 million games sold.

WHAT DO THE MUSHROOMS IN THE *MARIO KART* GAMES DO TO A KART?

GUINNESS WORLD RECORDS

Wipeout

THE FUTURISTIC RACER MIXES SPEEDY THRILLS, SLICK CRAFTS AND A SASSY SOUNDTRACK

LONGEST-RUNNING FUTURISTIC RACING SERIES

The first *Wipeout* (Psygnosis) came out in 1995, and more than 16 years later *Wipeout 2048* (Studio Liverpool, 2012) was launched on the PS Vita. Sci-fi racing competitor *F-Zero* (Nintendo) may have begun as early as 1990 but the series has been on hiatus since 2004's *F-Zero: Climax* (Suzak). *Wipeout* has always been at the cutting edge of Sony's technology, with *Wipeout HD* (pictured, Studio Liverpool, 2008) one of the first big-name games to be issued first as a download.

D.Y.K.?

The *Wipeout* series is today synonymous with the PlayStation brand, having made a good-looking appearance on every one of Sony's consoles. Yet it wasn't always only a Sony affair: the first two games in the series also appeared on other platforms, including the PC and the Sega Saturn, and in 1998 the Nintendo 64 got its own spin-off, *Wipeout 64* (Psygnosis).

FIRST GAME WITH PS3 AND PS VITA CROSS-PLAY

One of the smartest features of Sony's PS Vita allows players to go head-to-head with PlayStation 3 owners. Gamers with *Wipeout HD* on the PS3 can now play against a Vita equipped with *Wipeout 2048*. Online, up to eight players can take part in the same game, whether they're clutching their PS3 controller or their PS Vita.

FASTEST LAP OF KLIES BRIDGE IN *WIPEOUT 64*

On 28 March 2009, Wouter Jansen (Netherlands) completed a lap of the Klies Bridge track in *Wipeout 64* in a searing 13 seconds flat, making the programming glitches in the gameplay work to his advantage. Gamers coming to later series entry *Wipeout HD* (above) would have one extra track to play on, with eight. The overall accolade for **longest user-generated track in a driving game** goes to the mind-blowing concept that is *Forever Drive* (Supermono Studios, 2011). The iOS game allows users to generate their own tracks, which are pasted together into one ever-lengthening road.

FIRST RACING GAME SOUNDTRACK CD

The launch of the original *Wipeout* was accompanied by a CD featuring artists such as Leftfield (right) and The Chemical Brothers. A follow-up soundtrack, *Wipeout 2097*, accompanied the game of the same name in 1996. *Wipeout* failed to be the **first videogame with a soundtrack CD** by less than two months. That title went to *Killer Cuts*, which accompanied the SNES port of fighting game *Killer Instinct* (Rare, 1995).

MOST CRITICALLY ACCLAIMED FUTURISTIC RACER

As of 4 September 2012, *Wipeout 2097* (known as *Wipeout XL* in the USA) had a Metacritic score of 93%. Even *Wipeout 2048* (pictured) hasn't managed to improve on the critics' views of the 1996 game, one of the most widely praised titles of any kind on the original PlayStation.

THE DESIGNERS REPUBLIC WAS RESPONSIBLE FOR THE MEMORABLE *WIPEOUT* PACKAGING. WHICH CONTROVERSIAL GAME SERIES DID THEY ALSO DESIGN THE PACKAGING FOR?

TOMMY TALLARICO'S TOP 10 TUNES

Tommy Tallarico holds the record for the **most prolific videogame music composer**, and he is also an acclaimed veteran and pioneer of videogame audio, working on more than 300 games in a career that spans some 22 years. He is the founder of the Game Audio Network Guild (GANG), a non-profit organization for gaming audio professionals. Tommy is also the creator of Video Games Live, a touring concert experience that brings live performances of game music to audiences globally. We met with him during the E3 show in Los Angeles, USA, to find out about the pieces of videogame music that inspire him.

FINAL FANTASY VIII

Nothing stands out to me more than *Final Fantasy VIII*. From the incredible opening cinematic song "Liberi Fatali" to the highly emotional and beautiful "Eyes on Me", composer Nobuo Uematsu (Japan) has created one of the greatest game soundtracks of all time.

SUPER MARIO BROS.

The *Super Mario Bros.* theme, composed by Koji Kondo (Japan), spent more time in the *Billboard* Hot Ringtones chart than any tune in history. *Mario* music is the soundtrack of a generation who grew up in the 1980s.

FINAL FANTASY VII

Uematsu's score is the **best-selling videogame soundtrack**. The most requested song at Video Games Live is "One Winged Angel", aka "Sephiroth's Theme", while the incredible "Aerith's Theme" was recently voted No.16 in the Classic FM Classical Music Hall of Fame, alongside the likes of Holst and Vivaldi!

THE LEGEND OF ZELDA

I've seen grown, tough-looking men approach me after the show to say they cried like a baby when we started playing *Zelda*. The game's score [performed here, main picture], by *Super Mario*'s Koji Kondo, is so popular that it even had its own touring symphony!

WORLD OF WARCRAFT

The blaring horns, powerful strings, amazing choirs, incredible melodies, intense percussion and impeccable production quality make the music from this series, by composers Russell Brower and Jason Hayes (both USA), an all-time favourite.

SONIC THE HEDGEHOG

The first *Sonic* game was groundbreaking in many ways, and Masato Nakamura's (Japan) music was a great part of that. It was incredible, considering the Mega Drive/Genesis' limits, that every song for every level perfectly matched the action and was catchy!

RED DEAD REDEMPTION

This is one of the most authentic period videogame soundtracks of all time. Composers Bill Elm and Woody Jackson (both USA) hired some of the greatest western music performers, many of whom had worked on the famous "spaghetti westerns" of the 1960s.

CASTLEVANIA

Two female composers, Kinuyo Yamashita and Michiru Yamane (both Japan), worked on the *Castlevania* series, which is somewhat rare in the male-dominated game music industry. Considering the high quality, here's hoping more females get composing! Pipe organs in videogames = awesome!

HALO

The *Halo* theme, by Marty O'Donnell and Mike Salvatori (both USA), has the most memorable motif in modern gaming. As soon as those first few Tibetan monk choir notes start, the Video Games Live audience goes crazy, because they know what's coming.

BEYOND GOOD & EVIL

Although Ubisoft's 2003 action-adventure game was not a big commercial success, its music is a clear standout. French film composer Christophe Héral used a wide variety of languages and instruments from around the world to create the melodic score.

RPGs

Contents

9

Overview

An adventure to truly call your own, the role-playing game (RPG) has you step into the shoes of the farm boy, the street urchin or the lowly soldier to become a world-saving hero. Widely regarded as one of 2011's toughest games, action RPG *Dark Souls* (From Software) has proved popular with speed-runners, each looking to find a new glitch or strategy to go faster. As of August 2012, the **fastest completion of *Dark Souls*** was achieved by Japanese gamer "Youri_Ch" on 14 November 2011, with a single-segment completion time of 35 min 7 sec.

Biography

Kirsten Kearney has been a gaming journalist for more than a decade, writing for *GamesMaster*, *Official PlayStation 2 Magazine*, *360 Gamer* and the Pocket Gamer website. As well as contributing to the *Gamer's Edition*, Kirsten is currently working as the Editor of gaming site Ready-Up.

RPG Intro

How to spot this genre

HAS GOT:
- Bad guys with white hair
- Quests... lots and lots of quests
- Talking animals

HASN'T GOT:
- A final boss smaller than a building
- Polite dwarves
- A crystal that is just a crystal

MOST CRITICALLY ACCLAIMED RPG ON Wii
As of 25 September 2012, *Xenoblade Chronicles* (Monolith Soft, 2010) was rated 92% on Metacritic. Its lush graphics and involved gameplay were marked out for critics' praise and formed a showcase for the full potential of the Wii. Pictured right is Fiora, one of seven playable characters.

FASTEST TIME TO BEAT THE *DARK SOULS* ASYLUM DEMON
Steven Craig Epperson of Florida, USA, showed that speed-running *Dark Souls* is not the sole preserve of Japanese gamers when he posted a stunning 11-second completion of the game's Asylum Demon boss on the GWR Challengers website on 24 April 2012.

186,000 Character levels you can earn through repeated playthroughs of *Disgaea 3: Absence of Justice* (Nippon Ichi, 2008)

142

Falling out

Action RPG *Fallout 3* (Bethesda, 2008) received the highest rating of the series with an average of 91% on Metacritic, as of 25 September 2012. The first *Fallout* was developed by Interplay and released in 1997, and the most recent title is *Fallout: Las Vegas* (Obsidian/ Bethesda, 2010).

A very big adventure

RPGs have endured and evolved over 35 years to provide some of the richest gaming experiences. Players develop skills with their characters, battle with friends and constantly have to make choices as they journey through their adventures. It is this depth of gameplay that has made RPGs so well loved by generations of fans.

East meets West

RPGs come in two very different flavours, depending on their territory of origin. Developers in the West strive for a visceral experience where combat flows seamlessly from exploration and back again. You forge a path of your own, branching off according to your own beliefs, and may even play the bad guy.

Japanese RPGs have many of the same elements but you control a team rather than an individual. At the heart of JRPGs are the strategic battle systems which have to be mastered. Fights with enemies occur randomly, sometimes on a battlefield and otherwise in turn-based combat or on a grid.

Crossover success

In recent years the West has dominated with franchises such as *Dragon Age* (BioWare, 2009), *The Elder Scrolls* (Bethesda, 1994, see pp.144–145), *Mass Effect* (BioWare, 2007, see pp.146–147) and *Fable* (Lionhead, 2004) taking the genre out of the niche market. Japanese developers now chase bigger western audiences with simultaneous worldwide releases and games such as *Kingdom Hearts* (Square Enix, 2002–present), which mix Enix characters with more familiar Disney faces.

LONGEST RPG END SEQUENCE

Japanese RPGs are famed for substantial cutscenes and lengthy end sequences. Here is where all the loose ends are tied up and hopefully your hero gets a happily-ever-after ending – eventually. *Dragon Quest VIII: Journey of the Cursed King* (Level-5, 2004) has a popcorn-munching 50 minutes of cutscenes. Players can even take control of the story as they run off with the princess! The **longest end sequence** of any game is *Metal Gear Solid IV* (Kojima Productions, 2008), at 1 hr 8 min.

Stunner

Among the leaders in the resurgent Japanese RPG world is development studio Level-5. It achieved a visually stunning look for *Ni no Kuni* (2010) by working in partnership with award-winning anime producers Studio Ghibli. The game has its US and European releases in 2013.

The Elder Scrolls

EXPLORE THE LIVING, BREATHING WORLD OF TAMRIEL, WHERE EVERY PERSON YOU MEET HAS A STORY AND EVERYWHERE YOU GO THERE IS ADVENTURE TO BE HAD

MOST SIMULTANEOUS USERS ON STEAM

Download and community service Steam had its busiest day ever when *The Elder Scrolls V: Skyrim* (Bethesda, 2011) was released. *Call of Duty: Modern Warfare 3* (Infinity Ward, 2011), also released that week, languished with 78,000 gamers, but *Skyrim* had 274,410 concurrent players: a record for one game.

POWER UP!

NIRNROOTS

One of the biggest side quests in any of the *Elder Scrolls* games is the collecting of nirnroots in *The Elder Scrolls IV: Oblivion* (Bethesda, 2006). You'll need to collect at least 100 of the 300 nirnroots available to complete the quest and they don't grow back! You can find them next to water, glowing faintly blue. Make sure you turn up your sound or wear headphones – they make a humming noise when you get close.

MOST POPULAR GAMING MEME

Skyrim's most popular piece of dialogue is "I used to be an adventurer like you, then I took an arrow to the knee." By July 2012, the phrase was the fourth most popular meme of any kind on knowyourmeme.com, with over 3.2 million views, just seven months after being added. A meme is a cultural catchphrase, idea or symbol, and popular memes in videogaming have included "All your base are belong to us" in *Zero Wing* (Toaplan, 1989). More than 70 videos of knee-arrow meme compilations are viewable on YouTube.

FASTEST COMPLETION OF *SKYRIM*

Bethesda tester Sam Bernstein completed *The Elder Scrolls V: Skyrim* in a record time of just 2 hr 16 min 10 sec, some 20 seconds ahead of senior designer Jeff Browne. Having created the game, the colleagues had to outwit one another, as both of them knew all the possible shortcuts!

FLASH BACK

The Elder Scrolls II: Daggerfall (Bethesda, 1996) was one of the first large-scale 3D worlds. The map was actually twice the size of the UK at 487,000 km² (188,301 miles²), with 15,000 towns and 750,000 non-player characters to interact with.

FASTEST-SELLING OPEN-WORLD RPG

Despite *The Elder Scrolls IV: Oblivion* being a huge commercial success, it took sequel *The Elder Scrolls V: Skyrim* just 48 hours to sell 3.5 million copies. Within the first month of release it was just half a million copies short of matching *Oblivion*'s lifetime sales of 6.53 million. Total sales of *Skyrim* were 12.2 million, as of July 2012. The latest game in the series took the record from Bethesda's own *Fallout 3* (2008). Bethesda design director Todd Howard was presented with the company's latest GWR certificate in June 2012 at E3 in Los Angeles.

FIRST NON-JAPANESE GAME WITH A PERFECT *FAMITSU* SCORE

Only 19 games (by eight developers) have ever been rated 40/40 in the 26 years of *Famitsu*, Japan's most respected gaming magazine. *The Elder Scrolls V: Skyrim* was the first non-Japanese game to receive this esteemed honour.

IF you like The Elder Scrolls try...

Fallout 3 (Bethesda, 2008)
Dark Souls (From Software, 2011)
Dragon Age II (BioWare, 2011)
Baldur's Gate II: Shadows of Amn (Black Isle, 2000)
Fable III (Lionhead, 2010)
Neverwinter Nights (BioWare, 2002)
The Witcher 2: Assassins of Kings (CD Projekt RED, 2011)
Dragon's Dogma (Capcom, 2012)
Risen 2: Dark Waters (Piranha Bytes, 2012)
Dark Messiah: Might and Magic (Arkane/Floodgate/Kuju, 2006)

75 hours

The average overall time Bethesda said an estimated 10 million gamers spend playing *The Elder Scrolls V: Skyrim*.

IN WHAT FORMAT WAS THE WORLD OF TAMRIEL ORIGINALLY CREATED BY BETHESDA DEVELOPERS TED PETERSON, VIJAY LAKSHMAN AND JULIAN LEFAY?

GUINNESS WORLD RECORDS

Mass Effect

YOU'RE NOT JUST THE SAVIOUR OF THE WORLD; THE WHOLE GALAXY IS IN YOUR HANDS

"Just once I'd like to ask someone for help and hear them say, 'Sure. Let's go. Right now. No strings attached.'"

Commander Shepard – *Mass Effect 2*

MOST POPULAR MULTIPLAYER MODE IN A CONSOLE RPG

On both the PS3 and Xbox 360, gamers are able to play four-player co-operative matches within the *Mass Effect 3* (BioWare, 2012) universe. Players notched up over 1,800 years of combined playing time in the first two weeks alone, managing 22.84 million matches in six weeks, as of 2 August 2012. The multiplayer mode affects your "Galaxy at War" readiness rating in single-player mode, too.

The Kinect peripheral for the Xbox 360 version of *Mass Effect 3* allows gamers to use voice control. Players can command squad mates such as Jeff "Joker" Moreau, above, as well as choose dialogue options in conversations by reading the response aloud. The Xbox 360 is the most popular platform for *ME3*, with sales of 2.39 million as of August 2012.

MOST CRITICALLY ACCLAIMED RPG

Mass Effect 2 (BioWare, 2010) narrowly beat *The Elder Scrolls V: Skyrim* (Bethesda, 2011) to become the most highly rated RPG, with a Metacritic average of 96%, as of 2 August 2012. Its 70 perfect scores make it publisher EA Games' most critically acclaimed title in their 30-year history. The game enjoys artistic as well as critical acclaim; the Smithsonian American Art Museum in Washington, D.C., USA, featured the game in its 2012 exhibition, "The Art of Videogames".

HIGHEST RANK ON *MASS EFFECT 3* MULTIPLAYER

The N7 ranking is the total number of points a player has gained in *ME3* multiplayer mode. The more points accrued, the higher the player's ranking. "IAMxSHADRACH" (USA) is ranked first with 12,428 points. The more characters and classes a player unlocks and plays, the more levels they can add, and the higher their N7 rating becomes.

Mass Effect fans have speculated that the events depicted at the end of *ME3* are a hallucination. The theory goes that Shepard's over-exposure to Reaper technology exposed him to indoctrination.

FIRST DOWNLOADABLE ALTERNATIVE GAME ENDING

Disappointed by the multiple-choice conclusion to *Mass Effect 3*, fans launched the "Retake *Mass Effect*" campaign – an example of how gamers can mobilize to help shape the games they love. It resulted in the co-founder of BioWare, Dr Ray Muzyka (Canada), making a public apology and promising an "extended cut" to bring clarity to the game's ending. The new ending was released in June 2012 with additional cutscenes to explore players' in-game decisions. While downloadable content is frequently used to offer extra gameplay, this is the first instance of it being utilized to amend the ending of a game that had already been released.

50,000

Number of years the advanced race of Protheans has been extinct in the *Mass Effect* timeline.

MOST ADVANCED CHARACTER IMPORT SYSTEM

Mass Effect 3 allows gamers to import more than 1,000 of their decisions from the first two games, a significant increase on *Mass Effect 2*'s previous record of 400. Importing character details affects your abilities, how others treat you and how your new adventure will turn out. No other RPG boasts a more tailored experience for each player.

try...

IF you like *Mass Effect*

Binary Domain (Yakuza Studio, 2012)
Space Quest 6 (Sierra, 1995)
Dead Space 2 (Visceral Games, 2011)
Star Wars: Knights of the Old Republic (BioWare, 2003)
Harbinger (Silverback Entertainment, 2003)
Homeworld 2 (Relic Entertainment, 2003)
Phantasy Star Universe (Sonic Team, 2006)
Darkstar One: Broken Alliance (Ascaron, 2010)
Deus Ex: Human Revolution (Eidos Montreal, 2011)
System Shock 2 (Irrational Games, 1999)

WHAT ARE THE FOUR CATEGORIES OF POWERS IN THE *MASS EFFECT* GAMES?

Diablo

D.Y.K.?

FASTEST-SELLING PC GAME

After 12 long years of waiting, gamers were chomping at the bit to get their hands on the sequel to *Diablo II* (Blizzard North, 2000). In the event, *Diablo III* (Blizzard, 2012) sold 3.5 million copies in its first 24 hours after launch. This doesn't include the 1.2 million players who received the game for free as part of a *World of Warcraft* Annual Pass promotion. With a grand total of 4.7 million players on day one, it became the biggest PC game launch ever.

FIRST ONLINE SERVICE INCORPORATED INTO A GAME

Before the launch of Blizzard Entertainment's Battle.net, online gaming services used external interfaces and usually charged for the service. But Battle.net, launched on 30 November 1996 alongside *Diablo* (Blizzard, 1996), allowed gamers to access Blizzard's online services, and gave them the ability to join multiplayer games and chat without ever leaving their game. Battle.net Classic still hosts *Diablo* today, along with *Diablo II*, *StarCraft* (Blizzard, 1998) and several *Warcraft* titles, while Battle.net 2.0 hosts *Diablo III*, *World of Warcraft* (Blizzard, 2004) and *StarCraft II* (Blizzard, 2012).

FASTEST COMPLETION OF *DIABLO*

The fastest segmented speed-run through the original *Diablo* was achieved on 16 January 2009 by Maciej Maselewski (Poland), who played as the sorceror character and took only 3 min 12 sec to finish the game. The game takes most gamers between 10 and 20 hours to complete.

Following such a long wait for the launch of *Diablo III*, fans – including keen cosplayers – were left frustrated by technical problems. Gamers were unable to play due to the oversubscribed servers. This was especially unfortunate as *Diablo III* requires players to be online. Shown above is a costumed fan on launch day in Irvine, California, USA.

2,195,808 The number of experience points you get for killing Diablo, the Lord of Terror in *Diablo II*, on the "Hell difficulty" setting.

FASTEST TIME TO REACH LEVEL 60 IN *DIABLO III*

Using a "leeching" technique, Djhunterx (Sweden) gained invaluable experience by joining his friends' *Diablo III* games as they reached the end of specific quests and levels. He did this in order to level-up his Demon Hunter-class character. Djhunterx then immediately left the game so as to minimize the playing time he clocked up on each occasion. With plenty of organization and dedication in real life, he was able to progress his character to level 60 in just 15 minutes of logged in-game playing.

FASTEST COMPLETION OF *DIABLO III*

Just 5 hr 30 min after the *Diablo III* server opened on 15 May 2012, South Korean clan EHG had completed the game and killed the final boss. Due to server problems, however, they were unable to collect some of the best loot along the way. They still gained accolades for being both the fastest *Diablo III* players in the world, a record that stood as of July 2012, and also the **first players to complete *Diablo III***.

GAME OVER

The real-life concerns of gaming were highlighted in 2012 when a Taiwanese *Diablo III* player died after a 40-hour session. The 18-year-old, named as Chuang, went without food or sleep in an internet cafe's private room on 13–15 July. When a member of staff found him resting and woke him, Chuang took a few steps, collapsed and died in hospital. Authorities suspected that he had a fatal blood clot after being seated for so long.

Activision said, "We're saddened to hear this ... Moderation is clearly important and ... day-to-day life should take precedence over any form of entertainment."

FIRST "HARDCORE INFERNO" COMPLETION OF *DIABLO III*

Canadian gamer Kripparrian and his "wizard friend" Krippi (USA) claimed a major victory in the millions-strong *Diablo III* community when they achieved the first "Hardcore Inferno" completion of the game. This milestone was reached on 19 June 2012, a total of 37 days after the game's launch. "Inferno" is the game's highest difficulty level, while the "Hardcore" character mode means that when a character dies, the game ends and the player cannot reload his or her last save point.

If you like Diablo try...

Moria (RA Koeneke & JW Todd, 1994)
Angband (Angband Development Team, 1990)
Torchlight (Runic Games, 2009)
Fate (WildTangent, 2005)
Dungeon Siege III (Obsidian, 2011)
Dungeon Keeper (Bullfrog, 1997)
Sacred 2: Fallen Angel (Ascaron, 2008)
Neverwinter Nights (BioWare, 2002)
Baldur's Gate: Dark Alliance II (Black Isle Studios/Interplay, 2004)
Titan Quest (Iron Lore, 2006)

WHAT IS THE NAME OF THE FANTASY WORLD IN WHICH *DIABLO* IS SET?

GUINNESS WORLD RECORDS

Final Fantasy

THE VENERABLE SERIES IS LONG ON INVENTION, WITH AIRSHIPS, GIANT CHICKENS AND SPEEDY CACTI ADDING FUN TO COMPLEX STORIES AND COMBAT

MOST PROLIFIC RPG SERIES

As of September 2012, *Final Fantasy* (Square Enix, 1987–present) runs to 54 titles, including numbered entries and spin-offs (but not games outside of the RPG genre). *Final Fantasy XIII* (above) was released in 2009. The spin-offs have included movies and TV series. The games' Japanese creator Hironobu Sakaguchi put "Final" into the title because it was his last attempt at designing a hit game – he had planned to quit the industry and go to university.

The "Theme of Love" was composed by Nobuo Uematsu (Japan) for Rosa's scenes with Cecil in *Final Fantasy IV* (1991). From 2005, it was included in the musical curriculum taught to 11-year-olds in Japanese schools, meaning that students were learning about music from a game released before they were born. An anthem that has captured the popular imagination in Japan, it has also been included on five *Final Fantasy IV* soundtrack albums.

LONGEST ATTACK ANIMATION

Japanese RPGs are known for elaborate boss fights and complex attack animations. In the penultimate battle of *Final Fantasy VII* (1997) the boss Safer Sephiroth's SuperNova attack starts a cutscene that takes a record 2 min 16 sec to unfold. This is gaming's longest wait between the start and end of an attack, and cannot be skipped through.

By comparison, in *Borderlands 2* (Gearbox, 2012) some automatic weapons work quickly enough to produce 2,400 individual attacks in the same time it takes for just one SuperNova cutscene to finish!

ONE UP

Square Enix claims its Luminous Studio engine will close the gap in quality between what can be achieved with real-time game graphics and narrative cinematic sequences. The engine was unveiled at E3, USA, in June 2012, with a *Final Fantasy*-themed demo entitled *Agni's Philosophy*. Characters were incredibly detailed, down to the last hair and facial feature, and all attributes were definable. Full games have yet to be announced for the technology but the exquisite taster turned heads. It is likely that future titles will include *Final Fantasy*, and Square Enix are adapting the technology to run not only on consoles but also on smartphones, PCs and the web.

MOST PROLIFIC BOSS ENEMY IN AN RPG

Bahamut has appeared in 32 RPGs, of which 27 are *Final Fantasy* titles. In 1996 he got his own game, *Bahamut Lagoon* (Square). Bahamut features as a boss in every *Final Fantasy* game except the original, although he can sometimes be summoned to help players in battles. He also appeared in the 1970s *Dungeons & Dragons* pencil-and-paper RPGs.

Time to look down the back of the sofa for some extra small change. American videogame historian Frank Cifaldi (USA) was seeking offers in the region of $50,000 (£31,000) when he listed a sample *Final Fantasy II* cartridge on eBay in August 2012. It was claimed to be a rare example of the abandoned North American version of the game. The asking price dwarfed the $21,400 (£10,700) paid for a gold version of the special edition *Nintendo World Championship 1990* (Nintendo/Square/Alexey Pajitnov) on eBay back in 2007.

If you like Final Fantasy

try...

Blue Dragon (Mistwalker/Artoon, 2006)
Star Ocean: The Last Hope (tri-Ace, 2009)
Dark Chronicle (Level-5, 2002)
Dragon Quest VIII: Journey of the Cursed King (Level-5, 2004)
Eternal Sonata (Tri-Crescendo, 2007)
Xenoblade Chronicles (Monolith Soft, 2010)
Lost Odyssey (Mistwalker/feelplus, 2007)
Chrono Trigger (Square, 1995)
Tales of Vesperia (Namco Tales, 2008)
Kingdom Hearts II (Square Enix, 2005)

FASTEST COMPLETION OF *FINAL FANTASY IV*

Superfan Andrew Melnyk (Canada) broke his own speed-running record three times in *Final Fantasy IV*, most recently with a 3-hr 40-min 3-sec single-segment completion.

MOST CRITICALLY ACCLAIMED JRPG

Final Fantasy IX (2000) has a mighty Metacritic score of 94%, as of September 2012. The game – which features a light-hearted plot and has a protagonist with a tail – was a return to the style of the early series.

LONGEST DEVELOPMENT PERIOD FOR A JRPG

Final Fantasy Versus XIII is still in development more than six years after it was first announced at E3 in May 2006. It beats the previous holder of the record, *Final Fantasy XII* (2006), by nearly two years. Industry whispers in summer 2012 prompted a July tweet from Square Enix head Yoichi Wada: "There's someone making a false rumour that *Versus* was cancelled. Haha... Just a minute ago, the regular *Versus* meeting ended. If you saw the presentation of the city, it'd knock you off your feet~lol."

WHAT IS THE NAME OF THE PUDDING-LIKE ENEMIES THAT APPEAR IN THE *FINAL FANTASY SERIES*?

Skylanders

**IS IT A GAME? IS IT A TOY?
NO, IT'S BOTH – IN A WHOLE
UNIVERSE OF PORTAL-
POWERED FUN!**

BEST-SELLING INTERACTIVE GAMING TOYS

In June 2012, publisher Activision announced that *Skylanders: Spyro's Adventure* (Toys For Bob, 2011) had been the best-selling console game of the first half of 2012. Even more impressive is the meteoric rise of the *Skylanders* range of interactive toys, 30 million of which sold within seven months of the game's October 2011 launch. Pictured right is dragoness Cynder on a Portal of Power, a crucial *Skylanders* peripheral. The Portal connects the player's console with the toys, converting them from frozen figurines to all-action gaming heroes. The Portal glows in different colours according to which character is perched on it. Due for October 2012 release, *Skylanders: Giants* (Toys For Bob) is shown above.

FIRST CONSOLE GAME TO USE NEAR FIELD COMMUNICATION

"Near Field Communication" is a system whereby compatible electronic devices in close proximity can communicate using radio frequencies. Its origins go way back to 1983, although it wasn't utilized by mobile phone companies until 2004. The technology is used in the Portal of Power for *Skylanders: Spyro's Adventure*, which reads special chips within the toy figurines to send data to the game and receive data back in return.

£827 ($1,310)

The total price of six Silver and Gold *Skylanders* toys sold on eBay on 18 February 2012.

ONE UP

Originally, all Skylanders were set to use their own nonsense language rather than a real, comprehensible dialect. After testing, developers Toys For Bob decided to allow 14 characters to speak English, while the rest still use gibberish to communicate. Although fearless Gill Grunt, one of three figures bundled with the game, speaks mostly in English, he still has a single line of gobbledygook, used when he is placed on the Portal of Power.

FIRST ONLINE GAME TO USE TOY FIGURES AS PLAYABLE CHARACTERS

In webgame *Skylanders: Spyro's Universe* (Frima Studios, 2011), players can plug their Portal of Power into a PC's USB port to unlock new characters in the free online world. The Portal is also a transporter, taking Skylanders to distant parts of Spyro's universe.

MOST PLAYABLE CHARACTERS IN AN ACTION RPG

Skylanders: Spyro's Adventure has a total of 53 fearsome warriors to choose from: 40 regular Skylanders, four Legendary Skylanders (painted blue and gold), Dark Spyro and eight brand new "Giant" characters that tower over their regular-sized companions.

The game with the **most playable characters** overall is *Fire Pro Wrestling Returns* (Spike, 2005), which has 327 individual personas for gamers to control. The game's subsequent 2007 release on the PS2 marked the first USA port for this successful Japanese wrestling series.

FIRST GAME WITH CRACK PROTECTION

Before Spyro joined the ensemble cast of *Skylanders*, he was the star of his own game series for the PlayStation and PS2. *Spyro: Year of the Dragon* (Insomniac Games, 2000), the third entry in the *Spyro* series (Various, 1998–present), was the first game to feature a brand new copy-protection system that meant it was "booby-trapped" against piracy. As a result, it took far longer to find a way to crack the game's code.

WHICH ELEMENT IS TREE REX, FROM *SKYLANDERS: GIANTS*, PART OF?

Girl Power-Up

It is universally acknowledged in gaming that male videogame characters vastly outnumber their female counterparts, but quantity is not everything! While women are all too often relegated to the background or supporting cast as sidekicks or girlfriends, there are plenty of exceptions. Here we present our pick of landmark playable female characters through the years.

Feature

MS. PAC-MAN
According to creator Toru Iwatani (Japan), *PAC-Man* (Namco, 1980) was designed to appeal primarily to women. Two years later, the addition of a hair bow and lipstick to the munching mouth turned PAC-Man into *Ms. PAC-Man* (Bally/Midway, 1982), the **first playable female videogame character**. It sold 125,000 cabinets by 1988, the **most successful US-made arcade machine**.

JENNIFER HALE
Quest for Glory: Shadows of Darkness on CD (Sierra, 1994) marked the videogame debut of Jennifer Hale (Canada), the **most prolific videogame voice actor (female)**. That first character was not playable, but Hale went on to take leads in many of her 130 subsequent roles, including Samus Aran in *Metroid Prime* (Retro Studios/Nintendo, 2002).

SAMUS ARAN
Following in the mouth-steps of *Ms. PAC-Man* came Samus Aran, the female bounty hunter of *Metroid* (Nintendo R&D/Intelligent Systems, 1986). Undermining her strong role, however, was the way she appeared to be a male hero until the game was completed, at which point she stripped off her armoured suit (although she always kept something on).

Samus was the **first playable human female character in a mainstream videogame** and has proven to be enduringly popular. The *Metroid* series had sold over 17.44 million copies as of 22 September 2012.

CHUN-LI
Street Fighter II (Capcom, 1991) set the standard by which all 2D fighters are judged. It is the **most prolific fighting series**, with a total of 146 different versions, including *Street Fighter X Tekken* (Dimps/Capcom, 2012). It also boasted the **first female playable character in a fighting game** with ex-Interpol agent Chun-Li. She has featured in most later titles and is the character of choice for French gamer "Kayane" (see p.92), the **first woman to win a pro-*Street Fighter* videogame competition**.

LARA CROFT
Iconic Lara Croft (see *Tomb Raider*, pp.64–65) is the **best-selling videogame heroine** and a media star in her own right, appearing in magazines and adverts for soft drinks and fast cars. Her enduring popularity and wild adventures attract plenty of speed-runners, with the **fastest glitched single-segment speed-run of *Tomb Raider*** (Core Design, 1996) set at 1 hr 50 min 16 sec by Ali "AKA" Gordon on 25 May 2007.

VALENTINE
The **first female player character in a survival-horror game** was police officer Jill Valentine. Better equipped than male counterpart Chris Redfield, it was no surprise that in the **fastest completion of *Resident Evil*** (Capcom, 1996) Brandon "Ekudeht" Armstrong (USA) played her. He completed a run on 28 May 2005 in 1 hr 9 min 17 sec.

GLaDOS
Portal (Valve, 2007) is an oddity, a puzzler built like an FPS. It has attracted speed-runners such as Kevin "Monopoli" Marnell, who achieved the **fastest single-segment speed-run of *Portal*** on 6 September 2011, with 21 min 8 sec. The appeal of this uniquely engaging game is not hard to see. It's largely down to the main characters, all female or voiced by female actors, led by the malevolent, artificially intelligent computer GLaDOS, voiced by actress and opera singer Ellen McLain (USA, below). She recorded the game song "Still Alive", which was later performed live at the prestigious Press Start Symphony of Games concert in Japan, a celebration of gaming music.

AERITH GAINSBOROUGH
The *Final Fantasy* series has a long history of playable female characters. But *Final Fantasy VII* (Square, 1997) had a shocking twist when – spoiler alert – Aerith Gainsborough, a playable character, was unexpectedly killed in the middle of the game by Sephiroth. The unusual move didn't stop the game becoming the **best-selling JRPG**, with sales of 9.72 million.

BAYONETTA
Where Chun-Li is empowered, Bayonetta is all excess, a fighting witch who shoots both from the hip and from the guns integrated in her high heels. This is only to be expected of the over-the-top hack-and-slash genre, and Japanese gaming bible *Famitsu* gave *Bayonetta* (Platinum Games, 2009) a 40/40 score, the **first Xbox 360 game to get a perfect *Famitsu* score**. It is one of only three Xbox 360 titles to have made the grade.

FAITH CONNORS
Female characters such as Faith Connors of action-adventure *Mirror's Edge* (EA DICE, 2008) are often in the vanguard of gaming experimentation, and Faith was the star of the **first first-person game to feature free running**. *Mirror's Edge* received critical praise for its inventiveness and a Metacritic score of 81%, although some thought it too short. Yet the game still appeals to speed-running fans, among them David "Weatherproof" Streeter (USA), who recorded the **fastest single-segment speed-run of *Mirror's Edge***, with 57 min 23 sec on 23 September 2011.

Contents

10

Overview

Sporting videogames remain one of the most enduring genres, consisting of some of the longest-lasting franchises such as *NHL* (EA, 1991–present) and *FIFA* (EA, 1993–present). Soccer-mad Jacob Gaby (UK) is a *FIFA 12* expert. On 20 August 2012 he set the record for the **highest margin of victory against a computer**, winning 189–0 playing as Barcelona FC against Fulham FC, in Bushey, UK.

Biography

Joseph Ewens is a freelance videogame journalist and poker columnist. His scribblings can be read at institutions such as Kotaku, Den of Geek and Pokerati. Additionally, he once wrote about dwarves for Fantasy Flight Games, and has occasionally dipped his hand into the bubbling cauldron of immersive theatre.

MOST PROLIFIC VIDEOGAME SPORTSMAN
No real-life competitor comes close to matching the prowess of Mario. The Nintendo favourite has appeared in 30 sports titles over the years, starting with the Game & Watch title *Donkey Kong Hockey* (1984), followed by his console sports debut in *Golf* (Nintendo, 1984) on the NES. Mario has tried his hand at a huge range of sports including baseball, basketball, soccer, tennis, snowboarding, archery, fencing and gymnastics. With all that exercise it's difficult to believe he still hasn't managed to shift his trademark "pasta paunch"!

Sport for all
Picking up a controller to play *FIFA* (EA, 1993–present, see pp.164–165) or *Madden NFL* (EA, 1988–present, see pp.162–163) is as close as you can get to the action without strapping on some boots and getting muddy in the field. In many ways, it's a better experience. Gamers can play for several different teams in a single afternoon or craft a legendary managerial career in just a few months. They can be sinking free throws one minute and serving an ace the next. As a gamer, there's no sport that can't be mastered and no league that can't be conquered.

How to spot this genre

HAS GOT:
- Pros on the cover looking angrily into the middle distance
- Loud men shouting at each other
- Stilted speech from… "the commentators!"

HASN'T GOT:
- Health packs
- Player ratings that satisfy every fan
- Subtlety

Emulate success
The desire to emulate our sporting heroes has had a profound effect on sports games. Simulation games have become the most popular in the genre, with the likes of *FIFA* and *NBA 2K* (Visual Concepts, 1999–present) striving to provide ever more accurate renditions. In a more abstract way, *Football Manager* (Sports Interactive, 2004–present, see pp.166–167) recreates the day-to-day life of a top coach facing soccer's highest highs, lowest lows and all points between.

LONGEST NHL VIDEOGAME MARATHON

James Evans and Bruce Ashton (both Canada) played *NHL 10* (EA, 2009) for 24 hr 2 min in Orillia, Ontario, Canada, between 30 and 31 July 2011. Playing outside the town's Walmart superstore, Ashton's Winnipeg Jets fantasy team won the 45-game series against Evans and his Detroit Red Wings fantasy team by 32–13.

Wii can be heroes

Wii Sports (Nintendo, 2006) showed how more accessible games also capture the sense of competition delivered by simulation titles. There has also been a blending of the two styles, with EA's various *Street* series creating an arena in which flair is just as important as playing to win.

Pong time ago

When videogames were in their infancy, sports attracted pioneering programmers. Even the simplistic but seminal *Pong* (Atari, 1972) relied on an understanding of table tennis for its basic mechanics.

Today, the relationship between sports games and the players they depict is closer than ever. Many sports stars are regular gamers who grew up idolizing their heroes on pixelated pitches rather than through grainy TV images.

Sports videogames appeal to our real-life sporting heroes because, above all else, they encourage competition and there's only one thing that suits competition more than professional sports people: records.

MOST PERFECT GAMES OF Wii SPORTS BOWLING

With 14,000 perfect "300" games on *Wii Sports*, John Bates (USA) is the most accomplished bowling kingpin in videogames. Bates plays at least 50 matches every day and rarely drops a point – his longest winning streak is more than 350 perfect games! At the time of his last game count (in June 2012) he was 85 years 205 days old, making him the **oldest videogaming record-holder**.

BEST-SELLING SNOWBOARDING SERIES

Following the release of *SSX* (EA, 2012), the long-running alpine sports series took its total sales up to a staggering 9.47 million units, as of September 2012. Following a five-year wait since the last game, the high-octane 2012 edition debuted at No.1 in the UK chart in its week of release in March. *SSX* (Snowboard Supercross) began in 2000 and the most recent entry in the series brought its trademark features to HD consoles for the first time, with incredible tricks, combos, huge jumps and lethal peaks to conquer.

NBA

IN WHICH ATHLETES POWER HARD TO THE PAINT AND SLAM DUNK THEIR WAY INTO SPORTING FOLKLORE

BEST-SELLING BASKETBALL FRANCHISE

EA Sports hasn't released an *NBA Live* game since 2009, but that has not prevented the series from staying top of the list of b-ball franchises. An enormous 35 million games have been sold since *NBA Live 95* was released in 1994. An attempt to rename the brand *NBA Elite* fell through when the 2011 console release was cancelled due to "game polish" concerns. The franchise is back on track with a scheduled *NBA Live 13* reboot.

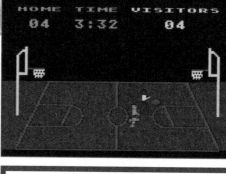

Atari's 1979 title *Basketball* (above) was one of the first hit b-ball games, even appearing in the 1980 American comedy film *Airplane!* Two pilots are seen playing *Basketball* instead of flying the plane. One of them is professional basketball player Kareem Abdul-Jabbar.

In PC and NES title *Harlem Globetrotters* (Softie, Inc., 1990), gamers could only play as either the Globetrotters or their rivals the Washington Generals. They could, however, perform multiple tricks and even pull down the referee's trousers!

BIGGEST BLOWOUT IN *NBA JAM* (SINGLE-PLAYER)

One of the most beloved basketball games ever to grace an arcade's neon halls, *NBA Jam* (Midway, 1993) brought an exaggerated flair to one of America's most electric sports. Competing in 3-on-3 matches, players could leap into the air to perform acrobatic dunks and literally catch fire during a hot streak. The biggest blowout – a term for the gap between the winning and losing score – on the MAME emulator version of the game is 50. The score was set by Nicola Matteuzzi (Italy). Pictured here is the 2010 port for the PlayStation 3, Wii and Xbox 360.

MOST PLAYS IN A BASKETBALL VIDEOGAME

To the casual observer, basketball can look like two teams of men taking turns to put a ball through some netting, but there are intricacies beneath the surface. A player's movements are often choreographed according to rehearsed "plays" that teams use to unlock the opposition's defence. The celebrated *NBA 2K11* (Visual Concepts, 2010) features an enormous 850 different plays to choose from.

FIRST GAME WITH AN NBA LICENCE

Numerous non-licenced basketball games appeared in the late 1970s and 1980s; organizations such as the NBA charge a hefty fee for their players' likenesses, so it took a brave developer to stump up the cash. That developer was Tecmo, and the game was *Tecmo NBA Basketball* (1992). Tecmo also developed the **first game with an NFL licence**, *Tecmo Super Bowl* (1991).

LONGEST-RUNNING BASKETBALL SERIES

The very first game in EA's *NBA Live* series was *NBA Live 95*. There have been 16 games so far, with the 17th, *NBA Live 13*, scheduled for an autumn 2012 release. The successful *NBA 2K* series didn't start until 1999, and EA's own *NCAA Basketball* first appeared in 1998 (as *NCAA March Madness*). *NBA Live* has featured numerous cover stars over the years, including American b-ballers Shaquille O'Neal, Dwyane Wade and Dwight Howard.

If you like NBA games try...

- *World Basketball Manager* (icehole, 2003)
- *NBA 2K12* (Visual Concepts, 2011)
- *NBA 2K2* (Visual Concepts, 2001)
- *NBA Ballers* (EA, 2004)
- *NCAA Basketball 10* (EA, 2009)
- *NBA Elite* for iOS (EA, 2010)
- *NBA Jam* (Midway, 1993)
- *NBA Street* (EA, 2001)
- *Wii Sports Resort* (Nintendo EAD, 2009)
- *Mario Hoops 3-on-3* (Square Enix, 2006)

TOP 10 MOST CRITICALLY ACCLAIMED *NBA* TITLES

Score	Game	Platform
93%	*NBA 2K1* (Visual Concepts, 2000)	Dreamcast
93%	*NBA 2K2* (Visual Concepts, 2001)	Dreamcast
90%	*NBA 2K12* (Visual Concepts, 2011)	Xbox 360
90%	*NBA 2K12* (Visual Concepts, 2011)	PS3
90%	*NBA 2K2* (Visual Concepts, 2002)	GameCube
90%	*NBA 2K2* (Visual Concepts, 2002)	Xbox
90%	*NBA Street: Vol. 2* (EA Canada, 2003)	PS2
89%	*ESPN NBA Basketball* (Visual Concepts, 2003)	PS2
89%	*NBA 2K2* (Visual Concepts, 2002)	PS2
89%	*NBA Street* (EA, 2001)	PS2

According to Metacritic, as of 2 August 2012.

FIRST CELEBRITY-ENDORSED BASKETBALL GAME

Basketball fans constantly argue about who was the greatest ever. Michael Jordan and Larry Bird (both USA) are two likely candidates. Although Chicago Bulls (USA) legend Jordan may now have a higher profile, it was Bird who got to the videogame party first, with EA's *Dr J and Larry Bird Go One on One* (1983), in which gamers can assume the roles of Bird and fellow NBA legend Julius Erving in 1-v-1 basketball matches.

Magic Johnson (USA) was the star of the **first game to feature a single professional basketball player** when he endorsed *Magic Johnson's Fast Break* (Arcadia, 1988). Jordan's first gaming appearance was in *Jordan vs Bird: One on One* (Arcadia, 1988).

24 Total number of games featuring basketball superstar Michael Jordan.

WHAT DOES NBA STAND FOR?

Madden NFL

THE BONE-CRUNCHING NOBILITY OF THE GRIDIRON IS PLAIN TO SEE IN AMERICAN FOOTBALL'S MOST CELEBRATED GAMING FRANCHISE

LONGEST-RUNNING SPORTS GAME FRANCHISE

While John Madden himself retired in 2009, the game series that bears the commentator's name shows no sign of slowing down. With a total of 27 games released in 25 years, the franchise is the longest-running in sports. Just as impressive is the unbroken run of annual launches: every year since 1990, gridiron fans have had a new *Madden* game to play for the start of the season. The latest release, pictured above, is *Madden NFL 13* (EA Tiburon, 2012).

FASTEST ROSTER UPDATE IN A SPORTS GAME

Dedicated sports fans are always desperate to get their hands on the latest players in sporting videogames. For the real-life NFL draft in April 2012, *Madden* developers EA Tiburon went to great lengths to ensure that updates were the timeliest, most accurate they've ever been. Rookie players were released into the card-based "Ultimate Team" mode of the game within minutes of their selection in the real draft. The Indianapolis Colts' new quarterback Andrew Luck (USA) was listed as one of six special "Future Stars" by EA Tiburon.

MOST PLATFORMS FOR A SPORTS FRANCHISE

Across its history, the *Madden* series has appeared on an impressive 33 different types of hardware, which puts it two ahead of closest challenger *FIFA* (EA Sports, 1993–present). *Madden*'s platform portfolio includes such ill-fated entries as the Tapwave Zodiac, pictured right, which sold fewer than 200,000 units, and the Gizmondo, which sold a mere 25,000 units. By comparison, the Nintendo DS has sold more than 150 million. As of April 2012 *Star Wars* (1982–present) holds the record for the **most platforms for a videogame series**, with 279 games across 41 platforms.

HIGHEST-RATED RUNNING BACKS IN *MADDEN NFL 13*

Rating	Player	Team
97	Maurice Jones-Drew	Jaguars
97	Adrian Peterson	Vikings
96	Arian Foster	Texans
95	LeSean McCoy	Eagles
95	Ray Rice	Ravens
93	Matt Forté	Bears
92	Frank Gore	49ers
92	Steven Jackson	Rams
91	Jamaal Charles	Chiefs
91	Michael Turner	Falcons

According to speed, truck, acceleration and elusiveness, from EA's survey of Madden fans.

BIGGEST BLOWOUT ON *MADDEN NFL ARCADE*

Jeffrey M Widzinski (USA) scored a stunning 35-point victory over a rookie AI on *Madden NFL Arcade* (EA Tiburon, 2009) on 21 April 2012. He may be further inspired by the newest game in the franchise, *Madden NFL 13*, which was released in August 2012 with a cover featuring Calvin "Megatron" Johnson, the wide receiver for Widzinski's local team the Detroit Lions.

LONGEST-SERVING VIDEOGAME COMMENTATOR

Although the first *Madden* game hit the shelves in 1989, gaming technology was not advanced enough to support John Madden's famous voice until the release of *Madden NFL 96* (Tiburon Entertainment, 1995). After 13 years of gaming commentary, he hung up his microphone in 2008 having completed work on *Madden NFL 09* (EA Tiburon, 2008).

ONE UP

The "Madden Curse" is a mythical affliction suffered by *Madden* cover stars in the season after they grace the box art, and EA are now developing a movie all about the phenomenon. Details are sparse, but the movie is believed to be a comedy based on a retired videogame champion. Examples of the curse? The 2004 cover featured Michael Vick, who then broke his leg in a pre-season game. Shaun Alexander suffered a broken foot after starring on the 2007 package, and Peyton Hillis's 2012 cover appearance was followed by a season hampered by injury.

POWER UP

DREAM TEAM

If you've ever wondered what the guys who work at EA Tiburon would look like on a football field, you need wonder no more. While selecting your team for an exhibition match, you can unlock the Dev Team by pressing **L2** five times (on a PlayStation 3) or **LT** five times (on the Xbox 360). The developers have generously rated themselves 99 in every stat.

WHICH US PRESIDENT APPEARS IN *MADDEN NFL 11* (EA TIBURON, 2010)?

7 million

Total sales across all platforms of *Madden NFL 2004* (EA Tiburon, 2003), the best-selling *Madden* series title as of 9 August 2012.

FIFA

THE BEAUTIFUL GAME NEVER LOOKED QUITE SO BEAUTIFUL...

FASTEST-SELLING SPORTS GAME

No sports title has launched more successfully than *FIFA 13* (EA Canada, 2012), which sold 4.5 million units in less than a week. This was made easier by the game's availability on a wide range of platforms, including major consoles as well as PC and even iOS seeing some action. Predecessor *FIFA 12* (2011) holds the record for **most official box art designs**, with a total of 17. In addition to the region-specific covers, EA put together a collection of downloadable box art for selected clubs from the English Premier League and the Championship, including (above, left to right) Manchester City, Chelsea and Fulham, which fans could download, print and insert into the box sleeve.

FIRST SOCCER GAME FOR KINECT

Shouting at your TV is a time-honoured tradition when it comes to watching sport, but it's unheard of to have the on-screen action react to your screams – until now. *FIFA 13* (EA Canada, 2012) integrates with the Kinect on Xbox 360 to allow you to call for substitutions and formations using just your voice, making it the **first voice-controlled soccer game**. Watch your language, though, as swearing at the referee could earn you a yellow card. While *Kinect Sports* (Rare, 2010) features a goalkeeping mini-game, *FIFA 13* is the first soccer-only game to support the Kinect.

MOST SPORTS GAMERS ONLINE SIMULTANEOUSLY

On 30 September 2012, just a few days after the release of *FIFA 13*, EA recorded 800,000 gamers logged in to play that one game alone. By 3 October 2012, more than 66 million online *FIFA 13* game sessions had been played, which adds up to more than 600 million minutes of game time.

MOST WINS OF *FIFA* INTERACTIVE WORLD CUPS

FIFA ace Alfonso Ramos (Spain, below) is the first and only person to win the *FIFA* Interactive World Cup more than once. Ramos played as Real Madrid in 2012 and claimed a narrow win on penalties against Bruce Grannec (France), the 2009 world champion who also played as Real Madrid. Ramos first won the title in 2008 at the age of 20 and has a lot to be proud of: he is the champion of the **largest gaming tournament**, which saw more than 1.3 million players registered for the 2012 competition.

RONALDO

MESSI

MOST FANS ON EA SPORTS FOOTBALL CLUB

When you boot up *FIFA 12* for the first time, the game asks you to select a favourite team. In previous releases this was little more than a courtesy, but the addition of "EA Sports Football Club" means that what you do in-game helps contribute to your club's stature. The team with the most fans is Manchester United (UK), who had 737,451 supporters as of 17 September 2012.

TOP TEN

BEST DRIBBLERS IN *FIFA 12*

Player	Club	Rating
Lionel Messi	Barcelona	97
Arjen Robben	Bayern Munich	94
Cristiano Ronaldo	Real Madrid	93
Franck Ribéry	Bayern Munich	93
Sergio Agüero	Man. City	93
Andrés Iniesta	Barcelona	91
Robinho	AC Milan	91
Alexis Sánchez	Barcelona	90
Ezequiel Lavezzi	PSG	90
Neymar	Santos	90

According to EA Sports, as of 17 September 2012.

D.U.K?

FIFA 12 became the focal point for a spate of Xbox 360 account hacks in late 2011, as hundreds of gamers found EA's soccer title appearing unexpectedly on their list of played games. Internet thieves were gaining access to players' accounts and then using their credit cards or Xbox Live points to buy stacks of cards for the *FIFA* Ultimate Team game mode.

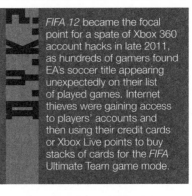

91% Metacritic score of *FIFA 10*, the series' most acclaimed title.

GUINNESS WORLD RECORDS

Football Manager

A STAGGERING COLLECTION OF STATISTICS AND DATABASES COME TOGETHER TO CREATE AN ENDLESSLY ADDICTIVE SIMULATOR

ONE UP

While many games developers are looking to mobile platforms as a way of bringing their work to a wider audience, piracy – particularly on Android phones – has become a big headache for the industry. Miles Jacobson (UK), studio director at Sports Interactive, wrote in *Wired* magazine that "more than 100,000 people were enjoying the new Android version of our game. The bad news is that only about 10% of them paid for it."

LARGEST SOCCER GAME DATABASE

The success of the *Football Manager* series (Intelek/Sports Interactive,1992–present) is based on its realism, achieved by collecting a huge amount of data about players, clubs and stadia around the world. Sports Interactive employs a team of scouts to travel the globe, recording the abilities of thousands of soccer players in almost every league. In the 2012 game, the database contained 501,451 entries.

MOST COUNTRIES IN A SPORTS GAME

Football Manager 2012 (Sports Interactive, 2011) features unparalleled potential for patriotic pride. Players can take the reins of national squads from 53 different countries and lead them to glory in competitions as varied as the Olympic Games and the Caribbean Championship, as well as the FIFA World Cup, of course.

MOST PLAYABLE LEAGUES IN A SPORTS GAME

Whether you prefer a second-tier Turkish side or the mighty Barcelona, *Football Manager 2012* has you covered. There are 117 different leagues to choose from, not to mention international competitions and continental tournaments.

MOST IN-GAME AWARDS

Gathering as many achievements and trophies as possible is par for the course for the gaming community, but it would take some serious dedication to win all of the 1,931 awards available in *Football Manager 2012*. Each accolade is based on a real prize from worldwide professional soccer, including "Belarusian Discovery of the Year".

CALL IT A LOAN

If you've signed a foreign player who doesn't yet have a work permit, the quickest way to secure one is to loan him out to a feeder club. The fastest clubs for securing a permit are in the Belgian, Spanish or Polish leagues. During his loan period, offer him a new contract at least once every month.

GAME OVER

When soccer coach Steve McClaren left Middlesbrough FC (both UK) to become the England team boss, avid *Football Manager 2005* (Sports Interactive, 2004) player John Boileau (UK) submitted his CV and covering letter to the club. Perhaps unsurprisingly, the chairman did not invite him for interview.

FIRST GAME DEVELOPERS AWARDED AN MBE

The *Football Manager* series is so beloved in the UK that even the Queen saw fit to recognize it. She awarded Paul and Oliver Collyer (UK), the creators of *Championship Manager* (Intelek, 1992), the Member of the British Empire (MBE) honour in 2010. *Football Manager* was known as *Championship Manager* until 2003, when SEGA took over as publishers. Miles Jacobson, studio director at Sports Interactive, was also awarded the OBE in 2011. The **first game developer to win an OBE** was Jez San (UK), in 2002.

CAN YOU NAME ALL FIVE SOCCER PLAYERS PICTURED ABOVE?

eSPORTS WORLD TOUR

eSports continued to grow in 2012, both in stature and numbers, and it shows no sign of letting up in 2013. Online streaming services such as Justin.tv and Twitch.tv continue to bring coverage of gaming's highest echelons to ever-increasing audiences. As eSports grows in global popularity, being a pro gamer has become a handy way for top players to see the world...

JÖNKÖPING, SWEDEN

Starting in a Swedish school in 1994, Dreamhack attracted some 20,000 people for its winter 2011 event, making it the **largest LAN party**. A LAN is a local area network that connects computers.

LOS ANGELES, USA

Riot Games' *League of Legends* is rapidly becoming a dominant force in eSports. The game's second competitive season, organized by developer Riot Games, consisted of hard-fought qualification for six regional finals in 2012. The top 12 teams from these finals went on to compete in the overall Championship Finals in Los Angeles, California, for a combined prize pool of $3 million (£1.9 million). Pictured above are the champions of season one in 2011 – Fnatic, a team made up of gamers from various countries, including Finland and Spain.

ANAHEIM, USA

Major League Gaming (MLG) has been running eSports tournaments since 2002, hosting a variety of games and formats. Is now regarded as the biggest eSports promoter in America. The 2012 Spring Championship in Anaheim, California, attracted 0,000 attendees, with a total prize pool for competitors of 00,000 (£127,000). A collaboration between KeSPA (the managing body of eSports in Korea) and MLG brought a selection StarCraft professionals to the USA for an exhibition tournament.

LAS VEGAS, USA

IGN.com has been involved with games since its founding in 1996, but 2011 saw the **most popular videogames website** enter the eSports scene in earnest with the IGN Pro League (IPL). The IPL4 competition took place in July 2012 at the Cosmopolitan Hotel in Las Vegas, Nevada, and saw more than 10,000 spectators and players attend.

HAMAR, NORWAY

The Gathering, the largest computer party in Norway, began in 1992 and has grown from an attendance of 1,400 to a sell-out crowd of 5,200 in 10 years. *StarCraft II: Wings of Liberty*, *Battlefield 3*, *League of Legends* and *Minecraft* are all in competition, and professional teams such as Team Dignitas (UK), Team Grubby (Netherlands) and mousesports (Germany) attended the 2012 event.

PARIS, FRANCE

Established in 2003, the Electronic Sports World Cup final in 2012 was hosted during Paris Games Week. An estimated 150,000 visitors attended, with a total of 45 countries represented by 400 pro players.

DUBAI, UAE

The FIFA Interactive World Cup 2012 saw 24 opponents from around the globe facing off in an extended *FIFA* tournament over three days in Dubai. A total of $20,000 (£12,746) was up for grabs, as well as tickets to the prestigious FIFA Ballon d'Or Gala in Zurich, Switzerland. Find out which gamer won the virtual World Cup on p.101.

SEOUL, SOUTH KOREA

The "premier league" for *StarCraft II* players is the prestigious Global *StarCraft II* League (GSL) in South Korea, which runs events and tournaments throughout the year. In a country where eSports is a national pastime, GSL competitions feature both Korean and English-language commentary. The 2012 season one prize pool was a huge 2.1 billion South Korean won ($1.9 million; £1.2 million).

LAS VEGAS, USA

When it comes to fighting games, one event stands out on the eSports calendar: the Evolution Championship Series (EVO). The 2012 tournament hosted competitions in nine games including *Super Street Fighter IV Arcade Edition*, *Ultimate Marvel vs Capcom 3* and newcomer *Skullgirls*. Over 30,000 players entered from all over the world, and it proved popular: spectator tickets sold out.

MELBOURNE, AUSTRALIA

The Australian Cyber League was started in 2006 by a group of gamers frustrated at the lack of *Halo 2* tournaments. By 2012, competitors were taking part in regional, national and online qualifiers and finals for events in *StarCraft II*, *Halo: Reach*, *Halo 3*, *Call of Duty: Modern Warfare 3*, *Gears of War 3* and *FIFA 12*.

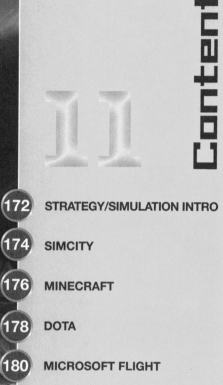

Contents

11

Overview

While sim games tend to involve complexity and life-like intricacy, strategy games are often about a bigger picture – one that includes warfare, battles and aggressive action.

In November 2011, developer Riot Games announced that its *League of Legends* (2009) had accumulated more than 11.5 million active users, making it the **most played action real-time strategy game**. This free2play title averages over four million players per day, with a peak of 500,000 concurrent online users. As of August 2012, *LoL* had been downloaded well over 30 million times.

Biography

Wesley Yin-Poole is currently obsessed with *League of Legends* and *Dota 2*, having spent hundreds of hours losing badly at both. But there's also time for some sandbox simulation with *Minecraft*, which he plays co-operatively with his nephew.

Strategy/Simulation Intro

How to spot this genre

HAS GOT:
- The chance to apply critical thinking skills to solve problems and win matches
- Resource gathering, whether it's from mineral patches or geysers
- Base building, for unit, vehicle and upgrade options

HASN'T GOT:
- A time-out option for when you desperately need to go to the toilet mid-match
- Bonus points for the player with the fewest commands per second
- AGTs, or, Alternative Game Titles

MOST CRITICALLY ACCLAIMED iOS STRATEGY GAME

A must-have title for iOS strategy lovers, *Anomaly: Warzone Earth* (11 bit studios, 2011) carried a highly impressive 94% average on Metacritic, as of September 2012, putting it in the top 0.5% of all games released for the platform. The winning combination of high production values and innovative "tower attack" gameplay put the game at the top of reviewers' and strategy gamers' lists.

Winning strategy

Strategy games are all about careful planning and meticulous attention to detail. Whether you're commanding an entire army of marines in an RTS (real-time strategy) or a powerful hero unit in an action RTS, without sound strategy, you simply cannot win.

Blizzard's hugely popular *StarCraft II* (2010) has successfully replaced the original *StarCraft* (1998) as the king of RTS games. Players gather resources as efficiently as possible and build vast armies in an attempt to out-muscle opponents. Professional *StarCraft* players bewilder with their commands per minute (often in the hundreds) and the skill with which they "micro-manage" units on the battlefield.

BIGGEST eSPORTS PRIZE POOL

The largest eSports prize fund is $5 million (£3.23 million). Riot Games fronted up the astonishing prize pool for its *League of Legends* (Riot Games, 2009) Season Two Championship, with money going to local, national and international tournaments throughout autumn 2012. Riot explained that its record-breaking prize was designed to "foster and grow" the *League of Legends* eSports scene.

But in recent years a strategy sub-genre has emerged that has taken the entire industry by storm...

Team games

In the "Defense of the Ancients" (DotA) mod for *Warcraft III: Reign of Chaos* (Blizzard, 2002), two teams of five players, each commanding a single hero unit, fight for control of a map. The goal is simple – destroy the enemy team's defences. Along the way, levelling up, "experience point gain" and item management put the emphasis on strategy, even if the on-screen action can seem chaotic.

The most popular game of this type is free2play title *League of Legends*. Developer Riot Games calls it a Multiplayer Online Battle Arena (MOBA) game, but in truth it plays similarly to the *Warcraft III* modification on which it is based.

League of Legends contests attract huge online and in-person crowds in East Asia and, now, via the Major League Gaming organization, in the USA and Europe. This sub-genre's popularity will only intensify with the scheduled 2013 releases of *Blizzard All-Stars* (Blizzard) and Valve's *DOTA 2*.

Simulations

Sim games dial down the aggro. Instead, they challenge the player to master complex systems in predominantly "player versus environment" situations. The *Sims* series has dominated the genre for decades, but fresh and exciting titles have prompted renewed interest, with titles such as monster indie hit *Minecraft* (Mojang, 2011), the return of *SimCity* (Maxis, 2013) and *Microsoft Flight* (Microsoft Studios, 2012), the reboot of one of the longest-running game series of all time, *Microsoft Flight Simulator*. Then there's German developers Astragon's vast array of esoteric sims, including *Camping Manager* and *Fire Engine Simulator*.

HIGHEST-RANKED *LEAGUE OF LEGENDS* TEAM

Following victory at 2011's Major League Gaming Spring Championship in Anaheim, California, USA, Team SoloMid (USA) is the top-ranked *League of Legends* team. SoloMid defeated rivals CLG NA two games to one in a tense final, taking home $20,000 (£12,932) in prize money.

Founded by Brandon "Ryze" Beck and Marc "Tryndamere" Merrill, Riot Games was established in 2006 and – unusually for a developer – hit the big time with its debut title: *League of Legends* boasted 11.5 million active users as of January 2012.

This front line hasn't moved in almost 1000 years. Whenever conventional forces start to make progress, they just get nuked. These cities often change hands but are never kept for long by either side.

LONGEST GAME OF *CIVILIZATION II*

Reddit user Lycerius showed his commitment to classic strategy title *Civilization II* (MicroProse, 1996) when he posted details of a game that he had been playing for more than 10 years in June 2012. Having taken his game far into the distant future of AD 3991, Lycerius' world is a bleak wasteland in which only three super-nations remain, locked in a 1,700-year stalemate with constant warfare.

WHICH OF THE FOLLOWING IS THE PLAYER ROLE IN CONSTRUCTION AND MANAGEMENT SIM SERIES *TROPICO* (POPTOP SOFTWARE, 2001–2011) – EL PRESIDENTE OR EL GENERAL?

SimCity

THE BIGGEST CITY-BUILDING SERIES RETURNS WITH A REBOOT, A NEW GAME ENGINE AND UPGRADED GRAPHICS

MOST PROLIFIC SIMULATOR GAME SERIES

Starting with *SimCity* (Maxis) in 1989, the *Sim* series – based around *The Sims* and *SimCity* franchises – has become the most prolific in the genre, with over 130 games bearing some variation of the name. Latest title *SimCity* (Maxis, 2013, above) utilizes the new and advanced GlassBox Engine. This visually represents every player's decisions in the game, rather than presenting them as statistics. So if lots of sim characters (or "agents") are working, the player will see traffic jams as they commute and the pollution that modern industry creates. Publishers EA say this will give gamers "the power to change a world together".

LONGEST-RUNNING CITY-BUILDING SERIES

The *SimCity* franchise began some 24 years ago, with regular releases appearing ever since. The much-anticipated reboot of the series in 2013 makes *SimCity* the longest-running city-builder franchise. Including spin-offs, 18 games have been released on a variety of platforms, such as the Commodore Amiga, SNES and iOS.

BEST-SELLING CITY-BUILDING SERIES

Although free2play *CityVille* (Zynga, 2010) is the most played city-building simulator, Maxis' *SimCity* series is still the best-selling, with 18 million units shipped worldwide since its launch in 1989. The top seller is *SimCity 2000* (1993), with sales of 2.14 million. Pictured above is the original *SimCity*, the **first city-building game**.

If you like *SimCity*

try...

Cities XL (Monte Cristo, 2009)

Stronghold 3 (Firefly Studios, 2011)

Dwarf Fortress (Bay 12 Games, 2006)

The Settlers 7: Paths to a Kingdom
(Ubisoft Blue Byte, 2010)

Tropico 4 (Haemimont Games, 2011)

Grand Ages: Rome
(Haemimont Games, 2009)

Anno 2070
(Related Designs / Ubisoft Blue Byte, 2011)

A World of Keflings (NinjaBee, 2010)

SimCity is the brainchild of US developer Will Wright, who co-founded Maxis in 1987. His biggest success to date has been *The Sims* (2000), which is the **best-selling PC game** of all time, with sales of over 16 million. More recently, he designed *Spore* (Maxis, 2008) before setting up an "entertainment think-tank" called Stupid Fun Club.

ONE UP

In June 2012, EA announced *SimCity Social* (Playfish, 2012), a Facebook version of the city-building series. Like its big brother, the game mirrors life, challenging the player to tackle fires, crime and pollution. Gamers are also able to interact with Facebook friends by visiting their cities and asking them to help complete tasks. However, *SimCity Social* will have a long way to go to catch up with sim social network sensation *CityVille* (see pp.84–85), which has over 100 million active users.

HIGHEST POPULATION IN *SIMCITY 3000*

Committed city-builder Vincent Ocasla (Philippines) spent four years trying to find the perfect design in *SimCity 3000* (Maxis, 1999). He completed his masterpiece, the city of Magnasanti, in 2010. Using an octagonal shape (above), he managed to attract a population of 6,005,407 to his metropolis. Former Buddhist Ocasla based his city's design on the Bhavacakra, the wheel of life and death in Buddhism.

Minecraft

SANDBOX SENSATION MINECRAFT IS ALL ABOUT USING BLOCKS TO BUILD ANYTHING YOU CAN IMAGINE

BEST-SELLING INDIE GAME

As of July 2012, *Minecraft* (Mojang, 2009) had notched up sales of 6,799,347 on the PC, with 35,915,045 registered accounts. On 25 May 2012, Mojang business developer Daniel Kaplan revealed that *Minecraft* had sold nine million units across all platforms – PC, Android, iOS and Xbox Live Arcade. This means that the Swedish sandbox title has sold more than any other independently developed videogame. This isn't *Minecraft*'s only mind-boggling statistic; the game's open-world surface area of 4,096,000,000 m² (44,088,977,066 ft²) comfortably makes it the **largest land-based videogame area**.

In August 2011, *Minecraft* designer Markus "Notch" Persson (Sweden) revealed that American developers Bethesda had sued his company, Mojang, over the similarity between the name of Bethesda's role-playing game series *The Elder Scrolls* (1994–2011) and Mojang's upcoming card game *Scrolls*. "Notch" offered to settle the dispute through a multiplayer deathmatch in *Quake 3* (id Software, 1999). Bethesda declined, and both parties settled out of court.

BETHESDA
GAME STUDIOS

FIRST LEGO SET FOR AN INDIE GAME

The 480-piece LEGO *Minecraft* Micro World set launched in June 2012 for £29.99 ($34.99 in the USA). A group of three *Minecraft* fans submitted their design for the set on the LEGO CUUSOO site, which encourages new ideas for LEGO designs. After receiving the 10,000 public votes required, LEGO began manufacturing the set. One *Minecraft* block is represented as one 1x1 LEGO plate with a tile on top. The set includes *Minecraft* character Steve and a Creeper, represented as Micro Mobs.

After moving on from *Minecraft* in December 2011, "Notch" (see left) took some time out before announcing in April 2012 that he was working on a new title called *0x10c*. It will be a space-themed sandbox game inspired by the American television show *Firefly* and seminal British space trading game *Elite* (David Braben and Ian Bell, 1984). The curiously titled game begins in the year AD 281474976 712644, in a parallel universe.

BEST-SELLING XBOX LIVE ARCADE GAME

The Xbox version of *Minecraft*, developed by 4J Studios, had sold more than three million copies in the Xbox Marketplace as of September 2012. This astonishing feat was achieved just two months after it went on sale, and eclipsed previous best-seller *Castle Crashers* (The Behemoth, 2008). *Minecraft* achieved one million of those sales in its first five days, making it the **fastest-selling Xbox Live Arcade game**, ahead of previous record holder *Trials Evolution* (Red Lynx, 2012). *Minecraft* on the Xbox became profitable after only one hour on sale.

HIGHEST-GROSSING INDIE GAME

According to the *Financial Times* (UK), *Minecraft* has made an incredible $80.8 million (£51.7 million) in revenue since it launched in alpha stage on 17 May 2009. Those figures were revealed by Mojang's financial filings for the 15 months from October 2010. After interest, tax and depreciation, the game's earnings were still an impressive $13.5 million (£8.7 million).

If you like *Minecraft* try...

Total Miner
(Greenstone Games, 2011)

FortressCraft
(ProjectorGames, 2011)

CastleMiner
(DigitalDNA Games, 2011)

Dwarf Fortress
(Bay 12 Games, 2006)

Blockland
(Blockland LLC, 2007)

Infiniminer
(Zachtronics Industries, 2009)

Manic Digger
(Various, 2011)

ROBLOX
(ROBLOX Corporation, 2006)

Ace of Spades
(Ben Aksoy, 2012)

LONGEST *MINECRAFT* TUNNEL

Australian gamer Jonathon Pepper took the mining elements in *Minecraft* very seriously when he committed himself to digging a 1,860-block in-game tunnel. Jonathon's tunnel measures 930 m (3,051 ft) in length and takes almost five minutes to walk through. He completed his creation in Brisbane, Australia, on 5 May 2011.

FLASH BACK

Before *Minecraft*, "Notch" was building a game inspired by *Dwarf Fortress* called *RubyDung*, and says he even considered making a zombie game in the vein of *Left 4 Dead* (Valve, 2008). "Notch" traces *Minecraft*'s origins back to *Infiniminer*, an open-source, multiplayer, block-based sandbox. He says it was *Infiniminer* that convinced him to create his own sandbox building title.

BIGGEST CONVENTION FOR AN INDIE GAME

MineCon 2011, held at the Mandalay Bay Hotel in Las Vegas, Nevada, USA, on 18 November 2011, celebrated the release of *Minecraft 1.0*, the full PC version of the game. Some 4,500 fans attended the sell-out event, which included a talk by "Notch" and a set by musician deadmau5 (inset above).

CRAFTY

One of the best ways to plan a creation in *Minecraft* is to grab some graph paper and draw out what you want to build. This helps you work out how much "resource" you'll need and where any scaffolds need to go. You'll save a lot of time and effort doing this out of the game rather than inside it!

IN WHICH EUROPEAN CAPITAL CITY ARE *MINECRAFT* DEVELOPERS MOJANG BASED?

DotA

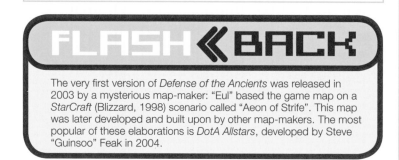

THE MULTIPLAYER
FANTASY ACTION OF
*DEFENSE OF THE
ANCIENTS* BEGAN LIFE
AS A *WARCRAFT III*
MODIFICATION

MOST PLAYED GAME BETA

DotA 2 (Valve, 2013) is currently the most played
game that hasn't had an official release, eclipsing
the achievement of previous record holder *Minecraft*
(Mojang, 2010), which finally left its beta-testing phase
in 2011. With an average of 82,423 concurrent players,
DotA 2 sat at the top of Valve's "games by current
player count" as of 4 September 2012, which is not
at all bad for a game that isn't even out yet!

FLASH « BACK

The very first version of *Defense of the Ancients* was released in
2003 by a mysterious map-maker: "Eul" based the game map on a
StarCraft (Blizzard, 1998) scenario called "Aeon of Strife". This map
was later developed and built upon by other map-makers. The most
popular of these elaborations is *DotA Allstars*, developed by Steve
"Guinsoo" Feak in 2004.

IF you like DotA 2 try...

Defense of the Ancients ("Eul", Steve
"Guinsoo" Feak, "IceFrog", all USA, 2003)

Smite (Hi-Rez Studios, 2012)

Guardians of Middle-earth
(Monolith Productions, 2012)

League of Legends (Riot Games, 2009)

Heroes of Newerth (S2 Games, 2010)

Rise of Immortals (Petroglyph Games, 2011)

The Witcher 2: Assassins of Kings
(CD Projekt RED, 2011)

Demigod (Gas Powered Games, 2009)

Warcraft III: Reign of Chaos (Blizzard, 2002)

Super Monday Night Combat
(Uber Entertainment, 2012)

StarCraft II (Blizzard, 2010)

STICK TOGETHER

Successful *DotA 2* players work as a team, especially at end-game, when assaults on enemy bases become more frequent. Rather than playing "lone wolf" style, players should try to co-ordinate their efforts, offering support to one another where necessary. This means that less glamorous heroes can potentially become game changers.

MOST BANNED HEROES IN *DotA 2*	
Lycanthrope	1,124
Nature's Prophet	1,063
Chen	1,037
Dark Seer	1,036
Broodmother	943
Invoker	832
Enchantress	676
Anti-Mage	604
Leshrac	552
Tidehunter	517

Number of bans according to DotA Academy, as of 13 September 2012.

LARGEST SINGLE eSPORTS PRIZE

The largest cash prize in electronic sports history is the $1 million (£630,000) awarded to the winners of The International, a *DotA 2* championship organized by developers Valve. In 2011, its inaugural year, the contest was held at the German videogame show Gamescom, while in 2012 it took place independently in Seattle, Washington, USA. The winners were Invictus Gaming (China, pictured below), who defeated 2011 champions Natus Vincere (Ukraine) 3–1 in a best-of-five final in September 2012.

MOST *DotA* TOURNAMENT WINS

Veteran *DotA* player Jacob "Melk" Toft-Andersen (Denmark) has led teams to 32 victories and 57 podium placements in major *DotA* tournaments since his debut in 2005. Jacob was born on Norfolk Island, a tiny annex of Australia in the South Pacific with a population of just 2,302, making it the **smallest territory to produce a gaming champion**.

One of the best kept secrets in gaming is the identity of *DotA* lead designer "IceFrog". He was hired by Valve to work on *DotA 2* in 2009, but there is still no confirmation of exactly who he is!

MOST POPULAR UNSUPPORTED GAME MOD

The unsupported game modification (or mod) *Defense of the Ancients* had 10 million players at its peak in 2008. *DotA* is a mod for *Warcraft III: Reign of Chaos* (Blizzard, 2002). The only competitor for the title is *Counter-Strike* (Valve, 2003), which was picked up and officially supported by Valve Software less than a year after it first became available. Videogame industry website Gamasutra conducted an analysis of *DotA*, concluding that as well as being the most popular game mod, it was also "the most discussed free, non-supported game mod in the world".

Microsoft Flight

TAKE TO THE SKIES AND EXPLORE WITH THE ESSENTIAL AVIATION SIMULATOR

FIRST FREE2PLAY FLIGHT SIM

When *Microsoft Flight* (Microsoft Game Studios) launched in February 2012, it brought a free2play, microtransaction-based revenue model to the simulation genre. Gamers are able to download the core game with a small selection of aircraft for free, but if they want access to the more exciting planes they can head to the online marketplace. The move was criticized by some flight sim fans, who had become accustomed to freely modifying and editing the game to get the experience they wanted – a system that was removed from *Microsoft Flight*.

BEST-SELLING FLIGHT SIM SERIES

The *Microsoft Flight Simulator* series has sold a phenomenal 22 million copies worldwide, as of 13 August 2012. Even with *Microsoft Flight Simulator X* (Microsoft Game Studios, 2006) reportedly shifting fewer than 1 million copies, and *Microsoft Flight* being ineligible for the count due to its status as a free2play title, no other flight sim has given as many aspiring pilots the chance to experience the thrill of virtual aviation. Sim pilots have been able to fly everything from a Sopwith Camel biplane to a Boeing 777 jet.

MOST EXPENSIVE FLIGHT SIM AT LAUNCH

Treading the fine line between fun videogame and training simulator, aerospace firm Lockheed Martin's *Prepar3d* cost a staggering $499 (£300) when it was launched in April 2011. The game uses the core code from *Microsoft Flight Simulator X* but enables a range of more advanced features, including ultra-high-resolution graphics, online multiplayer and even support for submarines with a realistically modelled sea floor! *Prepar3d* features 45 airports and 39 cities.

24,000

Total number of airports featured in *Microsoft Flight Simulator X*. Pilots can land and take off on every one of Earth's continents.

Flight Simulator T80-FS1
with BRITISH ACE 3D aerial battle game

TRS-80

subLOGIC
Communications Corp.

Games for Windows · PC DVD

Microsoft **Flight Simulator** X

LONGEST-RUNNING VIDEOGAME SERIES

Having spanned an impressive 32 years and three months between its first and most recent releases, *Flight Simulator* is the longest-running series of them all. Originally released by developer subLOGIC in October 1979 for the Apple II, the game was subsequently acquired by Microsoft and distributed for PCs as *Flight Simulator 1.00* in 1982. It now boasts a total of 16 main series titles. *Space Invaders,* the previous record holder, has not seen a new release since 2008, and the next closest, *Asteroids*, was released a month after *Flight Simulator.*

try...
If you like Flight Simulator

Jane's Advance Strike Fighters (Trickstar, 2012)

Falcon 4.0 (MicroProse, 1998)

Sky Odyssey (Cross, 2000)

Infinite Space (EA, 2009)

Ace Combat: Assault Horizon (Project Aces, 2011)

Pilotwings Resort (Monster Games, 2011)

Red Baron II (Dynamix, 1997)

Flight Gear (open source, 1996)

Space Shuttle Mission 2007 (Exciting Simulations, 2011)

ONE UP

Flight Simulator was created by Bruce Artwick (USA), who had worked for Hughes Aircraft in California, USA. Artwick's original Apple II flight simulator software only became *Microsoft Flight Simulator* after Bill Gates (USA), who had just set up his own small software company, defeated IBM in a bidding war for the licence in the early 1980s.

GAME OVER

In July 2012, Microsoft announced that it was ending development of the free2play *Microsoft Flight* after just five months, in order to "align with our long-term goals and development". The game will remain downloadable, and the online store will continue selling in-game planes and locations, but it will no longer be updated and no new content will be created.

TOP 10
BEST-SELLING FLIGHT GAMES

Game	Sales (in millions)
Microsoft Flight Simulator for Windows 95 (Microsoft, 1996)	5.12 m
Ace Combat 04: Shattered Skies (Namco, 2001)	3.17 m
Star Wars: Rogue Squadron (LucasArts, 1998)	2.17 m
Star Wars Rogue Leader: Rogue Squadron II (LucasArts, 2001)	1.9 m
Air Combat (Namco, 1995)	1.83 m
Star Wars: Starfighter (LucasArts, 2001)	1.76 m
Ace Combat 5: The Unsung War (Project Aces, 2004)	1.71 m
Nuclear Strike (EA, 1997)	1.19 m
Soviet Strike (EA, 1996)	1.17 m
Pilotwings (Nintendo EAD, 1990)	1.14 m

According to VGChartz, as of 20 August 2012.

LONGEST FLIGHT SIM SESSION

On 4–11 November 2007, a Boeing 777 took off from a virtual Sydney, Australia, and continued the flight for 39,848 miles across seven days. The whole journey, organized to raise money for Cancer Research UK, was undertaken by a team of 17 "pilots" working in shifts in a custom-built simulator inside a garage in Surrey, UK. Among the team was Iron Maiden singer Bruce Dickinson (UK), who has been flying real planes for 20 years.

AT THE MOVIES

The late 2012 release of the *Wreck-It Ralph* film (USA, right) and tie-in game marks the 30th anniversary of videogames at the movies. But throughout those three decades, games have been heavily influenced by films, too, mimicking plots, characters and scenery: titles such as *Red Dead Redemption* and *L.A. Noire* owe much to Hollywood classics. Here we take a look at some of the key films inspired by or based on videogames. Let's go to the movies!

TRON (USA)
A computer programmer gets sucked into his own virtual world in this, the very **first gaming-themed movie**.

THE MATRIX (USA)
Despite not being about games at all, this Keanu Reeves classic is the ultimate videogame movie. There's even a tutorial level.

THE WIZARD (USA)
A pair of brothers run away from home to compete in the supreme videogame championship.

| 1982 | 1983 | 1984 | 1985 | 1986 | 1987 | 1988 | 1989 | 1990 | 1991 | 1992 | 1993 | 1994 | 1995 | 1996 |

THE LAST STARFIGHTER (USA)
A boy spends hours playing an arcade game, without realizing it is actually a recruitment test for an alien defence force.

SNEAKERS (USA)
Hollywood legends including Robert Redford and Sidney Poitier star in this thriller about computer security experts who become embroiled in a sinister hacking plot.

Super Mario Bros. (USA, 1993), starring British actor Bob Hoskins as Mario the plumber and Colombian-born John Leguizamo as his brother Luigi, was the **first live-action film based on a videogame**. Although not a huge critical or commercial success at the time, the film has gone on to attain cult status. Hoskins and co-star Dennis Hopper (USA) also share the record for the **first Oscar-nominated actor to star in a game-licensed movie**. *Super Mario Bros.* started a mini-trend of adaptations in Hollywood: *Street Fighter* (1994) and box office hit *Mortal Kombat* (1995) followed.

WarGames (USA)
A teenage videogame fanatic thinks he's hacking into a software firm, but he actually breaks into the USA's nuclear defence control system.

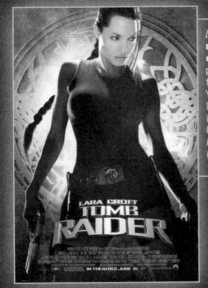

Lara Croft: Tomb Raider (USA) contains the **most Oscar winners in a movie based on a videogame**. Angelina Jolie (USA), who plays intrepid explorer Lara, won an Oscar for the movie *Girl, Interrupted* (1999). Jon Voight (USA), who plays Lord Richard Croft, Lara's father, won his Oscar for *Coming Home* (1978). Voight is Angelina Jolie's father in real life as well as in the movie. *Lara Croft: Tomb Raider* grossed an impressive $274,703,340 (£189,255,000) worldwide.

PRINCE OF PERSIA: THE SANDS OF TIME (USA)
With a budget of $200 million (£129 million), this is an epic blockbuster movie based on a hit videogame, from legendary Hollywood producer Jerry Bruckheimer.

THE KING OF KONG: A FISTFUL OF QUARTERS (USA)
When it comes to holding the *Donkey Kong* record, how far would you go? This critically acclaimed documentary shows that reality can sometimes be tougher than virtual reality.

WRECK-IT RALPH (USA)
The latest Hollywood movie inspired by gaming mixes old-school arcades, first-person shooters, comedy and modern animation as a gaming villain sets out to become the good guy.

1997	1998	1999	2000	2001	2002	2003	2004	2005	2006	2007	2008	2009	2010	2011	2012

eXistenZ (UK)
The worlds of gaming and reality blur in this thriller from acclaimed Canadian director David Cronenberg.

RESIDENT EVIL (USA)
The first of five live-action films based on the survival-horror videogames.

GAMER (USA)
A futuristic, mind-controlling videogame created by a psychopath forces death row convicts to battle each other for freedom.

RA.ONE (INDIA)
A shape-shifting indestructible virtual videogame creation finds its way into the real world. The ultimate villain – Bollywood style.

SPY KIDS 3-D: GAME OVER (USA)
Mexican-American Robert Rodriguez's movie, based around a 3D, virtual-reality videogame, performed well at the box office but was panned by critics. Much of the story takes place within the world of a game controlled by The Toymaker (Sylvester Stallone).

Tron: Legacy (USA, 2010) is the **highest-grossing game-centred movie**, smashing the competition with takings of $400,062,763 (£239,394,000) worldwide. *Tron: Legacy* centres on a young man who goes looking for his father, a virtual-world computer designer, and ends up inside the digital realm that his father created. It is the sequel to *Tron*, which only took $33,000,000 (£20,777,700) upon its release in 1982. But *Tron* went on to become a cult film with a dedicated fanbase on video and DVD, and a sequel had long been touted.

Readers' Polls

Evolution of gaming graphics

Thanks to all of you who voted in our **Top 50 Graphics** and **Top 50 Villains** polls. Before we reveal your winners on the following pages, we present the 30-year evolution of gaming graphics, from a cluster of chunky pixels to lifelike, 3D polygons.

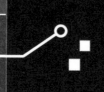

Fun Zoo (1972)

The Magnavox Odyssey was the **first cartridge-based console**. *Fun Zoo* players stuck coloured plastic overlays over the screen and guided dots along paths.

FIRST GENERATION 1972–76

The Nintendo Entertainment System had been launched in 1983 and the 8-bit revolution was an immediate hit, offering vivid colours.

Mega Man (1987)

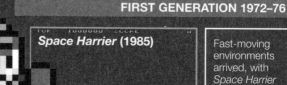

Space Harrier (1985)

Fast-moving environments arrived, with *Space Harrier* (Sega) offering frantic action and pseudo-3D visuals.

THIRD GENERATION 1983–87

Altered Beast (1988)

For the first time, home consoles began catching up on arcade machines, with *Street Fighter II* (Capcom) featuring huge sprites and detailed animations.

Street Fighter II (1991)

FOURTH GENERATION 1987–93

The fourth generation was the 16-bit era of gaming. It brought improvements to every department: bigger environments, brighter colours and faster action.

TimeSplitters (2000)

The generation began with the arrival of the SEGA Dreamcast, but is better remembered for the Xbox's debut and Sony's PS2, for which *TimeSplitters* (Free Radical Design) was an exclusive title.

Doom 3 (2004)

SIXTH GENERATION 1998–2005

Widescreen resolutions and open-world environments became available, along with real-time lighting effects to make games even more immersive.

HD graphics came with the Xbox 360 in 2005, followed by the PS3 in 2006, encouraging many gamers to upgrade their TVs in order to get the best visuals possible.

Uncharted 2 (2009)

SEVENTH GENERATION 2005–12

Pong (1975)

The first home consoles were simple and games were primarily centred on a bat-and-ball style of play.

Armor Battle (1979)

12

Different colours appeared on gaming screens at long last, along with more detailed controls and sound effects.

1899
19:38 **Pitfall! (1982)**

ACTIVISION

SECOND GENERATION 1976–83

The second generation of consoles was dominated by Atari in the USA, while the likes of *Armor Battle* (Mattel) set the blueprint for future multiplayer shooters.

Tomb Raider (1996)

FIFTH GENERATION 1993–98

With the runaway success of the PlayStation, CDs were introduced as games media, offering more storage than cartridges. The new technology allowed fully explorable 3D environments, though the cartridge-based N64 still competed.

LEFT **29** **F-Zero X (1998**
TIME 00`15"82
BEST 02'39"05

723km/h

We asked you
to tell us about your favourite games in our latest online poll at www.guinnessworldrecords.com/gamers. We received more than 12,000 votes and several surprises as we opened up the ballot box. You are a highly opinionated lot!

Turn to p.186 for our Top 50 Videogame Graphics run-down and find out which game you rate as the most visually stunning in the history of gaming. This year's results run the full range of beautiful games, from the perfect visual fidelity of modern shooters to the abstract, stylized shapes of leftfield puzzlers.

Your Top 50 Villains start on p.192 and readers with a mean streak should turn over now to see who was a bad enough dude to make it to the top of our reprehensible rogues' gallery.

From blocks to rich cinematic experiences and photo-realistic graphics in 40 years... Today, sprawling epics provide stunningly detailed environments.

The Wii U arrived in 2012, its power approximately equal to the PS3 and Xbox 360. Gaming's richest epoch is really still around the corner and its power remains to be seen.

The Legend of Zelda (demo)

Battlefield 3 (2011)

EIGHTH GENERATION FROM 2012

Top 50 Graphics

50-31

THE LEGEND OF ZELDA: OCARINA OF TIME 3D
(Grezzo, 2011)
The land of Hyrule is as lush as it's ever been in this hand-held retelling of the classic clash of good vs. evil. Enhanced graphics and a glasses-free 3D experience ensure this remake of the 1990s original looks as slick and impressive as it plays.

50

CHILD OF EDEN
(Q Entertainment, 2011)
Abstract, organic shapes move and swirl in time with the ambient music in this synaesthetic shooter.

49

43

HALO 4
(343 Industries, 2012)
With environments ranging from dense jungles to vast technological constructs, *Halo 4* paints its explosive action with a varied palette. This Xbox 360 exclusive provides a strong showcase for the console's capabilities.

OKAMI
(Clover Studio, 2006)
Using a style inspired by Japanese "sumi-e" ink painting, this mythological adventure is just as good to watch as it is to play. The game resembles a Japanese watercolour painting that has magically sprung into life.

44

PRO EVOLUTION SOCCER 2012
(Konami, 2011)
Near photorealistic, sharp re-creations of top-flight stars make this an accurate soccer simulation.

42

METRO 2033
(4A Games, 2010)
PC users looking to run this post-apocalyptic FPS survival horror on its maximum settings will need a serious gaming rig. The game has epic system requirements.

41

35

JUST CAUSE 2
(Avalanche, 2010)
Version 2.0 of the Avalanche Engine brings the azure seas and white beaches of tropical island Panau to life in this striking open-world actioner.

MARIO KART 7
(Nintendo EAD/Retro Studios, 2011)
The Mario Kart series' first outing in stereoscopic 3D offers blinding speeds and impressive vistas. Experiencing the tracks from the air is a neat visual extra, but for skilled Karters the Mushroom Kingdom's scenery will zip by too fast to be properly admired.

36

HALO: COMBAT EVOLVED ANNIVERSARY EDITION
(343 Industries, 2011)
Respectfully updating the original shooter for HD consoles, this gives a whole new perspective on *Halo*'s familiar locations, and includes a full stereoscopic 3D mode.

34

MORTAL KOMBAT
(NetherRealm Studios, 2011)
Mortal Kombat's brand of ultra-violent fighting might not be to all tastes, but there's no denying the game's gory sense of style and graphic X-ray moves.

33

HEAVY RAIN
(Quantic Dream, 2010)
Sharp motion-capture and noir-like environments give the Origami Killer story the feel of a Hollywood movie.

48

SUPER MARIO GALAXY
(Nintendo EAD, 2007)
Bright, colourful characters and bizarre distant stars populate this universe, leaving players expecting the unexpected in another dazzlingly imaginative Mario title.

47

RAGE
(id Software, 2011)
The makers of seminal shooter *Doom* showcase the power of the id Tech 5 engine with ravaged, high resolution deserts that are both beautiful and terrifying.

45

STAR WARS: THE OLD REPUBLIC
(BioWare, 2011)
Offering a stylized take on the classic "galaxy far, far away", *The Old Republic* explores a vivid, colourful and varied region of space.

46

MAX PAYNE 3
(Rockstar, 2012)
Rockstar's gritty crime drama may not conform to traditional standards of beauty, but it's certainly a stylish shooter. The game's grainy visuals reflect Max's troubled state of mind.

40

39

GOD OF WAR III
(SCE Santa Monica Studio, 2010)
A fitting showcase for the PS3's muscular Cell processor, Kratos' epic adventure includes some truly spectacular boss fights.

MASS EFFECT 3
(BioWare, 2012)
The climactic conclusion to the *Mass Effect* trilogy features explosive space battles, rich and detailed alien worlds and believable, compelling characters.

37

RAYMAN ORIGINS
(Ubisoft, 2012)
This original, quirky platformer brings hand-drawn environments to life with heaps of personality.

38

LIMBO
(Playdead, 2010)
The unique monochrome world of *Limbo* is populated by shadow puppets and visual tricks that create a potent sense of terror, leaving some players jumpy. This game looks like no other.

32

WWE '12
(Yuke's, 2011)
The legendary sports entertainment spectacle gets a fitting facsimile in its console games: the new "Predator Technology" makes the virtual wrestlers look more similar to their real-world counterparts than ever before.

31

IN WHICH CITY IS *MAX PAYNE 3* SET?

GUINNESS WORLD RECORDS

Top 50 Graphics

30

SHIFT 2: UNLEASHED
(Slightly Mad Studios, 2011)
This title from the *Need for Speed* racing series has gritty, stylized vehicles that sharply evoke the thrills of street racing.

NBA 2K12
(Visual Concepts, 2011)
With ever more accurate player re-creations, this seminal basketball sim series gets more life-like with every new title.

29

THE WITCHER 2: ASSASSINS OF KINGS (CD Projekt RED, 2011)
The continuation of Geralt of Rivera's adventures is atmospheric, action-packed and relentlessly dark and brooding.

23

INFINITY BLADE
(Chair Games, 2012)
The Unreal Engine 3 provides the power behind this impressive hack-and-slash game – the only iPad title in your top 50. A watershed game for Apple, it hints at what can be achieved on the tablet.

24

SUPER MARIO 3D LAND
(Nintendo EAD Tokyo/ Brownie Brown, 2011)
Drawing on 1988's *Super Mario Bros. 3* for inspiration, this visual extravaganza combines classic Mario stylings with shiny, new 3D technology.

22

21

PORTAL 2
(Valve, 2011)
A 1950s time capsule and the clean, white lines and winding corridors of the Aperture Science testing facility clash with wild, overgrowing nature in this puzzler.

15

GEARS OF WAR 3
(Epic Games, 2011)
The bleak planet Sera, complete with striking, gothic architecture and vast underground caves, erupts into conflict once more in the conclusion to the Marcus Fenix trilogy.

16

POKÉMON BLACK AND WHITE 2
(Game Freak, 2012)
Boasting some of the most iconic and recognizable character art in gaming, *Pokémon* remains a classic of visual design. *Black and White 2* breathed new life into the classic protagonists and kept the series looking fresh.

SONIC GENERATIONS
(Sonic Team, 2011)
The colourful fusion of old-school and brand new graphical styles seamlessly shifts from 2D to 3D, and makes this platform revival a superfast feast for the eyes.

14

HALO: REACH
(Bungie, 2010)
Vast, sweeping views of a planet under siege give the story of *Reach* a bittersweet beauty. From mountain ranges to alien ships, the graphical range here is huge and detailed.

13

28
THE LEGEND OF ZELDA: THE WIND WAKER
(Nintendo EAD, 2002)
Bringing more cartoon-like visual styles to the beloved series was controversial with fans, but this adventure has endured well.

27
METAL GEAR SOLID 4
(Kojima, 2008)
With its well-defined character animation, Solid Snake's globe-trotting, PS3 exclusive is a fitting showcase for the power of Sony's console.

25
FINAL FANTASY XIII–2
(Square Enix, 2011)
With their sweeping, epic vistas, the lands of Cocoon and Gran Pulse provide a beautiful backdrop for the New Tale of the Crystal.

26
GRAN TURISMO 5
(Polyphony Digital, 2010)
Realistically modelled race tracks and highly detailed cars, such as this Nissan 37OZ, make this one of the most attractive of all sim games.

20
ASSASSIN'S CREED: REVELATIONS
(Ubisoft, 2011)
The final chapter in the story of Ezio Auditore da Firenze explores an impressive, detailed recreation of 16th-century Constantinople.

19
CALL OF DUTY: BLACK OPS
(Treyarch, 2010)
Oppressive prisons, humid jungles and dazzling explosions create a strong and life-like visual identity in this Cold War thriller. Perhaps the most memorable visual is the deadly cloud of orange nerve gas.

17
CRYSIS
(Crytek, 2007)
The first-person shooter that inspired a generation of PC owners to upgrade their graphics cards, *Crysis* remains a benchmark in gaming visuals that was well ahead of its time.

18
GRAND THEFT AUTO IV
(Rockstar, 2008)
Rockstar's crime drama has a varied cast of characters, but all are upstaged by the majesty of the living, breathing, New York-like Liberty City.

12
MINECRAFT
(Mojang, 2011)
Who says pixels are ugly? The randomly generated, infinite worlds of *Minecraft* can create some truly impressive scenery. What's more, you never know what you'll find, and no two worlds are the same.

11
RED DEAD REDEMPTION
(Rockstar, 2010)
The most evocative Western in the history of videogaming, *Red Dead Redemption*'s finest moments happen at sunset and sunrise, when the game resembles an HD movie, complete with life-like cowboys, deep canyons and ultra-realistic horses and saloons.

HOW MANY YEARS OF SONIC THE HEDGEHOG DOES SONIC GENERATIONS CELEBRATE?

GUINNESS WORLD RECORDS

10-01

L.A. NOIRE
(Team Bondi, 2011)
This 1940s crime drama features some of the most detailed facial animation ever seen in a videogame, bringing an eclectic cast of characters to life. The game's rendering of Los Angeles through the eyes of gumshoe Cole Phelps is vivid and bright, making for some memorable exploring and unforgettable police chases.

10

UNCHARTED 3: DRAKE'S DECEPTION
(Naughty Dog, 2011)
Sharp, vibrant colours saturate Drake's environment and more citizens populate cities than in previous games. Detailed animations make hand combat as engrossing as weaponry. The developers have demonstrated a cinematic sensibility, giving time to appreciate evocative sandstorms and forests. Much thought has gone into every last rendered footfall of Drake's progress.

04

CRYSIS 2
(Crytek, 2011)
The ruins of a futuristic New York City look attractive as you fight in Manhattan's most iconic locations, including subways. A climactic shootout occurs in Central Park. While some critics found the action uninspiring, this shooter is a feast for the eyes.

05

02

THE ELDER SCROLLS V: SKYRIM
(Bethesda Softworks, 2011)
The northern province of Skyrim is the true star of this entry in the successful series of open-world role-playing games. Ranging from snow-capped peaks to lovely meadows populated with creatures both bizarre and familiar, the game has created a living, breathing fantasy land like no other. Chief among the game's pleasures is a simple exploration of the wilderness, where you might happen upon a forgotten cave, a peaceful village or a forbidding fortress. A unique visual treat.

03

CALL OF DUTY: MODERN WARFARE 3
(Infinity Ward, 2011)
This thrilling instalment of the series includes all the spectacle fans have come to expect: lightning-fast action, explosive set pieces and a plot that takes in locations from all over the wor Claiming refresh rates of 60 frames per second, the game's smooth animation is immersive, putting the player at the hear of a new World War as terrorists threaten democracy. Detaile interiors, bombed-out cities and Afghani villages serve as the picturesque and varied backdrop to electrifying shootouts.

09

FORZA MOTORSPORT 4
(Turn 10 Studios, 2011)
The iconic racing sim for consoles reproduces a host of desirable sportscars in meticulous detail and allows players to explore them in the game's showroom. Realistic recreations of race tracks and support for multiple screens bring aspiring racers closer to the asphalt.

08

FIFA 12
(EA, 2011)
The long-running sim offers realistic player behaviour and international stadiums reproduced to scale. A soccer game so realistic that you could almost believe you're watching the real thing on an HD screen.

06

THE LEGEND OF ZELDA: SKYWARD SWORD
(Nintendo, 2011)
Pushing the limitations of Wii hardware to the limit, Link's latest offers a breathtaking aerial view of the land of Hyrule. Its unique visual style sits between the cartoon aesthetic of *The Wind Waker* (2002) and the dark fantasy of *Twilight Princess* (2006).

BATMAN: ARKHAM CITY
(Rocksteady Studios, 2011)
The faded grandeur of Gotham City provides a stunning backdrop for the Dark Knight, complete with grinning gargoyles over the rundown streets, towering spires and tacky neon.

07

01

BATTLEFIELD 3
(EA Dice, 2011)
Your favourite in 2012 narrowly beat the competition to the greatest graphics accolade. *Battlefield 3* brings the military FPS on to a bigger stage, with support for up to 64 players wielding all the weaponry of modern conflict from pistols to fighter jets. Highlights of the game's enormous multiplayer maps include the Caspian Border level, featuring multiple military bases, slick green land and open skies ready to be torn apart by the clatter of machine guns or the shudder of explosives. The game shines on modern PCs, with ultra-high resolution and textures, gorgeous particle effects and realistic shadows.

WAS THE *ELDER SCROLLS* DEBUT, *ARENA*, RELEASED IN 1994, 2004 OR 2010?

GUINNESS WORLD RECORDS

Top 50 Villains

	VILLAIN	GAME SERIES			VILLAIN	GAME SERIES
50	Hades	Kid Icarus		30	The Locust Horde	Gears of War
49	Atlas	BioShock		29	Vanitas	Kingdom Hearts
48	Jacqueline Natla	Tomb Raider		28	Darth Vader	Star Wars
47	Shepherd	Call of Duty		27	Dr Wily	Mega Man
46	Herobrine	Minecraft		26	Team Rocket	Pokémon
45	Solidus Snake	Metal Gear Solid		25	Kefka Palazzo	Final Fantasy
44	Diablo	Diablo		24	Police	Grand Theft Auto
43	Dr Robotnik	Sonic the Hedgehog		23	Zombies	Call of Duty
42	Dr Neo Cortex	Crash Bandicoot		22	Aliens	Space Invaders
41	Shao Kahn	Mortal Kombat		21	The Reapers	Mass Effect
40	Zoran Lazarević	Uncharted		20	N	Pokémon
39	Tabuu	Super Smash Bros.		19	Zeus	God of War
38	Kaos	Skylanders		18	Alduin	Skyrim
37	Wheatley	Portal		17	M Bison	Street Fighter
36	Mother Brain	Metroid		16	The Covenant	Halo
35	Ghirahim	The Legend of Zelda		15	Andrew Ryan	BioShock
34	Dr Nefarious	Ratchet & Clank		14	Donkey Kong	Donkey Kong
33	Xehanort	Kingdom Hearts		13	Psycho Mantis	Metal Gear Solid
32	Kessler	Infamous		12	Albert Wesker	Resident Evil
31	The Flood	Halo		11	Vladimir Makarov	Call of Duty

10. CREEPER
Minecraft
(Mojang, 2011)
Cactus-shaped beasties that sneak up on players and explode. Often their tell-tale hiss is all you hear before your home is reduced to rubble.

9. LIQUID OCELOT
Metal Gear Solid
(Konami, 1998)
The most recurring villain in the series worked his way up from rookie double agent to world-threatening megalomaniac.

8. INKY
PAC-Man
(Namco, 1980)
Blinky, Pinky, Inky and Clyde, the lovable-yet-infuriating ghosts, have remained largely unchanged since their first appearance in 1980.

7. THE BORGIAS
Assassin's Creed II
(Ubisoft, 2009)
Lucrezia Borgia is just one of this extended clan of Templars. They aim to subvert the assassins and are utterly ruthless with their power.

6. SEPHIROTH
Final Fantasy VII
(Square, 1997)
Falsely believing himself to be a descendant of an extinct race, he wants revenge on those he considers responsible for its destruction.

GAMING'S GREATEST VILLAINS

GWR's latest poll was the first in which you got to vote for the bad guys (see pp.184–185). Enough chose Herobrine to take him to No.46, even though the character has long been known to be a *Minecraft* urban legend! Still, not to worry – there are enough real villains to keep the most dedicated gamers busy.

5. GARY OAK
Pokémon Red/Blue
(Game Freak, 1995)
The son of Professor Oak, Gary is a rival Pokémon trainer who manages to stay one step ahead of the player throughout the game. His penchant for pithy putdowns and ego have made him one of the most reviled figures in gamer culture – but he gets his comeuppance.

4. GANON
The Legend of Zelda **(Nintendo EAD, 1996)**
The Great King of Evil has been the eternal arch enemy of Link and Zelda. His attempts to gain control of the sacred Triforce and destroy the land of Hyrule have seen him take many forms, and he usually plans to kidnap the princess.

3. THE JOKER
Batman: Arkham Asylum **(Rocksteady, 2009)**
"It's okay to die, Bats. I'll be here to protect Gotham. I'll do a real good job!" The only thing you can be certain of with this villain: there's always going to be a punchline.

2. GLaDOS
Portal **(Valve, 2007)**
The insane computer is nothing new in popular culture – just ask Hal 9000 in the film *2001* (USA, 1968) – but the doyenne is GLaDOS. Acting as guide, narrator and then final boss, her sinister wit is an example to evil geniuses everywhere.

1. BOWSER
Super Mario Bros. **(Nintendo, 1985)**
The King of the Koopas takes our top slot. Mario's nemesis and occasional ally is persistent. Few other villains would attempt to kidnap the same princess twice, let alone eight times over the last 28 years.

WHICH BRITISH COMEDIAN PROVIDED THE VOICE FOR *PORTAL 2*'S WHEATLEY?

TWIN GALAXIES SCOREBOARDS

For more than 20 years, Twin Galaxies International has been verifying videogame scores on behalf of Guinness World Records. Founded by Walter Day (USA) in 1981, TGI continues to provide gamer stats and player rankings, maintaining an exhaustive database of record scores and times – a selection of which are listed here. We've opted for the most recent additions to the archive across classic arcade games, emulators and consoles.

THE GOOD, THE BAD AND THE SUPER

Classic arcade platformer *Bubble Bobble* (Taito, 1986) is the **first videogame to feature multiple endings**. The game has "good", "bad" and "super" endings, depending on player performance and the game modes used. Bub and Bob, the dragon stars, also featured in *Puzzle Bobble* (1994, also known as *Bust-a-Move*, below).

CLASSIC ARCADE AND EMULATORS

Game	Platform	Setting	Record	Gamer	Date
Arabian	Arcade	Points	244,850	Chris Mansfield (USA)	8-Jul-12
Berzerk [Set 1]	MAME	Fast Bullets (One Life Only)	128,530	Paolo Dyo Colman (Italy)	20-Nov-11
Bomb Jack [Set 1]	MAME	Marathon: Points	50,214,370	Paolo Dyo Colman (Italy)	12-Apr-12
Bubble Bobble	Arcade	Points [Super Bubble Bobble Mode]	9,999,990	Lonnie L Johnson (USA)	22-Apr-12
Daioh	Arcade	Points [Single Player]	333,060	Robert Racek (USA)	9-Jun-12
Death Race	Arcade	Points [Single Player Only]	28	Michael B Chase (USA)	2-Jun-12
Discs of Tron	Arcade	Points	589,900	Paul Hornitzky (Australlia)	3-Oct-11
Donkey Kong	Arcade	Points [No Hammer]	640,500	Estel J Goffinet (USA)	24-Oct-11
		Points [Hammer]	1,127,700	Hank S Chien (USA)	18-May-12
Donkey Kong [US Set 1]	MAME	Points	1,167,400	Dean Saglio (USA)	21-Apr-12
Donkey Kong 3	Arcade	Points [Marathon]	4,252,400	George Riley (USA)	14-Jan-12
Donkey Kong 3 [US]	MAME	Points [Marathon]	6,167,400	George Riley (USA)	28-Nov-11
Donkey Kong Junior [US]	MAME	Points	1,308,000	George Riley (USA)	12-May-12
Frogger	Arcade	Points [Tournament]	970,440	Michael Smith (USA)	15-Jul-12
GI Joe: A Real American Hero	MAME	Points [Single Player]	5,516	Travis Warnell (USA)	7-Feb-12
Galaga [Namco Rev B]	MAME	Points [Tournament]	940,580	Andrew K Barrow (New Zealand)	28-Jun-12
Joust	Arcade	Points [Marathon/Doubles]	40,120,150	Lonnie McDonald & Steve Sanders (USA)	12-Nov-11

Level 6 Next

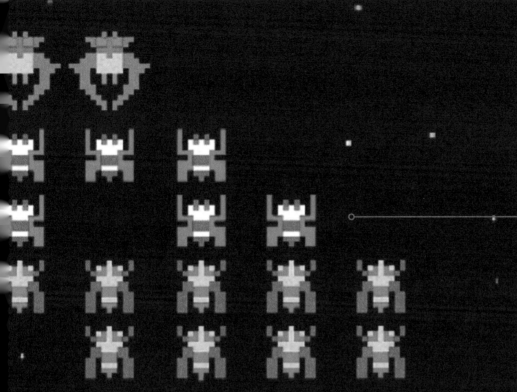

GOING GA-GA FOR *GALAGA*

One of the truly iconic and legendary arcade games, Namco's space shooter *Galaga* made its debut in 1981. It has stood the test of time: not only is it widely available to play for free online, but it has also appeared on the PS3, Xbox 360 and Wii as part of Namco's retro gaming collections. The plot is simple: gamers control a spaceship and must fire on aliens as they rapidly fill the screen. *Galaga* appeared three years after 1978 arcade classic *Space Invaders* (Taito) – the **first videogame to feature animated aliens**.

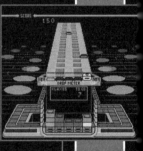

BLOCKING

Klax (Atari Games, 1989) is a puzzle game that started out as an arcade title and was eventually ported to numerous consoles, including the PlayStation and Game Boy. The aim is to organize blocks that are falling off a conveyor belt into rows of similar colours. If it sounds similar to *Tetris* (Alexey Pajitnov, 1985), that's because it was originally intended to be a coin-op sequel to the Russian block-builder blockbuster.

Kicker	Arcade	Points [Marathon]	46,276,700	Greg Laue (USA)	10-Nov-11
Klax	Arcade	Points	2,833,216	Paul Hornitzky (Australlia)	3-May-12
Make Trax	Arcade	Points	2,374,790	Greg R Bond (USA)	31-Jul-12
Mr Driller	Arcade	1,000 m – Points	826,530	Robert Racek (USA)	8-Jun-12
NBA Showtime: NBA on NBC	Arcade	Largest Point Spread – Doubles	29	Craig Dols and Rick Courchaine (USA)	12-Feb-12
Nibbler	Arcade	Points – 5 Life Limit (TGTS)	1,781,630	Tim McVey (USA)	24-Dec-11
Nibbler	Arcade	Points – Marathon	1,041,767,060	Tim McVey (USA)	25-Dec-11
Pang 3	Arcade	Points [Panic Mode, 1 Player]	400,400	Robert Racek (USA)	8-Jun-12
Sel Feena	MAME	Points [Single Player]	852,600	Paul R Ford (USA)	12-Jun-12
Space Fever	Arcade	Game C – Points	2,870	Brian Cady (USA)	1-Oct-11
Space Invaders	Arcade	Points	184,870	Richie Knucklez (USA)	5-Nov-11
Space Zap	Arcade	Points	244,250	Robert Lakeman (USA)	13-Jun-12
Spin Master	MAME	Points [Single Player]	656,200	Gerardo Molina Martinez (Mexico)	9-Feb-12
Street Fighter II: Hyper Fighting	MAME	Points [Tournament]	1,441,400	Thomas S Foster (New Zealand)	2-Apr-12
Super Mario Bros.	Arcade	Nintendo Play Choice 10 – Points [TGTS]	1,262,800	Isaiah "TriForce" Johnson (USA)	24-Sep-11
Tecmo Bowl	MAME	Biggest Blowout	90	Matthew N Runnels (USA)	1-Jun-12
Tetris	Arcade	Points	2,072,133	Jeff Craggy (USA)	24-Mar-12
Vs. Super Mario Bros.	Arcade	Points [Tournament]	3,404,400	Isaiah "TriForce" M Johnson (USA)	6-Aug-11
Zoo Keeper	Arcade	Points	63,061,100	John A Petric (Australlia)	14-Nov-11

GAMING WITH LEGS

Arcade Classics 2 brought Atari retro title *Centipede* (1981) and sequel *Millipede* (1982) to Nintendo. Along with games such as *PAC-Man* and *Joust*, *Millipede* was part of the **first videogame world championships**, an event co-sponsored by Twin Galaxies in January 1983. The **first person to become a videogaming world champion** was Ben Gold (USA).

SNAPPY SNAP

Rondo of Blood is the tenth title in Konami's successful *Castlevania* series of platform horrors, and originally appeared on the PC and SNES prior to its 2010 port to the Wii. Super-fan Rikardo Granda (Colombia) has taken 17,000 screenshots of the game – the **largest collection of videogame screenshots**. *Castlevania* first appeared on the Famicom Disk System in 1986.

NINTENDO

Game	Platform	Setting	Record	Gamer	Date
101-in-1 Explosive Megamix Sports	DS	Fencing – Points	22,750	Tom Duncan (USA)	1-Jan-11
10-Yard Fight	NES	NTSC – Biggest Blowout	56	Matthew S Miller (USA)	26-May-12
1943: The Battle of Midway	NES	NTSC – Points	3,173,400	JD Heins (USA)	21-Jun-11
A Nightmare on Elm Street	NES	NTSC – Points	640,075	Ryan Sullivan (USA)	9-Jul-12
An American Tail: Fievel Goes West	SNES	NTSC – Points	339,440	John Pompa (USA)	8-Feb-12
Arcade Classics 2	Game Boy/Color	Centipede – Points	119,951	John M Brissie (USA)	31-Jul-11
Baseball Stars 2	Wii Virtual Console	Neo-Geo – Biggest Blowout	11	Lance E Swegart (USA)	19-May-12
Bejeweled Twist	Nintendo DS	Classic Mode – Points	1,001,800	Daniel M Phillips (USA)	22-Apr-11
Boomer's Adventure in ASMIK World	Game Boy/Color	Points	5,860	Jeff Sumerlin (USA)	25-May-12
Break 'em All	DS	Quest Mode – Single Play – High Score	617,420	John M Brissie (USA)	15-Oct-11
Bubble Bobble	Wii Virtual Console	NES – Points [Normal Mode]	3,676,940	Michael H Brady (USA)	2-Feb-11
Bubble Bobble Plus!	WiiWare	Arrange – 3 player	2,372,490	Ryan Johnson, Jon Adams & Brandon Bean (USA)	23-Nov-11
		Arrange – 4 player	3,532,460	Jason Brotski, Jodi McFarlane, Joshua Schwalbe & Dan Phillips (USA)	10-Aug-11
		Expert 2 – 2 player	1,142,870	Jackie Bartlett & Michael Sroka (USA)	26-Oct-11
Bust-a-Move Bash!	Wii	Puzzle Mode – Points	156,113,600	Shawne Vinson (USA)	26-Jun-12
California Games	NES	NTSC – Flying Disk – Points	640	James Schuenemeyer (USA)	11-Jun-12
				Marc Cohen (USA)	13-Jul-12
		NTSC – Half Pipe – Points	25,496	James Schuenemeyer (USA)	11-Jun-12
				Marc Cohen (USA)	13-Jul-12
California Games II	SNES	NTSC – Snow Boarding – Points	162,300	Jonathan Adams (Canada)	3-Jun-12
Castlevania: Rondo of Blood	Wii Virtual Console	TG-16 – Points	87,780	John Pompa (USA)	17-Jan-12
Centipede/Breakout/ Warlords	Game Boy Advance	*Breakout* – Breakthru – Points	1,226	John M Brissie (USA)	5-Jul-11
Contra Advance: The Alien Wars EX	Game Boy Advance	Points	75,180	Ryan Sullivan (USA)	9-Jul-11
Cybernator	Wii Virtual Console	SNES – Points	865,270	David C Kinnick (USA)	6-Jan-11
Darkwing Duck	NES	NTSC – Fastest Completion	28 min 14 sec	Ryan Clement (Canada)	21-Jun-12
		PAL – Fastest Completion	25 min 5 sec	Fredrik Svensson (Sweden)	22-Jul-12

THE EMPIRE STRIKES QUACK

Capcom's 1992 platformer *Darkwing Duck*, released for the NES and Game Boy, was based on Disney's TV series of the same name, which ran for 91 episodes, from 1991 to 1992. The hero is Darkwing, ably accompanied by a pilot named Launchpad McQuack. The hero was voiced by Jim Cummings (USA), whose other credits include *Star Wars: The Old Republic* (BioWare, 2011) and *World of Warcraft* (Blizzard Entertainment, 2004).

Defender of the Crown	NES	NTSC – Fastest Completion	2 min 53 sec	Jeffery McQuiston (USA)	17-Dec-11
Donkey Kong	Game Boy/Color	Points [TGTS]	317,600	John Pompa (USA)	26-Jan-11
	NES	Fastest Completion (Kill Screen)	5 hr 44 min 19 sec	Tom Votava (USA)	6-Jun-12
Donkey Kong Country Returns	Wii	NTSC – Fastest 200% Completion	5 hr 47 min 50 sec	John Lundrigan (USA)	11-Aug-11
Dream Pinball 3D	DS	Amber Moon [Points]	238,850,960	John M Brissie (USA)	20-Aug-11
	Wii	Amber Moon [Points]	229,919,400	John M Brissie (USA)	19-Nov-11
Duck Tales	NES	NTSC – Most Money	14,780,000	Antonio Filho (Brazil)	26-Nov-11
Elf Bowling 1 & 2	DS	Elf Bowling – Points	153	John M Brissie (USA)	23-Jul-11
Elite Beat Agents	DS	NTSC/PAL – Avril Lavigne – "Sk8er Boi" – Breezin' – High Score [Points]	61,692	John M Brissie (USA)	1-Jul-11
Faceball 2000	SNES	NTSC – Cyberscape – Points	12,889	John Pompa (USA)	28-Mar-12
Furu Furu Park	Wii	Swan Runner – High Score	5,825,399	Shawne Vinson (USA)	15-May-12
GI Joe: A Real American Hero	NES	NTSC – Points	2,214,670	D Russel Archey (USA)	3-Mar-12
Game & Watch Collection	DS	NTSC – Green House – High Score	485	John M Brissie (USA)	6-Jul-12
Game & Watch: Ball	Nintendo DSiWare	Game A – High Score	257	Ryan McDonagh (UK)	18-Aug-11
Game Boy Gallery: 5 Games in 1	Game Boy/Color	Vermin – Game A – Points	2,349	Daniel Pompei (Australia)	14-Jun-12
Golden Axe II	Wii Virtual Console	Sega Genesis/Mega Drive – The Duel – Fastest Completion	7 min 28 sec	Shawne Vinson (USA)	21-May-12
Gradius Galaxies	Game Boy Advance	Points	147,100	Ryan Sullivan (USA)	9-Jul-12
Hal's Hole in One Golf	SNES	NTSC – Lowest Amount of Strokes	59	Jonathan Adams (Canada)	25-Apr-11
Harley's Humongous Adventure	SNES	NTSC – Points	170,390	D Russel Archey (USA)	25-May-12
Intellivision Lives!	GameCube	NTSC – Astrosmash – Peak Score	858,410	Matt Siegfried (USA)	26-Sep-11
		NTSC – Pinball – Points	55,720	John M Brissie (USA)	2-Jul-11
James Bond Jr	SNES	NTSC – Points	84,200	John Pompa (USA)	15-May-12
Just Dance 3	Wii	Lena – "Satellite"	1,526,152	Matt Siegfried (USA)	13-Nov-11
		Nelly Furtado feat. Timbaland – "Promiscuous"	11,141	Michelle Ireland (USA)	4-Jun-12
Ken Griffey Jr's Winning Run	SNES	NTSC – Home Run Derby – Most Home Runs	36	Ryan Reed (USA)	14-May-12
Kid Icarus	NES	NTSC – Points	2,487,800	Ian Wright (USA)	9-May-12
Kirby Super Star Ultra	DS	Gourmet Race – Course 1 – Fastest Completion	21.2 seconds	Michael Craig (USA)	16-Jan-12
Klax	NES	NTSC – Points	2,403,600	Roger Gray (USA)	20-Sep-11
Knights of the Round	SNES	NTSC – Points	89,390	Jonathan Adams (Canada)	13-Apr-11
The Legend of Zelda II: The Adventure of Link	NES	PAL – Fastest Extreme Rules Speedrun	1 hr 35 min 18 sec	John Nurminen (Sweden)	23-Jul-11
Lords of Thunder	Wii Virtual Console	TurboGrafx-16 – Points	1,359,400	Ryan W Genno (Canada)	20-Jan-12

BEAT IT
Sharply dressed and imaginatively coiffeured, the *Elite Beat Agents* (iNiS, 2006) help those in need by inspiring them through dance and music. This tongue-in-cheek Nintendo DS title requires players to tap circles and spin a stylus to the rhythm of songs by various artists including Avril Lavigne, The Rolling Stones and Madonna, with unlockable songs by Cher, The Jackson 5 and Destiny's Child. The game had an impressive 87% Metascore, as of 10 September 2012.

AXE TO GRIND
Fighting classic *Golden Axe* (Sega, 1989) and its two main sequels have enjoyed a renaissance recently with appearances in retro collections on the Xbox 360 and PS3. American Daniel Lee Strickland Perea holds the record for the **fastest completion of "The Duel" in** *Golden Axe* on the Sega Mega Drive/Genesis, with a speedy time of 5 min 32 sec, on 17 April 2011.

SCUMMY HOUSE

Lucasfilm Games' first full point 'n' click adventure was *Maniac Mansion* (1987). It was the **first game to use the SCUMM game engine**. SCUMM stands for Script Creation Utility for *Maniac Mansion*. Over the next decade, the SCUMM engine was used to create 13 more games.

PARTY FOR YOUR RIGHT TO FIGHT

The good times have truly rolled for *Mario Party* (Hudson Soft/Nd Cube, 1998–2012), the **most prolific party videogame series**. With nine main series titles, and a further three spin-offs, the franchise has kept gamers entertained through its dozens of mini-games. The most recent title, and second for the Wii, is *Mario Party 9* (Nd Cube, 2012).

COPPING AN EARFUL

NES boxing sim *Punch-Out!!* (Nintendo, 1987) was released as *Mike Tyson's Punch-Out!!* in the USA and it remains the **best-selling boxing videogame**, with 3 million units sold. The real Mike Tyson (USA) is still the **youngest world heavyweight boxing champion** ever, having won the WBC title aged 20 years 144 days.

Maniac Mansion	NES	NTSC – Fastest Completion	8 min 3 sec	Christoff Bemis (USA)	13-Jun-12
Mario Bros.	NES	NTSC – Points	10,777,770	Tom Votava (USA)	28-Jun-12
	NES	NTSC – Points – 2 Player Co-Op	2,443,650	Ryan Johnson & Jonathan Adams (Canada)	13-Apr-11
	Wii Virtual Console	NES – Points – 1 Player only	14,900,990	Chad Brevik (USA)	12-Jul-12
Mario Golf: Toadstool Tour	GameCube	Stroke Play – Congo Canopy	41	Jonathan Adams (Canada)	5-Jun-12
Mario Party 6	GameCube	NTSC – Block Star – Points, Single Player only	71	Jake Patzer (USA)	15-Jul-11
Mario Party 7	GameCube	NTSC – Monty's Revenge – Longest Surface Time	16.16 seconds	Jake Patzer (USA)	15-Jul-11
Mario Party DS	Nintendo DS	Study Fall – Shortest Distance	0.0 m (perfect landing)	Ryan H Reed (USA)	23-Jun-12
Mario Strikers	GameCube	NTSC – Domination Mode – Biggest Blowout	7	Jeremy Zsupnik (USA)	21-Aug-11
Mega Man 3	NES	NTSC – Fastest Completion	39 min 49 sec	Daryl Kiddey (USA)	7-Jun-03
Mega Man 4	NES	NTSC – Fastest Completion	46 min 55 sec	Daryl Kiddey (USA)	16-Jul-11
Mendel Palace	NES	NTSC – Points – Extra Mode	395,200	Ryan Johnson (Canada)	1-Sep-11
Metroid Prime Pinball	Nintendo DS	Fastest Completion – Single Mission – Impact Crater (Normal Difficulty)	1 min 25.05 sec	Lance E Swegart (USA)	23-Mar-12
Midway's Arcade Hits: Joust/Defender	Game Boy/ Color	Joust – Points	43,350	John M Brissie (USA)	16-Sep-11
Midway's Greatest Arcade Hits	Game Boy Advance	Joust – Points	104,050	John M Brissie (USA)	5-Apr-11
Mike Tyson's Punch-Out!!/Punch-Out!!	NES	NTSC – Normal Circuit – Fastest Overall Completion	32 min 35 sec	Matthew Ziolkowski (USA)	22-Jan-12
Millipede/ Super Breakout/ Lunar Lander	Game Boy Advance	Millipede – Points	66,139	John M Brissie (USA)	20-Jul-11
Mortal Kombat: Deadly Alliance	GameCube	NTSC – Factory Default	15 min 16 sec	Michael Valenti (USA)	28-Sep-11
Mr Gimmick	NES	PAL – Fastest Completion	26 min 35 sec	Fredrik Svensson (Sweden)	21-Jul-11
Namco Museum: 50th Anniversary	Game Boy Advance	Galaga – Tournament Settings – Points	162,250	John M Brissie (USA)	20-Jul-11
	GameCube	NTSC – Ms. PAC-Man [Points]	33,530	John M Brissie (USA)	4-Jul-11
Namco Museum DS	Nintendo DS	NTSC/Pal – Dig Dug II	42,000	John Pompa (USA)	8-Oct-11

Namco Museum Remix	Wii	Cutie-Q – High Score	102,640	John M Brissie (USA)	24-Oct-11
NBA Jam	Wii	Play Now Mode – Biggest Blowout – Two-Player Team	47	Matthew S Miller & Michelle Ireland (USA)	4-Jul-12
Nemesis	Game Boy/ Color	Points	59,000	Jeff Sumerlin (USA)	25-May-12
NFL Quarterback Club	Game Boy/ Color	Accuracy Competition – Points	64	Jonathan Adams (Canada)	2-Feb-11
Nigel Mansell's World Championship Racing	Game Boy/ Color	Italy – Fastest Lap	1 min 37.3 sec	Jonathan Adams (Canada)	1-Feb-11
	Super NES	NTSC – San Marino – Fastest Race	7 min 20.9 sec	Jonathan Adams (Canada)	23-Jan-11
North & South	NES	PAL – Fastest Completion (TGTS)	2 min 30 sec	Fredrik Svensson (Sweden)	23-Jul-11
Penguin Wars	Game Boy/ Color	Points	1,527,400	Ryan Johnson (Canada)	9-Jul-11
Pilotwings	Super NES	NTSC – Points	1,133	James Cooper (Canada)	2-Nov-11
Pinball Deluxe	Nintendo DS	Sports Mode – Basketball Hard – Points	673,940	John M Brissie (USA)	20-Aug-11
Pinball Hall of Fame: The Williams Collection	Wii	Taxi – Points	20,741,260	Brian Mundo (USA)	1-May-12
Point Blank DS	Nintendo DS	Arcade – Insane [Points]	75,467	Lance E Swegart (USA)	23-Mar-12
		NTSC/PAL – Arcade – Practice [Points]	21,126	John M Brissie (USA)	27-Jul-11
Polarium	Nintendo DS	NTSC/PAL – Challenge – High Score	57,075	John M Brissie (USA)	20-Aug-11
Pong/Asteroids/ Yar's Revenge	Game Boy Advance	Asteroids – Points	18,810	John M Brissie (USA)	6-Apr-11
		Yars' Revenge – Points	58,808	John Pompa (USA)	19-Jan-11
Pop	WiiWare	1 Player – Normal Mode – High Score	11,176,592	Shawne Vinson (USA)	1-May-12
Power Rangers Zeo: Battle Racers	Super NES	NTSC – South Island 1 [Fastest Race]	53.31 seconds	Jonathan Adams (Canada)	5-Jun-12
Rayman Raving Rabbids 2	Nintendo DS	USA – Rabbid Bands [Points]	5,074	John M Brissie (USA)	24-Jul-11

BIRD WARS
Penguin Wars (UPL) started life as an arcade title in 1985 before making the jump to the NES and, in 1990, the Game Boy. It had a host of alternative titles: in Europe it was called *King of Zoo*, and in Japan it was known as *Penguin-Kun Wars Vs*. The gamer controls an animal, such as a cow, rat or penguin, and has to play a ball game with other animals, in a variety of locations. To complicate things, a jelly bean is thrown into the mix to interfere with the balls' movements.

KOMBAT AND CLARET
Mortal Kombat: Deadly Alliance (Midway, 2002) allowed players to choose the amount of blood on screen. There were four settings, from "Off" to "Maximum".

Two years after the release of *Deadly Alliance*, *Mortal Kombat: Deception* (Midway) on the PS2 and Xbox became the **first online 3D fighting game**. It offered one-on-one fighting between two players over the internet.

MAD AS A HATTER
The second title in the *Rayman Raving Rabbids* series (2006–present) of party games is made up of 54 mini-games. Its sales were fairly hefty, too, with 2.55 million units shifted on the Wii and DS, as of 10 September 2012. Its successor, *Rayman Raving Rabbids TV Party* (2008), is the **first videogame to be controlled by the player's posterior**. The "Beestie Boarding" snowboarding mini-game is controlled by the player sitting on the Wii Balance Board and shifting weight from cheek to cheek.

Resident Evil 4	GameCube	NTSC – Fastest Completion – New Round	2 hr 24 min 21 sec	Nolan Baucom (USA)	4-Oct-11
Retro Atari Classics	DS	NTSC/PAL – *Lunar Lander*	240	John M Brissie (USA)	23-Jun-11
RoboCop	NES	NTSC – Points	143,456	Antonio Filho (Brazil)	26-Nov-11
Rock Band [Nintendo Wii]	Wii	NTSC – Red Hot Chili Peppers – "Dani California" – Drums – Expert – 1 Player [Points]	161,750	Michelle Ireland (USA)	11-Apr-12
Rollerball	NES	NTSC – Points	8,253,400	Eric Bailey (USA)	19-Oct-11
Roundball: 2-on-2 Challenge	NES	NTSC – Biggest Blowout	779	Rudy Ferretti (USA)	1-Aug-12
Sonic Mega Collection	GameCube	NTSC – *Sonic & Knuckles* – Knuckles [Fastest 100% Completion] [TGTS]	38 min 7 sec	Jared E Oswald (USA)	27-Apr-12
Sonic Spinball	Wii Virtual Console	Sega Genesis/Mega Drive – Points	15,735,000	John Pompa (USA)	14-Dec-11
Space Invaders Extreme	DS	Stage Select – Normal Mode – Stage 2 – Points	889,460	John M Brissie (USA)	29-Jun-11
Space Invaders Extreme 2	DS	Score Attack – Points	10,802,360	John M Brissie (USA)	24-Jul-11
Space Invaders Revolution	DS	Classic Version – Points	4,510	John M Brissie (USA)	14-Jul-11
Spider-Man and The X-Men in Arcade's Revenge	Game Boy/ Color	Points	58,700	Jarrod McClanahan (USA)	15-May-12
StarTropics	NES	NTSC – Fastest Completion	1 hr 32 min 7 sec	Jonathan Adams (Canada)	16-Feb-11
Super Batter Up	SNES	NTSC – Biggest Blowout	17	Jonathan Adams (Canada)	11-Jan-12
Super C	NES	NTSC – Points	14,033,990	JD Heins (USA)	7-Dec-11
Super Mario Bros.	NES	PAL – Fastest Minimalist Completion	5 min 9 sec	Ribeiro Casaleiro Aurelio (Belgium)	16-Feb-12
	Wii Virtual Console	NES – Minimalist Speed Run	5 min 12 sec	John J Lundrigan (USA)	29-Aug-11
Super Mario Land	Game Boy/ Color	Points	999,999	Rudy Ferretti (USA)	9-Nov-11
Super Mario World: Super Mario Advance 2	Game Boy Advance	Points [TG Extreme Settings]	1,034,170	John Pompa (USA)	29-Jan-11

HIT ZOMBIES

German gamer Robert Brandl made use of glitches to achieve the **fastest completion of *Resident Evil 4* (New Game + mode)** in just 1 hr 37 min 35 sec. The fourth movie in the zombie franchise, *Resident Evil: Afterlife* (USA, 2010), incorporated elements of *Resident Evil 5* (Capcom, 2009) and became the **highest-grossing zombie film** of all time, taking $296 million (£203 million) at the worldwide box office by 4 November 2010. The 3D blockbuster was directed by Paul W S Anderson (USA), who has helmed three *Resident Evil* movies and the original *Mortal Kombat* (USA, 1995).

ALL IN A SPIN

Sonic the Hedgehog gets everywhere – in 2010 he even got his own roller coaster ride at Alton Towers theme park, UK. Just like the game of the same name, which was released on the Mega Drive/Genesis in 1993, the attraction spins its riders around as well as taking them up and down along the track. Although the roller coaster itself had been operational since 2004, the rebranding introduced new features such as Sonic's favourite tunes being played for thrill-seekers.

Super Monkey Ball 2	GameCube	NTSC – Main Game – Challenge Mode – Beginner	128,987	Jake Patzer (USA)	25-Jul-11
Super Smash Bros. Brawl	Wii	NTSC – Stadium – Multi-Man Brawl – Endless Brawl – Kills	525	Andrew Furrer (USA)	2-Sep-11
Super Street Fighter II Turbo Revival	Game Boy Advance	Points [Tournament Settings]	619.3	Jordan L Bean (Canada)	31-Aug-11
Swamp Thing	NES	Fastest Completion	18 min 40 sec	Lamar Mitchell (USA)	2-May-12
	NES	NTSC – Fastest Completion	18 min 40 sec	Lamar Mitchell (USA)	2-May-12
Target; Renegade	NES	NTSC – Points	543,410	Rudy Ferretti (USA)	8-Jul-12
Tetris	3DS Virtual Console	Game Boy/Game Boy Color – Lines	157 lines	John Pompa (USA)	10-Jul-12
	3DS Virtual Console	Game Boy/Game Boy Color – Points	74,472	John Pompa (USA)	10-Jul-12
Tetris Attack	Game Boy/Color	Endless – Points	13,768	John Pompa (USA)	22-Feb-11
Tetris DS	DS	NTSC/PAL – Points [Standard – Marathon]	1,584,000	Isaiah "TriForce" Johnson (USA)	2-May-12
Tetris Party	WiiWare	Beginner's Tetris – Marathon (Endless) – Points	35,356,680	Shawne Vinson (USA)	1-May-12
The Incredible Hulk	SNES	NTSC – Points	370,400	John Pompa (USA)	10-May-12
The Legend of Zelda: The Wind Waker	GameCube	NTSC – Squid Battleship	16	Jake Patzer (USA)	24-Jul-10
The New Tetris	N64	NTSC – Sprint – Lines	195	Matthew Straka (USA)	12-Jun-12
The Simpsons: Bart vs. the World	NES	PAL – Fastest Completion	28 min 17 sec	Fredrik Svensson (Sweden)	22-Jul-11
Thunder Spirits	SNES	NTSC – Points	314,850	Jared E Oswald (USA)	31-Aug-11
Tiger Woods PGA Tour 10	Wii	Banff Springs – Least Amount of Strokes	63	Matthew Runnels (USA)	5-May-12
Tiny Toon Adventures: Wacky Sports Challenge	Game Boy/Color	Carnival – Fifi's Water Squirting Challenge	8,940	Jonathan Adams (Canada)	7-Sep-11
Tony Hawk's Pro Skater 4	GameCube	NTSC – Shipyard [Points, Single Session]	912,319	Michael Dudley (USA)	27-May-11
Toobin'	NES	NTSC – Points	3,868,300	Mason Cramer (USA)	27-Apr-12
Total Recall	NES	NTSC – Points	451,420	Antonio Filho (Brazil)	26-Nov-11
Track & Field	Game Boy/Color	Discus Throw – Farthest Distance	83.32 m	Jonathan Adams (Canada)	7-Mar-11
Trauma Center: Under the Knife	DS	Operation 01 – Standard Procedure – Points	3,030	John M Brissie (USA)	30-Jun-11

MONKEY BUSINESS

The original Super Monkey Ball (Amusement Vision/SEGA EAD, 2001) was a popular launch title for the GameCube. Sequel Super Monkey Ball 2 (Amusement Vision, 2002) added four-player party game options to the rolling gameplay action.

GREAT SKATES

American skater and nine-times X Games gold medallist Tony Hawk first lent his name to a videogame in 1999, with Tony Hawk's Pro Skater. With sales of 53.7 million as of 10 September 2012, the Hawk franchise is the **best-selling action sports series**. There have been a total of 15 titles in the series, including Pro Skater 4 (Neversoft, 2002, above) and most recent release Tony Hawk's Pro Skater HD (Robomodo, 2012).

NINTENDO

OUT OF THE WOODS

Wario's Woods (Nintendo, 1994) features mushroom-headed hero Toad, who attempts to defeat Mario's old enemy Wario. The puzzler aspects of the gameplay owe a debt to *Tetris* (Alexey Pajitnov, 1984), the **most ported videogame**, with versions on more than 65 platforms including mobile phones.

CALL OF THE WILD

Zoo Keeper (Success, 2003) is an addictive tile game in which players have to line up pictures of animals in rows or columns for points. Tile puzzlers remain hugely popular and one of the best known in the genre is *Bejeweled* (PopCap, 2001–present). The **first perfect score on Bejeweled 2** (2004) was achieved by Mike Leyde (USA), who reached the maximum 2,147,483,647 points on 23 March 2009. Mike played for an hour or so a day for three years until he passed the point that the developers thought no gamer could reach – and the score reset.

Game	Platform	Category	Record	Holder	Date
WarioWare, Inc.: Mega Party Game$!	GameCube	NTSC – Time Attack – 20 Games	1 min 15.36 sec	Nicholas J Reymann (USA)	19-Sep-11
Wario's Woods	NES	NTSC – Fastest Completion [Fastest Total Completion/ Hard Mode]	11 min 30 sec	Daniel Dock (USA)	5-Mar-12
	SNES	NTSC – Fastest Total Completion/Hard Mode	9 min 45 sec	Daniel Dock (USA)	5-Mar-12
	Wii Virtual Console	NES – Fastest Completion [Fastest Total Completion/ Hard Mode]	17 min 43 sec	Ryan W Genno (Canada)	26-Jan-12
Wii Fit/Wii Fit Plus	Wii	NTSC – Aerobics – Rhythm Boxing – 03 Minutes [Points]	392	Marc Cohen (USA)	17-Jul-11
Wii Music	Wii	Handbell Harmony – My Grandfather's Clock – Points	100	Shawne Vinson (USA)	26-Jun-12
Wii Play	Wii	Find Mii – Stages Completed	78	Kevin M Conner (USA)	20-Sep-11
		Fishing – Points	3,480	Andrew Pete Mee (UK)	11-Mar-12
		Table Tennis – Most Volleys	291	Andrew Pete Mee (UK)	29-Feb-12
		Tanks! – Single Player Only – Tanks Destroyed	540	Paul Hornitzky (Australia)	8-Oct-11
		Tanks! – Two Player Team – Tanks Destroyed	65	Matthew S Miller & Michelle Ireland (USA)	4-Mar-12
Wii Play: Motion	Wii	Teeter Targets – Challenge Mode – Stage 3 – Points	1,256	Matthew S Miller (USA)	19-Dec-11
Wii Sports	Wii	Training – Golf – Hitting the Green	shy by 0 ft	Stanley Lauskey (USA)	21-Sep-11
Yoshi's Cookie	SNES	NTSC – Points	76,430	D Russel Archey (USA)	25-May-12
Zoo Keeper	DS	NTSC/PAL – Points – Time Attack	398,240	John M Brissie (USA)	23-Jul-11

CLASSIC CONSOLES

Game	Platform	Setting	Record	Gamer	Date
After Burner	Sega Master System	NTSC – Points	14,443,700	Antonio Filho (Brazil)	26-Nov-11
Alien 3	Sega Genesis/Mega Drive	NTSC – Points	250,310	Ryan Sullivan (USA)	22-Dec-11
American Gladiators	Sega Genesis/Mega Drive	NTSC – Points	138	Ryan Sullivan (USA)	22-Dec-11
Arcus Odyssey	Sega Genesis/Mega Drive	NTSC – Points	55,010	Ryan Sullivan (USA)	12-Jun-12
Bio-Hazard Battle	Sega Genesis/Mega Drive	NTSC – Points	26,450	David A Ray (USA)	18-Jul-12
Bomberman	TurboGrafx-16	Default	21,741,110	Ryan Genno (Canada)	3-Jun-11
Cabbage Patch Kids: Adventure in the Park	ColecoVision	NTSC/PAL – Skill 1	97,550	Stephen Wilkie (USA)	9-Feb-12
Carnival	Atari 2600	NTSC – Game 1, Difficulty B	1,500,130	Kyle Goewert (USA)	20-Apr-12
Castle Blast	Atari 5200	Default	4,234	Troy Whelan (USA)	20-Jan-11
Centipede	Sega Dreamcast	Points [Classic Version]	22,854	Jared E Oswald (USA)	17-Aug-12
Chew Man Fu	TurboGrafx-16	Points (Single Player Only)	573,720	Ryan Genno (Canada)	2-Jun-11
Crack Down	Sega Genesis/Mega Drive	NTSC – Points	147,350	Ryan Sullivan (USA)	6-Dec-11
Dead Moon	TurboGrafx-16	Points	3,319,900	Ryan Genno (Canada)	7-Jun-11
E.T. the Extra-Terrestrial	Atari 2600	NTSC – Game 1, Difficulty BB	1,058,399	Glenn Case (USA)	22-Dec-11
Elemental Master	Sega Genesis/Mega Drive	NTSC – Points	118,940	Ryan Sullivan (USA)	6-Dec-11
Forgotten Worlds	Sega Genesis/Mega Drive	NTSC – Points	1,699,100	Ryan Sullivan (USA)	22-Dec-11
Galaga '90	TurboGrafx-16	Points	341,730	Matthew Straka (USA)	29-Mar-11
Galaxy Force II	Sega Genesis/Mega Drive	Points	1,460,270	Matthew Straka (USA)	10-Feb-12
Gauntlet 4	Sega Genesis/Mega Drive	NTSC – Points	28,650	Ryan Sullivan (USA)	6-Dec-11
Horse Racing	Intellivision	NTSC/PAL – Most Money Won	$9,999	Jeff Coyle (USA)	9-Feb-12
Ice Cold Beer	Novelty	Points	350,000	Zach T Kaczor (USA)	30-Jul-11
Joust	Atari 2600	NTSC – Skill – Skilled	4,027,800	Craig A Queen (USA)	8-Jul-12

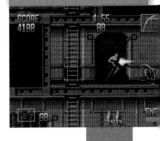

Jurassic Park	Sega Genesis/ Mega Drive	NTSC-Fastest Completion [Dr Grant]	17 min 17 sec	Ryan R Schempp (USA)	1-Aug-12	
Knuckles' Chaotix	Sega 32X	NTSC – Default Setting	423,900	Charles Ziese (USA)	16-Mar-12	
Legend of Hero Tonma	TurboGrafx-16	Points	69,600	Ryan Genno (Canada)	7-Jun-11	
Magical Chase	TurboGrafx-16	Points	2,912,730	Ryan Genno (Canada)	1-Jun-11	
Megamania	Atari 2600	NTSC – Game 1, Difficulty B [Guided Missiles]	999,999	Marc Cohen (USA)	19-Feb-11	
Mercs	Sega Genesis/ Mega Drive	NTSC – Points [Original Mode]	706,800	Jeffrey Bell (USA)	12-Jul-12	
Mighty Morphin Power Rangers: The Movie	Sega Genesis/ Mega Drive	Fastest Completion	0:30:20	Charles K Ziese (USA)	18-May-12	
Musha	Sega Genesis/ Mega Drive	Points	135,250,220	Chase A Dimino (USA)	17-Jul-12	
Namco Museum	Sega Dreamcast	NTSC – Ms. PAC-Man [Points]	26,820	Matthew Straka (USA)	22-Apr-11	
Ninja Golf	Atari 7800	Default	168,560	Mark Stacy (USA)	19-Jun-11	
Ordyne	TurboGrafx-16	Points	374,340	Ryan Genno (Canada)	2-Jun-11	
PAC-Man Collection	Atari 7800	PAC-Man [Fast Mode]	221,430	Ron Weston (UK)	26-Nov-11	
Psychosis	TurboGrafx-16	Points	303	Ryan Genno (Canada)	1-Jun-11	
Q*bert	ColecoVision	NTSC/PAL – Skill 2	77.270	Stephen Wilkie (USA)	18-May-12	
Rampart	Atari Lynx	Default	29,612	Jeremy Woodworth (USA)	9-Nov-11	
	Sega Genesis/ Mega Drive	Points	26,007	Jeremy Woodworth (USA)	5-May-12	
Road Rash	Sega Genesis/ Mega Drive	PAL – Grass Valley – Fastest Time	2 min 39.7 sec	Andrew Pete Mee (UK)	23-Jan-11	
Rocket Knight Adventures	Sega Genesis/ Mega Drive	Fastest Completion	54 min 18.8 sec	Jared E Oswald (USA)	11-May-12	
Samurai-Ghost	TurboGrafx-16	Points	31,600	Ryan Genno (Canada)	7-Jun-11	
Sega Bass Fishing	Sega Dreamcast	Cape [Heaviest Fish]	20.38	Troy Whelan (USA)	26-Mar-12	
Sega Marine Fishing	Sega Dreamcast	Original – Free Fishing – The Offing [Heaviest Fish]	375.13	Troy Whelan (USA)	9-Jul-11	
Sinistron	TurboGrafx-16	Points	288,800	Ryan Genno (Canada)	2-Jun-11	
Slaughter Sport	Sega Genesis/ Mega Drive	NTSC – Points	189,900	Ryan Sullivan (USA)	6-Dec-11	
Soldier Blade	TurboGrafx-16	Points (Normal Mode)	1,628,700	Ryan Genno (Canada)	4-Jun-11	
Sonic & Knuckles	Sega Genesis/ Mega Drive	Fastest Full Completion – Sonic	52 min 58 sec	Charles K Ziese (USA)	22-May-12	
Sonic & Knuckles and Sonic the Hedgehog 2	Sega Genesis/ Mega Drive	Fastest Minimalist Completion	43 min 3 sec	Jared E Oswald (USA)	21-May-12	
		Fastest Minimalist Completion – Knuckles	1 hr 3 min 31 sec	Jared E Oswald (USA)	12-May-12	

KARA-TEE KID

With its deadly human opponents, to say nothing of the mutant frogs and attacking gophers, *Ninja Golf* (BlueSky Software, 1990) always made getting a hole in one more tricky than most golf games. Nintendo's more orthodox *Golf* (1984) remains the **best-selling golf game**, with more than 4 million copies sold.

DYNAMIC DUO

Knuckles was designed as a rival to the speedy blue hedgehog, but nothing could shift Sonic in the public imagination. *Sonic the Hedgehog 2* (Sega, 1992) is the **best-selling game on any Sega platform**, with 6 million copies sold. As recently as September 2012, Sonic was still doing it, helping Sega achieve the record for the **best-selling third-party Wii platformer**, with 2.55 million sales of *Sonic and the Secret Rings* (Sega, 2007).

Sonic 3D Blast	Sega Genesis/ Mega Drive	Fastest Full Completion	1 hr 10 min 5 sec	Charles K Ziese (USA)	18-May-12
Sonic CD	Sega CD	NTSC – Points	349,300	Jared Oswald (USA)	5-Jan-11
Sonic the Hedgehog	Sega Genesis/ Mega Drive	Minimalist Speed Run	28 min 22 sec	Charles K Ziese (USA)	13-May-12
Sonic the Hedgehog 2	Sega Genesis/ Mega Drive	Minimalist Speed Run – Sonic	43 min 32 sec	Charles K Ziese (USA)	13-May-12
		Points	3,261,620	Eric Schafer (USA)	16-May-12
Sonic the Hedgehog 3	Sega Genesis/ Mega Drive	Minimalist Speed Run – Sonic	37 min 45 sec	Charles K Ziese (USA)	12-May-12
Space Panic	ColecoVision	NTSC/PAL – Skill 1	156,570	Leigh Pearce (USA)	3-May-12
Star Wars Arcade	Sega 32X	NTSC – Default Setting	40,581	David A Ray (USA)	18-Jul-12
T2: The Arcade Game	Sega Genesis/ Mega Drive	NTSC – Points – Single Credit Only	1,373,350	Ryan Sullivan (USA)	6-Dec-11
Taz Mania	Sega Genesis/ Mega Drive	Fastest Completion	16 min 32 sec	Jared E Oswald (USA)	21-May-12
Tecmo Super Bowl	Sega Genesis/ Mega Drive	NTSC – Biggest Blowout	38	Ryan Sullivan (USA)	6-Dec-11
The Terminator	Sega Genesis/ Mega Drive	NTSC – Points	30,000	David A Ray (USA)	18-Jul-12

Tiny Toon Adventures	Sega Genesis/ Mega Drive	Points	152,500	Daniel O Romero (Argentina)	6-Aug-11
Triggerheart Exelica	Sega Dreamcast	NTSC/J – Arcade Mode [Points]	7,837,087	Matthew Straka (USA)	29-Feb-12
Two Crude Dudes	Sega Genesis/ Mega Drive	NTSC – Points	74,750	Ryan Sullivan (USA)	22-Dec-11
Virtual Racing Deluxe	Sega 32X	NTSC – Big Forest	3 min 17 sec	Matthew Straka (USA)	10-Jun-11
Williams Arcade's Greatest Hits	Sega Genesis/ Mega Drive	NTSC – Robotron: 2084 – Marathon – Points	133,880	Ryan Sullivan (USA)	6-Dec-11
Yars' Revenge	Atari 2600	NTSC – Game 2, Difficulty B	7,001,715	Mike Tracy (USA)	13-Aug-11
Zillion II: The Tri Formation	Sega Master System	Points	134,700	Matthew Straka (USA)	22-Jan-12

MACHINE MUSIC

Tommy Tallarico (USA) worked on *The Terminator* (Probe Software, 1992) among countless other game soundtracks. He reveals his personal Top 10 on pp.138–139 and his success is proof that game music is an increasingly celebrated form. On 13 February 2011 *Civilization IV* (Firaxis, 2005) became the **first videogame theme to win a Grammy award**. Back in 1998, *Heart of Darkness* (Amazing Studio, 1998) had the **first orchestral recording of a videogame soundtrack** when its score by Bruce Broughton (USA) was performed by the Sinfonia of London.

DREAM SHOOTER

Sega's ill-starred Dreamcast might have been discontinued by 2001 but games continued to be produced. The old-school scrolling shoot-'em-up *Triggerheart Exelica* (Warashi) was ported over from the arcade to arrive on the machine in 2008.

GONNA MAKE YOU A STAR

Lumines (Q Entertainment, 2005) was the PSP launch title with block-dropping addictiveness that became the **most critically acclaimed puzzle game for PSP**. As of September 2012 it had a Metacritic score of 89%. By June 2011, it had sold over a million copies, making it the **best-selling PSP puzzle game**. The *Lumines* franchise also recorded the **first virtual pop star to launch a global fundraising event**, with Lumi from *Lumines II* (2007) at the 2007 Live Earth Tokyo concert for the environment. The lead singer of Genki Rockets also introduced a hologram of former US Vice President Al Gore to launch the show.

STARDUST

A 2D cartoon dog was the titular star of *PaRappa the Rapper 2* (NanaOn-Sha, 2001). The action was all about following his raps by hitting buttons in sequence. It was simple but fun, like the first game in the series, which in 1996 set a record by becoming the **first rhythm-action videogame**.

SONY

Game	Platform	Setting	Record	Gamer	Date
Activision Anthology	PS2	NTSC – *River Raid II* – Game 1, Difficulty B [Points]	7,900	Matt Siegfried (USA)	10-Sep-11
Atari Classics Evolved	PSP	NTSC/PAL – *Warlords Evolved* [Points]	783,710	Ryan Sullivan (USA)	31-Dec-11
Call of Duty: Modern Warfare 3	PS3	Special Ops – Solo – Missions – Stay Sharp – Fastest Completion	20.8 seconds	Adam Woodson (USA)	13-Nov-11
Critter Crunch	PS3 PSN	Survival Mode – Single Player	106,574	Daniel J Sampsel (USA)	13-Oct-11
Gran Turismo 4	PS2	NTSC – License Center Test B-05 – Lap Guide Run (Tsukuba) – Fastest Completion	1 min 39.8 sec	Matthew Runnels (USA)	5-May-12
Grand Theft Auto III	PS2	NTSC – Entire Game – Fastest Minimalist Completion	1 hr 29 min 8 sec	Jay Thomas (USA)	5-Sep-11
Guitar Hero Encore: Rocks the 80s	PS2	NTSC – 1. Opening Licks – 18 and Life – Medium Difficulty – 1 player [Points]	94,755	Jared E Oswald (USA)	28-Jul-11
Intellivision Lives!	PS2	NTSC – *Buzz Bombers*	51,100	Matt Siegfried (USA)	25-Sep-11
Lumines	PSP	NTSC/PAL – Time Attack – 60 Seconds [Most Blocks Cleared]	31	Ryan Sullivan (USA)	31-Dec-11
Marvel vs. Capcom	PlayStation	Points	2,200,100	Ryan Sullivan (USA)	29-May-12
Metal Gear Solid: VR Missions	PlayStation	NTSC – VR Training – Special Mode – Variety Mode – Time Attack – Level 10 [Fastest Completion]	1 min 14.5 sec	Ryan Sullivan (USA)	27-May-12
Midway Arcade Treasures	PS2	*Joust* – 1 player – Tournament [Points]	95,750	Ryan Sullivan (USA)	29-May-12
Midway Arcade Treasures: Extended Play	PSP	NTSC/PAL – *Rampart* [Points]	14,184	Jeremy N Woodworth (USA)	9-Nov-11
Namco Museum: 50th Anniversary	PS2	*Galaga '88* [Points]	191,620	Ryan Sullivan (USA)	29-May-12
Namco Museum Battle Collection	PSP	NTSC/PAL – *Bosconian* [Points]	119,940	Michael E Sroka (USA)	18-May-12
PAC-Man: Championship Edition DX	PS3 PSN	Championship II – Score Attack – 5 Minutes	2,067,050	Matt Siegfried (USA)	13-Nov-11
PaRappa The Rapper 2	PS2	NTSC – Stage 2 – Level 4 Difficulty – Strictly for Adults [Points]	2,622	Marc Cohen (USA)	30-Jan-11
Pinball Hall of Fame: The Gottlieb Collection	PSP	NTSC/PAL – Ace High [Points]	7,140,000	Ryan Sullivan (USA)	31-Dec-11

Game	Platform	Category	Score	Player	Date
Rock Band 2 [PlayStation 3]	PS3	NTSC – Alice in Chains – "Man in the Box" – Drums – Expert – 1 Player [Points]	131,350	Michelle Ireland (USA)	29-Dec-11
Rock Band 3	PS3	Faith No More – "Midlife Crisis" – 1 Player – Vocals	102,291	Elizabeth Bolinger (USA)	13-Nov-11
		Foreigner – "Cold as Ice" – 1 Player – Drums	64,350	Michelle Ireland (USA)	1-May-12
		Huey Lewis & The News – "The Power of Love" – 1 Player – Vocals	70,927	Chaz Kaczor (USA)	13-Nov-11
		Joan Jett & The Blackhearts – "I Love Rock'n'Roll" – 1 Player – Guitar	54,835	Matt Siegfried (USA)	13-Nov-11
		Lynyrd Skynyrd – "Free Bird" – 1 Player – Drums	232,901	Michelle Ireland (USA)	29-Dec-11
Sega Genesis Collection	PSP	NTSC/PAL – *Altered Beast* [Points]	339,100	Michael E Sroka (USA)	1-Jun-12
Shatter	PS3 PSN	Story Mode – 5 Life Limit – Points	29,633,590	Daniel J Sampsel (USA)	13-Oct-11
Snoopy vs the Red Baron	PS2	NTSC – Campaign – Aerodrome Island – Mission 1 [Fastest Completion]	2 min 18.6 sec	Troy Whelan (USA)	25-Feb-12
Super Stardust HD	PS3 PSN	Arcade Mode – Points	20,450,680	Wouter TM Lugtennar (Netherlands)	6-Feb-12
Taito Legends 2	PS2	*Chack'n Pop* [Points]	49,650	Ryan Sullivan (USA)	29-May-12
Taito Legends Power-Up	PSP	NTSC/PAL – *Raimais* [Points]	1,506,060	Kevin S Brisley (USA)	4-Mar-12
Tetris	PSP PSN	NTSC/PAL – Main Game – Points	216,622	John Pompa (USA)	10-Sep-11
Tony Hawk's Pro Skater 3	PS2	NTSC – Foundry – Single Session [Points]	1,020,419	Matt Siegfried (USA)	29-Aug-11
World Series of Poker	PS2	NTSC – Entire Game	44	Steve Germershausen (Canada)	19-Jan-12
Zen Pinball	PS3 PSN	Ninja Gaiden Sigma 2 – Points	6,091,000	Marc Cohen (USA)	31-Jan-11

MICROSOFT

BOOGIE NIGHT

The **longest marathon on a dance game** lasted 24 hr 2 min 44 sec and was achieved by Carrie Swidecki (USA), who played *Dance Central 2* (Harmonix, 2011) from 16 to 17 June 2012 in California, USA.

GEARED UP

The third game in the trilogy that made up the initial *Gears of War* (Epic Games, 2006–present) sold 3 million copies worldwide in its first week. This makes the *GoW* series the **first third-person shooter series to make $1 billion**. Back in 2006, the first instalment was also the **first console game to use the Unreal Engine 3**, developed and updated since 1998 by Epic Games.

XBOX AND XBOX 360

Game	Platform	Setting	Record	Gamer	Date
Bubble Bobble Neo!	Xbox Live Arcade	Single Player – Classic Mode	279,890	Ryan Sullivan (USA)	31-Mar-12
Burnout Revenge	Xbox	Crash – Crashaoke [Dollars]	$17,727,750	Troy Whelan (USA)	21-Mar-12
Child of Eden	Xbox 360	Stage 1 – Points	921,800	Matt Siegfried (USA)	13-Nov-11
Contra	Xbox Live Arcade	Points	290,400	Ryan Sullivan (USA)	30-Mar-12
Dance Central 2	Xbox 360	David Guetta feat. Akon – "Sexy Chick"	2,172,402	Elizabeth Bolinger (USA)	2-Jul-12
Decimation X	Xbox Live Arcade	Points	74,582	Ryan Sullivan (USA)	31-Mar-12
Decimation X3	Xbox Live Arcade	Normal Mode	624,271	Ryan Sullivan (USA)	31-Mar-12
Dig Dug	Xbox Live Arcade	Points	167,750	Tim McVey (USA)	30-Dec-11
Discs of Tron	Xbox Live Arcade	Points	41,400	Ryan Sullivan (USA)	29-Mar-12
Forza Motorsport 4	Xbox 360	Points – Alfa Romeo MiTo Spec Series	16,665	Nathan Leffler (USA)	11-Nov-11
		Points – Camaro Club	13,425	Scott Kazcor (USA)	11-Nov-11
		Points – Class A European Tour – Lotus Esprit	21,103	Jeff Wheaton (USA)	11-Nov-11
Frogger	Xbox Live Arcade	Points	15,200	Tim McVey (USA)	30-Dec-11
Galaga Legions	Xbox Live Arcade	Adventure Mode – Points	2,174,820	Ryan Sullivan (USA)	30-Mar-12
Game Room	Xbox Live Arcade	*Shark! Shark!* – Points	32,250	Matt Siegfried (USA)	2-Feb-11
Gears of Wars 3	Xbox 360	Campaign (Arcade) Act 1: One – Chapter 1: Anchored	47,349	Matt Siegfried (USA)	13-Nov-11

The Gunstringer	Xbox 360	Points – Act 3	20,918	Zach Kaczor (USA)	11-Nov-11
		Points – Act 4	27,796	Matt Siegfried (USA)	11-Nov-11
Intellivision Lives!	Xbox	*Thin Ice* [Points]	114,120	Troy Whelan (USA)	21-Jun-12
Joust	Xbox Live Arcade	NTSC – Points	88,950	Tim McVey (USA)	30-Dec-11
Kinect Adventures	Xbox 360	Points – Ralleyball Treasure Chest	200	Matt Siegfried (USA)	11-Nov-11
Madden NFL Arcade	Xbox Live Arcade	Play Now – Biggest Blowout	35	Jeffrey M Widzinski (USA)	21-Apr-12
Namco Museum Virtual Arcade	Xbox Live Arcade	*Bosconian* – Points	85,090	Ryan Sullivan (USA)	31-Mar-12
OutRun Online Arcade	Xbox Live Arcade	Points – Outrun Mode 15 Continuous Course	1,652,210	Ryan Sullivan (USA)	29-Mar-12
PAC-Man Championship Edition DX	Xbox Live Arcade	Spiral – Score Attack – 5 Minutes	2,295,160	Charlie D Wehner (USA)	10-Sep-12
Pinball Hall of Fame: The Williams Collection	Xbox 360	Medieval Madness – Points	1,243,820,370	Anthony Curran (USA)	12-Mar-12
Portal 2	Xbox 360	Time Trial – Chapter 1–1 to 1–5	4 min 12.1 sec	Matt Siegfried (USA)	13-Nov-11
Pure Pinball	Xbox	Excessive Speed	100,208,600	Troy Whelan (USA)	29-May-12
Puzzle Bobble Live!/ Bust-a-Move Live!	Xbox Live Arcade	Single Player – 1P Puzzle – Points	19,127,070	Michael E Sroka (USA)	30-Jan-12
Robotron: 2084	Xbox Live Arcade	Points	187,225	Tim McVey (USA)	30-Dec-11
Shinobi	Xbox Live Arcade	Points – Hardcore	39,820	Ryan Sullivan (USA)	30-Mar-12
Space Ark	Xbox Live Arcade	Mission Mode – Somewhere Under the Rainbow	69,215,200	Matt Siegfried (USA)	5-Mar-11
Super Contra	Xbox Live Arcade	Points	191,300	Ryan Sullivan (USA)	30-Mar-12
Super Street Fighter IV: Arcade Edition	Xbox 360	NTSC – Arcade Mode – Points – Tournament	1,144,000	John Lapsey (USA)	13-Nov-11
Time Pilots	Xbox Live Arcade	Points	129,900	Tim McVey (USA)	30-Dec-11
Triggerheart Exelica	Xbox Live Arcade	Points	13,174,325	Ryan Sullivan (USA)	29-Mar-12
Tron	Xbox Live Arcade	Points	36,268	Ryan Sullivan (USA)	30-Mar-12
UFC Undisputed 2010	Xbox Live Arcade	Exhibition Mode – Fastest Victory	3 seconds	Ryan H Reed (USA)	1-Jul-12
Xevious	Xbox Live Arcade	Points	43,610	Ryan Sullivan (USA)	31-Mar-12

DEAD SHOT

The bony outlaw hero of *The Gunstringer* (2011) added a dash of humour to the Western shooter genre and was an innovative and unique use of Kinect. Its developer, the witty house of Twisted Pixel Games, previously set a record for having the **first simultaneous four-player mode in a 2D platformer**, with *'Splosion Man* (2009).

MARTIAL ARTISTRY

There is no shortage of fighters and styles to choose from in *UFC Undisputed* games (Yuke's, 2009–present). The commentary isn't bad either, with the 2009 edition of the game running to 36 hours – the **most recorded commentary in a fighting game**.

Index

Quiz Answers

DID YOU GET A CRICK IN THE NECK FROM READING QUESTIONS SIDEWAYS UP THE PAGE? FIND OUT IF IT WAS WORTHWHILE AS WE REVEAL THE ANSWERS.

Page 7
72%, according to an Entertainment Software Association survey from July 2011

Page 23
1889

Page 25
Gomez

Page 27
The PlayStation 2 has sold 153.68 million units worldwide

Page 29
True. Nintendo say 73.2 million Euro Miis were made by the end of 2011

Page 31
Sackboy

Page 33
Tyria

Page 35
Google Chrome

Page 37
10 July 2008

Page 39
HTC Dream

Page 45
Adolf Hitler

Page 47
John "Soap" MacTavish

Page 49
On the map de_dust2, the name "Goose" is sprayed on the wall at bombsite A. His nickname is "Gooseman"

Page 51
Pandora

Page 53
The Covenant

Page 55
Andrew Ryan

Page 61
Sam & Max: Freelance Police

Page 63
Grand Theft Auto: San Andreas

Page 65
Angelina Jolie

Page 67
T-virus (or Tyrant virus)

Page 69
Robin Williams

Page 71
Jak and Daxter

Page 77
Cut the Rope: Experiments

Page 79
Lexiko

Page 81
"Night Boat to Cairo"

Page 83
Cruella de Vil, the villain of *The Hundred and One Dalmatians* by Dodie Smith

Page 85
Santa Claus

Page 87
False. It was created in Robstown, Texas, USA

Page 93
Kylie Minogue

Page 95
Akuma and Fei Long

Page 97
Raidou

Page 99
Resident Evil

Page 105
True

Page 107
At the Frozen Throne inside the Ice Crown Citadel

Page 109
Amarr Empire, Caldari State, Gallente Federation and Minmatar Republic

Page 111
(Earnest) Gary Gygax and David Arneson

Page 117
Tails

Page 119
True: two seasons from 1994–1995

Page 121
Luigi and Yoshi

Page 123
Craftworld, starring Mr Yellowhead

Page 129
SNES

Page 131
Force

Page 133
Micro Machines

Page 135
Mushrooms give karts a speed burst

Page 137
The first *Grand Theft Auto* (Rockstar, 1997)

Page 143
Dragon Quest came out in 1986

Page 145
Pencil and paper! The developers created Tamriel for weekly *Dungeons & Dragons* games

Page 147
Ammo, biotic, combat and tech

Page 149
Sanctuary

Page 151
The pudding-like enemies are Flans

Page 153
Life

Page 159
1958

Page 161
National Basketball Association

Page 163
President Barack Obama

Page 165
45

Page 167
Cristiano Ronaldo (Portugal), Mario Balotelli (Italy), Wayne Rooney (England), Lionel Messi (Argentina), Andres Iniésta (Spain)

Page 173
El Presidente

Page 175
Cat, dog and horse

Page 177
Stockholm, Sweden

Page 179
Basshunter

Page 181
Hawaii

Page 187
São Paulo, Brazil

Page 189
20 (1991–2011)

Page 191
1994

Page 193
Stephen Merchant

HOW DID YOU DO? FIND OUT IF YOUR SCORE MAKES YOU A BASIC BUNCH OF PIXELS OR A 3D VISION OF BEAUTY...

0:	The left-hand bat from *Pong*
1–10:	One of the pointy aliens from *Space Invaders*
11–20:	Ryu from the original *Street Fighter* coin-op
21–30:	The floating traffic lights at the start of *Mario Kart 64*
31–40:	An explosion in Stalingrad from the first *Call of Duty*
41–50:	A shiny red Infernus from *Grand Theft Auto IV*
51–60:	The watch Artyom wears in *Metro 2033*
61+:	A stylishly retro zombie from *The Organ Trail*

Cutscene	Non-playable sequence in a game used to advance the plot
DLC	Downloadable content
FPS	First-person shooter, with its action shown from the player's point of view. Can also mean frames per second
GB	Nintendo Game Boy, a hand-held launched between 1989 and 1990
HDD	Hard disk drive
iOS	Apple's mobile operating system (see OS definition)
Isometric	A form of rendering objects in games so that they are viewed from a perspective that makes them seem 3D
JRPG	Japanese role-playing game
MAME	Multiple Arcade Machine Emulator: an emulator – either hardware or software – that uses contemporary technology to replicate the original arcade game
Metacritic	Website that collates the scores from videogame reviewers
MMO	Any kind of Massively Multiplayer Online game – includes (and is often used interchangeably with) MMORPG (see definition). These "massive" games feature persistent "worlds" rather than just the multiplayer functions of a game such as *Call of Duty*
MMORPG	A type of MMO game that is specifically role-playing (RPG, see definition)
Mod	Modification made to a game by a fan or a developer, from the smallest in-game tweak to a complete new version of a game (such as *Counter-Strike* – Minh Le and Jess Cliffe's take on *Half-Life*)
NES	Nintendo Entertainment System, a third-generation console launched between 1983 and 1986
NPCs	Non-player characters, controlled by the computer rather than the gamer
NTSC	National Television System Committee: the TV system used in North America. Consoles are produced for both NTSC and PAL (see definition) territories
OS	Operating system, such as Windows, Mac OS or Linux – the software that runs the basic functions of a computer or device
PAL	Phase Alternating Line: the TV system used in Europe. Consoles are produced for both NTSC (see definition) and PAL territories
PS2	The Sony PlayStation 2, a sixth-generation console launched in 2000, is the **best-selling console ever**, with sales of 150 million
PS3	The Sony PlayStation 3, a seventh-generation console launched in 2006
PSP	Sony PlayStation Portable, a hand-held launched between 2004 and 2005, precursor to the PS Vita
RPG	Role-playing game
RTS	Real-time strategy game
Sandbox	An open-ended game or game world in which you can wander as well as attempt specific missions
Sim	A simulation game – one that aims to recreate a real-world scenario, such as a football match or jet flight
SNES	Super Nintendo Entertainment System, a fourth-generation console launched between 1990 and 1992
TGTS	Twin Galaxies Tournament Setting, the official game settings for Twin Galaxies International
Top-down/ top-downer	Gameplay viewed from a third-person, overhead perspective
TPS	Third-person shooter
VGChartz	Website of game sales charts

GUINNESS WORLD RECORDS

Picture Credits

6: James Ellerker/Guinness World Records
7: Paul Michael Hughes/Guinness World Records
7: Richard Bradbury/Guinness World Records
8: James Ellerker/Guinness World Records
9: Dan Griliopoulos
10: BAFTA
14: Gabriel Bouys/Getty Images
14: Mario Tama/Getty Images
15: Robin Marchant/Getty Images
16: Gabriel Bouys/Getty Images
16: Spencer Platt/Getty Images
16: BAFTA
18: James Ellerker/Guinness World Records
20: James Ellerker/Guinness World Records
24: Joe Kohen/Invision for Xbox
26: Startreks/Rex Features
28: Franck Fife/Getty Images
36: Tony Avelar/Getty Images
40: Desirai Labrada
40: The Goodness
41: Bobbi Slagter
41: Gary Hudston
42: James Ellerker/Guinness World Records
46: Jason Merritt/Getty Images
46: Activision
48: Filip Kubski
49: Rick Dahms
50: Elizabeth Tobey
66: Twitter
67: Davis Films/Impact Pictures
70: Hulton Archive/Getty Images
74: Ryan Schude/Guinness World Records
76: BBC
77: Alex Lentati
79: Tom Fox/Dallas Morning News
81: Michael Buckner/Getty Images
82: David Paul Morris/Getty Images
82: Bestofdrawsomething.com
83: Ramin Talaie/Getty Images
85: Gareth Cattermole/Getty Images
85: Juan Naharro Gimenez/Getty Images
85: David Paul Morris/Getty Images
88: Richard Heathcote/Getty Images
92: Kayane.Fr
96: Emmanuel Rodriguez
100: Samir Hussein/Getty Images
100: John Thys/GettyImages
100: Michael Desmond/ABC via Getty Images
101: Loic Venance/Getty Images
101: Kevin Winter/Getty Images
101: Image Bank/Getty Images
102: Trion
104: Daniel Dociu
105: Jagex
106: NarmiCreator/Deviant Art
107: Top200KOTH
112: Robyn Beck/Getty Images
112: Getty Images
112: Frederic J Brown/Getty Images
113: Frederic J Brown/Getty Images
113: Kevork Djansezian/Getty Images
113: Charley Gallay/Getty Images for SEGA
122: Eckehard Schulz/AP/PA
124: iStock
124: DC Comics
124: Archie Comic Publications
125: id Software
126: Richard Bradbury/Guinness World Records
132: Justin Towell
132: Rainer W Schlegelmilch/Getty Images
133: Rainer W Schlegelmilch/Getty Images
134: Paul Michael Hughes/Guinness World Records
137: Nick Pickles/Getty Images
138: Tommy Tallarico Studios
148: Blizzard
152: Tamara Muth King/Activision
154: Jennifer Hale
155: Lucozade/Animal Logic
156: Paul Michael Hughes/Guinness World Records
162: Todd Rosenberg/Sports Illustrated/Getty Images
163: Scott Halleran/Getty Images
164: FIFA Interactive World Cup
166: Jasper Juinen/Getty Images
166: Cavan/Getty Images
167: Martin Rose/Getty Images
167: Christof Stache/GettyImages
167: Michael Regan/FA/Getty Images
167: Rich Schultz/Getty Images
167: Laurence Griffiths/Getty Images
167: Stefan Rousseau/WPA Pool/Getty Images
168: Mattis Larsson/Dreamhack
168: Daniel Marklund/Dreamhack
168: MLG
168: IGN
169: Kara Leung/EVO
169: ACL
169: GOM TV
169: FIFA Interactive World Cup
169: ESWC
169: V Halvorsen
172: Lycerius
173: Neofelis/Deviant Art
176: Emma Johansson/Scanpix/PA
179: DotA2/Valve
179: Kunkka/Deviant Art
181: SSPL/Getty Images
181: Newspix/Rex Features
182: Walt Disney/Kobal
182: Walt Disney Animation
182: Moviestore/Rex Features
182: SNAP/Rex Features
182: Warner Bros/Everett/Rex Features
183: Paramount
183: Picturehouse
183: Walt Disney Pictures
183: Eric Charbonneau/Getty Images
200: Alton Towers Resort

Acknowledgements

Guinness World Records would like to thank the following for their help in the creation of *Guinness World Records Gamer's Edition* 2013:

2KGames; Ahmed Al Derazi; Danni Amos; Apple Inc; Arcade Flyer; Alison Beasley; Nicky Biscuit; Mike Bithell; Pete Bouvier; Andy Brown; Jonnie Bryant (at Blizzard); Tom Butler; Simon Byron; Capcom; Harry Cole; Timothy Courtney (at LEGO); Ste Curran; Frazer Davidson; DreamHack; EA; Dave Fade; FJT Logistics Limited; Flickr; FMG, London; Games Press; Kirsty Greenhill; Dan Griliopoulos; Will Guyatt; Mark Hardisty; Jim Hawker; Jon Howard; IGN; Integrated Colour Editions Europe; Ironside; Resmiye Kahraman; Geoff Keighley; Kickstarter; Dan Kilby; Lee Kirton; Kate Kneale; Gorm Lai; Ollie Macefield; Moby Games; Damien Moore and minesweeper.info; Lindsay Morle; Nintendo; Michael O'Dell; Cathy Orr; Play Expo; PlayStation; PopCap; Greg Rice; Matt Roche; Tim Schafer (at Doublefine); Chris Schmidt; SEGA; Greg Short; Iain Simons; Gordon Sinclair; Che'von Slaughter; Grace Snoke; Square Enix; Robert Taylor; Arlene Thornton; Trion Worlds; Adam Tuckwell; Turbine; Ubisoft; Alex Verrey; Ember Wardrop; Ryan Whelan; Lydia Winter (at Mojang); Zynga